Financial Forecasting, Analysis, and Modelling

Financial Forecasting, Analysis, and Modelling

A Framework for Long-Term Forecasting

MICHAEL SAMONAS

WILEY

This edition first published 2015
© 2015 Michael Samonas

Registered office
John Wiley & Sons Ltd, The Atrium, Southern Gate, Chichester, West Sussex, PO19 8SQ, United Kingdom

For details of our global editorial offices, for customer services and for information about how to apply for permission to reuse the copyright material in this book please see our website at www.wiley.com.

Library of Congress Cataloging-in-Publication Data
Samonas, Michael.
  Financial forecasting, analysis, and modelling : a framework for long-term forecasting / Michael Samonas.
      pages cm
  Includes bibliographical references and index.
  ISBN 978-1-118-92108-1 (cloth)
  1. Corporations–Finance–Mathematical models.   2. Corporations–Finance–Forecasting.   I. Title.
  HG4012.S26 2015
  658.1501'12–dc23
                                                                                2014040071

Cover Design: Wiley
Cover Image: Top:©iStock.com/MarsBars;
Bottom: ©iStock.com/studiocasper

Set in 10/12pt Times by Laserwords Private Limited, Chennai, India

Printed in the UK

To Konstantinos, Eleftheria, my Mom and Dad

Table of Contents

Preface

Over the past several years, spreadsheet models have been the dominant vehicles for finance professionals to implement their financial knowledge. Moreover, in the aftermath of the recent financial crisis the need for experienced Financial Modelling professionals has steadily increased as organizations need to plan and adjust to the economic volatility and uncertainty. The level of risk in taking certain decisions needs to be projected using proper financial models and the alternative possible outcomes need to be analyzed. One benefit of this type of analysis is that it helps companies to be proactive instead of reactive. They can avoid or at least mitigate potential negative results that may stem from influences in their industry or within the business itself.

This book provides a step-by-step guide that takes the reader through the entire process of developing long-term projection plans using Excel. In addition, by making use of various tools (Excel's Scenario Manager, sensitivity analysis, and Monte Carlo simulation) it provides practical examples on how to apply risk and uncertainty to these projection plans. Although these projections are not guarantees they can help organizations to be better informed, and thereby provide peace of mind.

Financial Forecasting, Analysis and Modelling: A Framework for Long-Term Forecasting covers financial models in the area of financial statement simulation. It provides clear and concise explanations in each case for the implementation of the models using Excel. It is relevant to a variety of situations. At the most fundamental level, it can help:

- Project a company's financial performance;
- Forecast future cash flows and perform a DCF valuation;
- Present the good, basic, and bad scenarios of the evolution of the company's debt covenants.

At a more advanced level it ensures that the financial analyst or decision-maker is properly informed and comfortable when called to decide the following types of question:

- What will be the double impact on the liquidity of the organization of a simultaneous increase of 35% in turnover and a decrease of 10 days in the credit period provided to clients?
- What will be the range of the company's net debt at a 95% confidence level based on selected assumptions?

Acknowledgments

I owe a debt of gratitude to many individuals who helped me with this book. Foremost is my wife Eleftheria for the support and encouragement she provided to me. Furthermore, I would like to thank my parents for their tireless efforts to support me in every step of my life. Their determination and drive have been a constant inspiration. My special thanks go to Nikos Karanikolas, a magnanimous reviewer, who provided detailed written suggestions in a response to the publisher's request for his review. Also I really appreciate the insightful comments of my esteemed colleague Carmen Mihaela Bulau on many of my manuscripts in spite of her hectic schedule.

Finally, I appreciate the efforts of all the people at John Wiley & Sons who have helped make this book happen. In particular I would like to thank Werner Coetzee (Commissioning Editor), Jennie Kitchin (Assistant Editor), Caroline Quinnell (Copy Editor), and last but not least Kelly Cracknell and Abirami Srikandan - Hoboken (Production Editors), who guided me through the production process.

About the Author

Michael Samonas is a finance professional with extensive experience in Financial Planning, Analysis and Modelling. He is currently the Group CFO of SIDMA S.A., a member of the Viohalco Group of companies. He has worked in the past for various multinationals including Vodafone S.A. and the Hellenic Telecommunications Organization conducting a range of models for business planning, valuations, mergers, projects, and data analysis. For a number of years Michael was an instructor at the School of Business & Economics of the University of Laverne, Athens Campus. A regular contributor to financial and business journals, Michael has taught specialized courses in Financial Analysis & Business Modelling, Credit Analysis & Cash Flow Forecasting, and Investment Evaluation & Appraisal.

Michael holds both MSc and PhD degrees from the Department of Physics and the Electronic & Electrical Engineering Department of University of Surrey as well as an MBA from the University of La Verne California. He also holds a BSc degree in Applied Accounting from University of Oxford Brookes (with honours) and is a Fellow of the Association of Chartered Certified Accountants (ACCA).

one

Developing Corporate Finance Models

1

Introduction

Chapter 1 answers some simple questions about financial modelling, such as: What is it? Who does it? What are the steps in building a financial model? But above all, why is financial modelling the single most important skill-set for the aspiring finance professional?

The framework for the development of a spreadsheet-based financial model is illustrated by using a simple concrete example. A spreadsheet is used in order to calculate the funding needs of a 2/10 net 30 credit policy on a certain turnover. The inputs and the output of the model are defined. Building this model is relatively straightforward. The model-builder needs to input estimates for certain items (i.e. turnover) and then make sure that the mathematical formulae are correct. From this simple base, the steps of the financial modelling process are described in order to build sophisticated and interconnected models for the income statement, balance sheet, and cash-flow statement, as well as "good/bad/base" scenarios that can be changed with a simple click or two. This ability of spreadsheets to deal with a lot of numbers, work with them, and produce answers is stressed, as well as the use of Excel as the ideal tool for financial modelling.

1.1 WHAT IS FINANCIAL MODELLING?

If you Google the term "financial model" you will get approximately 350 million hits. Yes, that's right. Financial modelling has become the single most important skill-set for the aspiring finance professional. But what exactly is a financial model and what does financial modelling do? *Investopedia*[1] defines financial modelling as the process by which a firm constructs a financial representation of some, or all, aspects of it. The model is usually characterized by performing calculations, and makes recommendations based on that information. Moreover, *Moneyterms*[2] defines a financial model as anything that is used to calculate, forecast, or estimate financial numbers. Models can range from simple formulae to complex computer programs that may take hours to run. Finally, according to *Wikipedia*,[3] financial modelling is the task of building an abstract representation (a model) of a real-world financial situation. This is a mathematical model designed to represent (a simplified version of) the performance of a financial asset. Similar definitions exist on other financial websites like *BusinessDictionary.com*, *Divestopedia*, etc. Financial modelling is a general term that means different things to different people. In the context of this book it relates to accounting and corporate finance applications and usually involves the preparation of detailed company-specific models used for decision-making purposes and financial analysis. While there has been some debate in the industry as to the nature of financial modelling – whether it is a tradecraft, such as welding, or a science – the task of financial modelling has been gaining acceptance and rigour over the years.

Financial models can differ widely in complexity and application: some are simple 1-page sheets built to get a "quick-and-dirty" estimate of next year's net income. Some span more than 40 worksheets and project various scenarios of the value of a company.

Although financial models vary in scope and use, many share common characteristics. For example:

1. **Reported financials for past years are the basis for most projection models.** To forecast financial statements we make use of key performance drivers derived from historical records.
2. **Projecting future years for the 3 main financial statements** – the income statement, the balance sheet, and the cash flow statement – is typically the first step. Income statement estimates for EBITDA and interest expense as well as balance sheet leverage statistics such as debt/equity and interest coverage are often the most important model outputs.
3. **Incorporating financial statement analysis through the use of ratios.** More often profitability, liquidity, and solvency ratios are calculated in order to pinpoint any weaknesses in the financial position of a company.
4. **Performing valuation.** Valuation involves estimating the value of a company using various techniques although the most commonly used are comparable company multiples and discounted cash-flow modelling.
5. **Conducting various forms of sensitivity analysis after a forecast model has been built.** These analyses are often the real reason a model was built in the first place. For example, sensitivity analysis might be used to measure the impact on one model output – say free cash flow – from the changes of one or more model inputs, say revenue growth or the company's working capital needs ("What happens to free cash flow if we increase sales growth by an extra 2% next year and at the same time reduce the payment terms to the suppliers by 5 days?").

Financial modelling is about decision-making. There is always a problem that needs to be solved, resulting in the creation of a financial model.

Financial modelling is about forecasting. In the post 9/11 environment, forecasting has become much more difficult because the economic environment has become much more volatile. Since profit is not the only important variable, a projected financing plan into the future is imperative for a business to succeed.

Financial modelling is the single most important skill-set for the aspiring finance professional. It is as much an art as a science. Financial modelling encompasses a broad range of disciplines used across many fields of finance. A good financial modeller must first of all have a thorough understanding of Generally Accepted Accounting Principles (GAAP) and the statutory accounting principles. They must know how the 3 financial statements work and how these are linked together. They need to know corporate finance theory and be able to apply it in valuation exercises. They will have to be adequate in forecasting. Finally, they will have to think analytically, be good at business analysis, possess industry-specific knowledge and, last but not least, have strong Excel skills. The applications of the above skill-sets are immense and somebody can develop them by applying and also by practising them.

In this book we look at the basics of most of these disciplines. In Chapter 2 we cover the fundamentals of accounting theory and the interrelationship of the 3 financial statements. In Chapter 3 we apply this theory in practice to build the proforma financial statements of a sample company of interest. In Chapter 4 we examine various forecasting techniques related to sales, costs, capital expenditures, depreciation, and working capital needs. In Chapter 5 we cover the theory behind Discounted Cash Flow (DCF) valuation.

During the financial crisis, the G20 tasked global accounting standard-setters to work intensively towards the objective of incorporating uncertainty into International Financial Reporting Standards (IFRS) (e.g. favourable and unfavourable scenarios are requested in estimating the fair value of an investment). In addition businesses are asked to prepare various scenarios in order to prove that they will be financially viable into the future and thus secure funding from their lenders or raw materials from their suppliers. Chapters 6, 7, and 8 deal with these types of uncertainty. Chapter 6 deals with sensitivity analysis, Chapter 7 elaborates on building multiple scenarios, and Chapter 8 introduces the Monte Carlo simulation and deals with building up a simulation model from scratch.

For the *Finance and the Accounting professional* in corporate finance and investment banking, financial modelling is largely synonymous with cash-flow forecasting and is used to assist the management decision-making process with problems related to:

- Historical analysis of a company
- Projecting a company's financial performance
- Business or security valuation
- Benefits of a merger
- Capital budgeting
- Scenario planning
- Forecasting future raw material needs
- Cost of capital (i.e. Weighted Average Cost of Capital (WACC)) calculations
- Financial statement analysis
- Restructuring of a company.

The same applies to the *equity research analyst* or the *credit analyst*, whether they want to examine a particular firm's financial projections along with competitors' projections in order to determine if it is a smart investment or not, or to forecast future cash flows and thus determine the degree of risk associated with the firm.

Furthermore, for the *small business owner* and *entrepreneur* who would like to project future financial figures of his business, financial modelling will enable him to prepare so-called proforma financial statements, which in turn will help him forecast future levels of profits as well as anticipated borrowing.

Finally, as more and more companies become global through the acquisition/establishment of international operations, there is an imminent requirement for sophisticated financial models. These models can assist the *business/financial analyst* in evaluating the performance of each country's operations, standardize financial reporting, and analyze complex information according to the various industry demand–supply patterns.

Financial modelling, unlike other areas of accounting and finance, is unregulated and lacks generally accepted practice guidelines, which means that model risk is a very real concept. Only recently certain accounting bodies, such as the Institute of Chartered Accountants in England

and Wales (ICAEW), published principles for good spreadsheet practice based on the FAST Standard which is one of the first standards for financial modelling to be officially recognized.[4] The FAST (Flexible Appropriate Structured Transparent) Standard is a set of rules on the structure and detailed design of spreadsheet-based models and provides both a clear route to good model design for the individual modeller and a common style platform upon which modellers and reviewers can rely when sharing models amongst themselves.[5] Other standards include SMART, developed by Corality, which provides guidance on how to create spreadsheets with consistency, transparency, and flexibility[6] and the Best Practice Modelling (BPM)[7] published by the Spreadsheet Standards Review Board (SSRB).[8] Nevertheless the above standards have not yet been widely adopted and the reader should be aware of the scope, benefits, and limitations of financial modelling. Always apply the "Garbage in Garbage out" principle.

1.2 DEFINING THE INPUTS AND THE OUTPUTS OF A SIMPLE FINANCIAL MODEL

A good model is easily recognizable. It has clearly identifiable outputs based on clearly defined inputs and the relationship between them can be tracked through a logical audit trail. Consider the following situation. Think of a wholesale company that wants to use a financial model to assess the financial implications of its credit policy. Let us say that the company has a 2-term trade credit agreement. In this agreement it offers a discount to its buyers if payment is made within a certain period, which is typically shorter than the net payment period. For example, a "2/10 net 30" agreement would give the buyer a discount of 2% if payment is realized by the 10th day following delivery. If the buyer fails to take advantage of the discount, there are still 20 additional days in which to pay the full price of the goods without being in default, that is, the net period has a total duration of 30 days. Finally, as with net terms, the company could charge penalties if the buyer still fails to meet the payment after the net term has expired. It is expected that 30% of the company's buyers would adopt the discount. Trade credit can be an attractive source of funds due to its simplicity and convenience. However, trade credit is like a loan by the company to its customer. There are 2 issues associated with loans: (a) what is the necessary amount of the loan and (b) what is the cost of it?

Therefore, the company needs to build a model in order to estimate:

(a) the cost of the trade credit it provides to its customers, and
(b) the funding impact of it, on the basis that 70% of the company's customers will not adopt the discount,

given that it has an annual turnover of €10,000,000.
So the model outputs should look like this:

Cost of the Discount

     Effective Annual Rate (EAR) :
     In absolute terms (€):

Funding impact of the credit period

     Funding needs (€):
     Cost of funding per year (€):

The Effective Annual Rate (EAR) is the cost of the discount offered by the company to encourage buyers to pay early and is given by the following formula:

$$EAR = \frac{\text{Discount percent}}{(100 - \text{Discount percent})} \times \frac{360}{(\text{Days credit is outstanding} - \text{Discount period})}$$

As far as the above situation is concerned:

$$EAR = \frac{2}{100 - 2} \times \frac{360}{30 - 10} = 36.7\%$$

This cost is really high and means that the company offering the discount is short of cash. Under normal circumstances it could get a bank loan much more cheaply than this. On the buyer side, as long as they can obtain a bank loan at a lower interest rate, they would be better off borrowing at the lower rate and using the cash proceeds of the loan to take advantage of the discount offered by the company. Moreover, the amount of the discount also represents a cost to the company because it does not receive the full selling price for the product. In our case this cost is:

$$(1 - 70\%) \times €10,000,000 \times 2\% = €60,000$$

Apart from the above cost, if we assume that the company's customers would wait until the last day of the discount period to pay, i.e. the 10th day, then the company should fund 10 days of receivables for turnover equal to:

$$(1 - 70\%) \times €10,000,000 \times (1 - 2\%) = €2,940,000$$

The factor (1–2%) takes into account the discount. These 10 days of receivables, assuming a 360-day financial year, are equal to the following amount (as we will see in Chapter 2):

$$10 \text{ days} \times €2,940,000/360 = €81,667$$

If the €81,667 are financed by debt and the cost of debt is 8% per year, then the company will bear interest of:

$$8\% \times €81,667 = €6,533/\text{year}$$

That is, the company will bear a cost of €60,000 per year arising from the discount of 2% plus a further cost of €6,533 as interest arising from the funding needs of the 10-day credit period.

Concerning the 70% of the company's customers that prefer the credit period of 30 days, this is equivalent to turnover of:

$$70\% \times €10,000,000 = €7,000,000$$

This turnover, if funded for 30 days, gives rise to receivables equal to:

$$30 \text{ days} \times €7,000,000/360 = €583,333.$$

Again, if the €583,333 are financed by debt and the cost of debt is 8% per year, then the company will bear interest of:

$$8\% \times €583,333 = €46,667/\text{year}.$$

To summarize: the company will bear a cost of €60,000 per year arising from the discount of 2% plus a further cost of €6,533 as interest arising from the funding needs of the 10-day credit period plus another cost of €46,667 as interest arising from the funding needs of the 30-day period.

All the numbers that feed into the above formulae should form the *inputs of the model* and all the formulae will be part of the *workings of the model* as we discussed in the previous paragraph.

Then, the *inputs* of the model should look like this:

Particulars	UOM	Values
Discount offered:	(%)	2%
First term of credit:	(days)	10
Second term of credit:	(days)	30
Percentage of clients choosing to take the discount:	(%)	30%
Company's annual turnover:	(€)	10,000,000
Company's annual cost of debt:	(%)	8%

and the *outputs* of the model will look like this:

Cost of the Discount	
Effective Annual rate (EAR) :	36.7%
In absolute terms (€):	60,000
Funding impact of the credit terms	
Funding needs (€):	665,000
Cost of funding per year (€):	53,200

where the funding impact of €665,000 is the sum of both the 10-day discount period and the 30 credit days (€81,667 + €583,333) and €53,200 is the cost of these funds per year at 8%.

So far you may have the impression that financial modelling is purely maths and finance. However, for a model to be effective, precise financial calculations are not enough and are only part of the equation. The second and equally important part is the appropriate application of subjectivity. Financial models that combine both maths and art become the models that are relevant and are actually used in business.[9] In this direction we have used a common style for the headings of both the inputs and the outputs. Moreover we could have used blue colour for the inputs. We have used 3 columns to separate the particular inputs from their relevant unit of measure (UOM) and their proposed value. We started by defining first *the outputs* of the model that will answer the business question the model will need to address. Then we identified any additional information required in order to complete the model (i.e. the cost of funds/debt for the company). Only then did we write down all the particular formulae and calculations that the model needs to perform.

As a final note to this specific modelling exercise, we mentioned previously that there was no need for any decision making. The model was constructed simply to enhance the business understanding of a particular company policy. Should any decision need to be taken about which credit policy is more efficient, we could model a number of different scenarios each with various credit policies. For example we could examine 3 different policies (2/10 net 30, 2/10 net 45, and 2/10 net 60) in order to choose the most favourable one.

1.3 THE FINANCIAL MODELLING PROCESS OF MORE COMPLEX MODELS

The financial modelling process is comprised of 4 steps as shown in Exhibit 1.1:

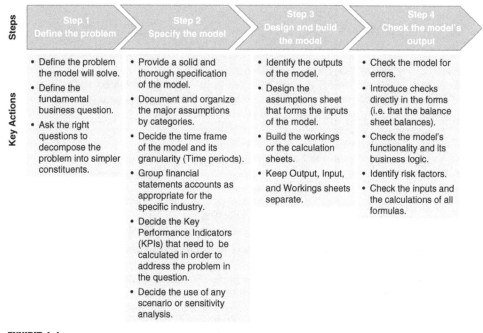

Steps	Step 1 Define the problem	Step 2 Specify the model	Step 3 Design and build the model	Step 4 Check the model's output
Key Actions	• Define the problem the model will solve. • Define the fundamental business question. • Ask the right questions to decompose the problem into simpler constituents.	• Provide a solid and thorough specification of the model. • Document and organize the major assumptions by categories. • Decide the time frame of the model and its granularity (Time periods). • Group financial statements accounts as appropriate for the specific industry. • Decide the Key Performance Indicators (KPIs) that need to be calculated in order to address the problem in the question. • Decide the use of any scenario or sensitivity analysis.	• Identify the outputs of the model. • Design the assumptions sheet that forms the inputs of the model. • Build the workings or the calculation sheets. • Keep Output, Input, and Workings sheets separate.	• Check the model for errors. • Introduce checks directly in the forms (i.e. that the balance sheet balances). • Check the model's functionality and its business logic. • Identify risk factors. • Check the inputs and the calculations of all formulas.

EXHIBIT 1.1 The 4 fundamental steps of the financial modelling process

Let us examine each of the above steps in detail.

1.3.1 Step 1: Defining the Problem the Model Will Solve: The Fundamental Business Question

Financial modelling is used, as we mentioned previously, in order to solve various problems. The first step of the process includes teams or individuals asking the right questions at the start of the problem-solving process. This is sometimes hard to believe as it often seems that people are trying to solve a problem before they have properly defined it. Asking the right questions helps break down the problem into simpler constituents.

For example the commercial manager of the company requests the financial analyst to present the impact on the bottom line results of the company of a New Product Development (NPD).

Let us say that the costs of the whole NPD process are available and can be largely funded through government subsidy. In order to tackle the problem the financial analyst needs to ask the following questions:

1. What will be the forecast sales volume of the new product per year?
2. What will be the unit price?
3. What will be the credit terms?
4. What will be the inventory needs of the product?
5. What will be the payment terms of the suppliers of the raw materials?
6. What will be the incremental variable and fixed cost per year for the proposed production?
7. When is it anticipated that the governmental subsidy for the initial investment costs will be received?

The problem, then, can be broken down as per Exhibit 1.2:

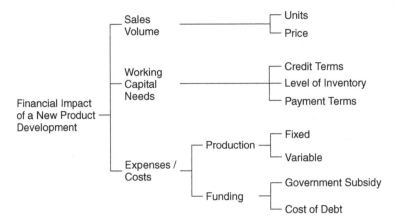

EXHIBIT 1.2   Breaking down a business problem into simpler constituents

1.3.2 Step 2: Specification of the Model

Now we have identified the variables of the problem, we need a solid and thorough specification for a successful financial modelling process. The major assumptions should be documented and organized by category (such as market prices, sales volumes, costs, credit terms, payment terms, capital expenditures, and so on). All assumptions should be placed separately on a single sheet so that we do not have to hunt through formulae to figure out where a number came from.

Moreover, the specification of the model, depending on the problem we have to address, might include the following:

- To formulate the standard financial statements, including the income statement, balance sheet, and statement of cash flow. For the problem described in Step 1, the balance sheet and cash-flow statements are used to determine the level of additional borrowing, although they are more time consuming than a plain income statement, provided that the new product development will be funded by debt. The interest expense of this borrowing is an expense line in the income statement that we need to forecast in order to answer the original question. In other cases, i.e. where a valuation is required, we would have to derive both the free cash flow and the Weighted Average Cost of Capital schedules as well.

- To decide the time frame of our forecast and its granularity (time periods). This refers to whether calculations will be done at the monthly level of detail or on a yearly basis. This is important when projecting cash flows in order to ensure enough liquidity to withstand cash-flow spikes due to factors such as inventory replenishment, slow accounts receivable cycles, large quarterly tax payments, major capital purchases, and other events. Output results are normally monthly for the first forecast year, quarterly for the next, and annual for the rest of a full 5-year plan.
- To group operating expenses by departments as appropriate for the specific industry. Typical departments might be General and Administrative, Sales & Marketing, Research & Development, or Operations. This allows a comparison of departmental expenses as a percentage of total expenses with other companies in the industry.
- To decide which Key Performance Indicators (KPI) need to be calculated in order to address the problem in question. KPIs expressed as ratios such as revenue EBITDA cover or the quick ratio allow projections to be benchmarked against other companies in the industry.
- To create various scenarios, in order to assess the impact of different strategies. That is, to evaluate a series of different model output variables given a set of different input variables.
- To create a sensitivity analysis that shows what will be the impact of changing the major assumptions by equal amounts, in percentage terms. This allows us to determine which assumptions have the greatest impact on our forecast, and must therefore be thought out most carefully. It will also allow us to focus on the important model variables rather than getting lost among all model variables.
- Finally, to create a control panel, i.e. a one-page summary where we can change the most important assumptions and see immediately how this impacts on the KPIs of interest.

The importance of this step is to ensure that the proposed model is easy to read, easy to understand, easy to change, and simply easy to use. The way to make a model useful and readable is to keep it simple. The complexity of the transaction which has to be modelled and the complexity of the model itself are 2 different things.

1.3.3 Step 3: Designing and Building the Model

Designing and building the financial model is the next phase of the process. The specification phase (Step 2) should lay out the structure of the model in detail. In this step we first identify the *outputs* of the model. It is good practice to present the output of the model on a separate sheet. This output sheet is a combination of model inputs and formulae and should read directly from the *workings* sheet of the model. There may be more than one output sheet in case the resolution of step 1 requires the handling of uncertainty and creating sensitivity analyses. Moreover, the control panel described in the specification part of the modelling process, if any, is part of the output of the model. Next we build the *assumptions* sheet that forms the *inputs* to our model. If our model needs past data to build on, i.e. historic financial statements, we collect them and adjust them to the right level of detail. Depending on the problem we have to solve we will not need all of the income statement, balance sheet, and cash flow statement accounts, and thus some will need to be grouped together. Finally we build the *workings* or *calculation sheets* and fill their cells with formulae. Thus, the sheets where the calculations are taking place should always be separate from both the input and the output sheets. Also no hard-coded values should be typed directly into the calculations of the workings sheet. In case the purpose of the model is to forecast future financial statements, all the relevant key drivers of the historic financial statements are calculated and forecast into the future. The forecast key drivers will make the building blocks of the future financial statements as we will see in Chapter 3 where we will build a financial model from scratch in order for the reader to grasp all the aforementioned abstract rules.

The following indicate best practices that will help you build models that are robust, easy to use, easy to understand, and painless to update. Best practices are of greatest concern when documents are used by more than one person:

- Use a modular design to divide your model into sections such as: Documentation, Data, Assumptions/Inputs, Workings, and Outputs, as we have already mentioned above. The first sheet of the model should serve as a user guide, step-by-step documentation as to how the model works. It may seem time-consuming, but it greatly increases the productivity of the whole team, and frees up time when, at a later stage, as you try to remember how you built the model, you will need to revise it.
- Always avoid hard-coding numbers into formulae and try to keep your formulae as short as possible. Always split complex formulae into multiple, simple steps.
- Use formatting for description rather than decoration. For example use different colour text for assumptions compared with formulae and output results. Use consistency in colours (e.g. blue for inputs) to highlight cells where data must be entered. When using more colours do not forget to add a legend explaining what each colour means. Always keep in mind the KISS principle: Keep It Simple Stupid.
- Present the data as clearly and in as uncluttered a form as possible. Always separate inputs into at least 3 columns, one with the particular inputs, the second describing the Units of Measure (UOM) of each input, and the last one with the values of each input.
- If you distribute your model to others, do protect it to prevent inadvertent changes. By default, anyone can change anything on any spreadsheet. To prevent unauthorized changes you should either protect your worksheets or your workbook as a whole. As a workbook owner you should always keep one copy of your original model in a directory that only you can change.
- Designate ownership and track who is changing what. If you decide not to prevent changes in your model then try at least to monitor them. To do so you can simply make use of the Track Changes tool in Excel 2010 and 2013. Microsoft's Track Changes function allows revisions to be made to a document and keeps a complete record of all changes made. Track Changes can be invaluable if you have created a business document and you distribute it to others to work with it.
- Design your worksheets to read from left to right and from top to bottom, like a European book. This is a common recommendation in the literature. Perhaps it is a remnant of paper-based documents, but it seems that following such a design does make spreadsheets easier to navigate and understand.
- Finally when incorporating charts in your model, always label the axes and use titles.

Although this is not a book on how to build good spreadsheets, the interested reader could visit the site of The European Spreadsheet Risks Interest Group – EuSpRIG[10] where they can find plenty of information and research papers about spreadsheet best practices. Perhaps one of the most important papers on this site is that of IBM – Spreadsheet Modelling Best Practice. This is a 100-page guide on how to develop high quality spreadsheets. This guide is of interest to anyone who relies on decisions from spreadsheet models. The techniques described include areas such as ensuring that the objectives of the model are clear, defining the calculations, good design practice, testing and understanding, and presenting the results from spreadsheet models.

1.3.4 Step 4: Checking the Model's Output

The model is not ready until we ensure that it produces the results it was designed to. Errors in the data or formulae could be costly, even devastating. The received wisdom is that about 5% of all formulae in spreadsheet models contain errors, and this rate is consistent across spreadsheets. Errors may occur at the functionality level, the logic level, the design level, etc. A simple way to check our model is to introduce checks directly in the forms. Some of these checks will be very generic and will therefore be included early. For example in case of a balance sheet the obvious check is the sum of assets vs the sum of equity and liabilities. In case of a cash flow statement the cash and cash equivalents at the beginning of a period should be equal to the cash and cash equivalents at the end of the previous period. Moreover the cash and cash equivalents at the end of a period should be the same as the cash account of the balance sheet of that period. Other checks will be more model-specific, and the need for them will not be obvious at the beginning – therefore, new checks will be included throughout the model building phase.

As a minimum, we can test our model subsequent to the building phase by playing with the inputs and see if this produces reasonable results (reasonableness tests). For example, if a formula is supposed to add a set of values then we can test it by providing known data, and checking that the answer is the expected one. Moreover we can change each of the input parameters and see if the output results change accordingly.

There is free textbook on Wikibooks (*Financial Modelling in Microsoft Excel/Testing*)[11] which provides a detailed checklist of the best practices on how to error-check a spreadsheet. From checking its functionality, i.e. whether the model does what it is supposed to do, to checking the business logic in the model. From identifying the risk factors, i.e. what could go wrong, and how serious that could be, to checking the inputs of the model and its calculations, i.e. examining all formula cells, where they read from, and where they feed their result to.

Of course there are error-checking tools that can make our life easier. Excel 2003 and later versions have a built-in error-checking tool. For example in Excel 2003 under the Tools menu, just select Error Checking. If the Excel Error Checking tool detects a possible error, it pops up a dialog box. This box gives several choices, which range from ignoring the warning to taking action. The more updated the version of Excel the better the error-checking tools that have been incorporated. However, the error-checking tools built into Excel are simple but limited. A number of more sophisticated error-checking products are available on the market.

1.4 EXCEL AS A TOOL OF MODELLING: CAPABILITIES AND LIMITATIONS

Microsoft Excel is the ideal tool for the kind of modelling covered in this book. Its immense popularity throughout the business world today for processing quantitative data and developing analytical solutions is widely acknowledged. One could argue that it is one of the most powerful and most important software applications of all time. It would not be an exaggeration to claim that if civilization were about to vanish and somebody could pass future generations a single wonder of our time, this should be Excel. Excel is everywhere you look in the business world – especially in areas where people are handling numbers, such as marketing, business development, sales, and finance. In a 2011 study, Weiser Mazars found that Excel was the favorite tool of insurance finance and accounting. Teams relied heavily on Excel to compensate for shortcomings in the information flow. Most leaders they questioned did not have plans to change this process. Moreover, they found that 87% of companies rely on Excel in their planning, budgeting, and other performance management processes.[12] In a different survey performed by *gtnews* during 2014 in relation to the technology that Financial Planning and Analysis (FP&A) professionals are using, almost three-quarters (73%) of those surveyed indicated that Excel is still the primary tool they use in more than half of all their analytical work, even if they also have a standalone system.[13]

But while Excel is reasonably robust, the spreadsheets that people create with Excel are incredibly fragile. For starters, there is no way to trace where your data came from, there is no audit trail (so you can overtype numbers and not realize it), and there is no easy way to test spreadsheets. The biggest problem is that anyone can create Excel spreadsheets – badly. Because it's so easy to use, the creation of even important spreadsheets is not restricted to people who understand programming and do it in a methodical, well-documented way. That is why one should be aware of Excel's limitations. Tim Worstall, a *Forbes* contributor, proclaimed recently in a *Forbes* article that "Microsoft's Excel Might Be The Most Dangerous Software on the Planet" after JP Morgan's loss of several billion dollars due to a spreadsheet error.[14] Moreover, a *CFO.com* article states that the error rates in spreadsheets are huge; Excel will dutifully average the wrong data right down the line and there's no protection against that.[15] Finally, an article entitled "Beware of the Spreadsheet" appeared in the international edition of *Accounting and Business*, in which David Parmenter argued that the use of large spreadsheets for reporting, forecasting, and planning should be abandoned because of their susceptibility to errors.[16] Excel is a tool and as such its use should be underpinned by proper controls as we mentioned earlier in this chapter.

In this direction both the Switzerland-based Basel Committee on Banking Supervision (BCBS) and the Financial Services Authority (FSA) in the UK have recently made it clear that when relying on manual processes, desktop applications, or key internal data flow systems such as spreadsheets, banks and insurers should have effective controls in place that are consistently applied to manage risks around incorrect, false, or even fraudulent data. The citation by the BCBS is the first time that spreadsheet management has ever been specifically referenced at such a high level, a watermark in the approach to spreadsheet risk.

Readers of this book should bear in mind that, although Excel is an incredible tool and without it we would not have had the incredible financialization of the world economy over the past 30 years, errors can easily happen while trying to model real life situations. Proper controls put in place can minimize possible errors and prevent wrong decisions.

BIBLIOGRAPHY AND REFERENCES

1. Investopedia, http://www.investopedia.com/terms/f/financialmodeling.asp.
2. Moneyterms, http://moneyterms.co.uk/financial-model/.
3. Wikipedia, http://en.wikipedia.org/wiki/Financial_modeling.

4. Institute of Chartered Accountants in England and Wales (ICAEW) "Twenty principles for good spreadsheet practice", June 2014, http://www.icaew.com/home/technical/information-technology/excel/twenty-principles.

5. The FAST Standard, http://www.fast-standard.org/.

6. The SMART Standard, Corality, http://www.corality.com/financial-modelling/smart.

7. Best Practice Spreadsheet Modeling Standards http://www.bestpracticemodelling.com.

8. Spreadsheet Standards Review Board-SSRB, http://www.ssrb.org/.

9. Juan Arangote, "Subjective Viewpoint. Financial Modeling: The math and art of painting the future today" (July/August 2014) 34(6) AFP *Exchange* 40–42, http://www.afponline.org/exchange/.

10. The European Spreadsheet Risks Interest Group – EuSpRIG, http://www.eusprig.org/index.htm.

11. WIKIBOOKS, http://en.wikibooks.org/wiki/Financial_Modelling_in_Microsoft_Excel/Testing.

12. Weiser Mazars, 2011, Insurance Finance Leadership Study, http://www.weisermazars.com/images/2011_Insurance_Finance_Leadership_Study.pdf.

13. 2014 gtnews FP&A Technology Survey, http://gtnews.afponline.org/Research/2014_gtnews_FP_A_Technology_Survey.html.

14. Tim Worstall, "Microsoft's Excel Might Be The Most Dangerous Software on the Planet", *Forbes*, 13 February 2013, http://www.forbes.com/sites/timworstall/2013/02/13/microsofts-excel-might-be-the-most-dangerous-software-on-the-planet/.

15. "Imagine there is no Excel", CFO.COM, 18 January 2012, http://ww2.cfo.com/analytics/2012/01/imagine-there-is-no-excel/.

16. "Beware of the Spreadsheet", *Accounting and Business International*, May 2014, http://issuu.com/accaglobal_publications/docs/ab_int_may14_comp_rgb.

2

A Short Primer in the Accounting of Financial Statements

Chapter 2 explains the basics of the financial statements and the Generally Accepted Accounting Principles (GAAP) that underlie their construction. Financial statements are the primary source of information for most investors and analysts. While an understanding of every detail and International Accounting Standards Board (IASB)[1] rule is not necessary, it is important that the reader understands at least the basics. The accounting equation is used to prepare the balance sheet, the income statement, and the statement of cash flows and the interrelationships among these statements are explained. A sample company's financial statements highlight the abovementioned articulation by using a proper graphical exhibit. Finally the most important financial ratios are described as a means of financial statement analysis and interpretation.

2.1 THE ACCOUNTING EQUATION

Any aspiring financial modeller should be familiar with the basic accounting principles and how they are reflected in the so-called financial statements. Financial statements are standardized forms developed by accountants and financial managers in order to record business transactions. They follow the fundamental principle of accounting: matching costs and expenses with the revenues they have created. In order for costs and expenses to be matched with revenues, accountants devised what is known as the double entry system of accounting. In other words, every transaction is listed in 2 places. Double entry accounting is largely attributed to the Italian mathematician and Franciscan monk known as Luca Pacioli who lived from 1445 to 1517. Pacioli is credited with the first publication of the "Venetian method" of keeping accounts, a system for maintaining financial records.

For example, when you purchase an asset for €100 using cash, you should increase your assets by €100 while at the same time decreasing your cash by €100. Moreover, when a company borrows money from a bank, the company's assets will increase and its liabilities will increase by the same amount. When a company purchases inventory for cash, one asset will increase and one asset will decrease. Double entry accounting refers precisely to the fact that

2 or more accounts are affected by every transaction. Frequently the notion of a T-account is used to describe the above transactions.

T-accounts have a left (debit) side and a right (credit) side. Exhibit 2.1 shows an example of a T-account:

Any Account

DEBIT	CREDIT
(LEFT SIDE)	(RIGHT SIDE)

EXHIBIT 2.1   The basic notion of a T-account

With the double entry system, debit merely means the left side of an account, while credit means the right side. Each transaction recorded must have the same number of euros on the left side as it does on the right side. Several accounts could be involved in a single transaction, but the debits and credits must still be equal. Double entry accounting is very simple to understand as soon as you remember that the accounting equation that we will see in a minute must always be balanced.

The debit and credit approach is a technique that has gained acceptance over a long period of time. The double entry system revolves around the *accounting equation* which simply measures the financial position of company in terms of the following items:

1. Assets (what it owns)
2. Liabilities (what it owes to others)
3. Owner's equity (the difference between assets and liabilities).

The *accounting equation* offers a simple way to understand how these 3 amounts relate to each other. The accounting equation for a corporation is shown in Exhibit 2.2:

$$Assets = Liabilities + Owner's\ Equity$$

EXHIBIT 2.2   The accounting equation

Assets are a company's resources – things the company owns. Examples of assets include cash, accounts receivable, inventory, investments, land, buildings, equipment, and goodwill. From the accounting equation, we see that the amount of assets must equal the combined amount of liabilities plus owner's equity.

Liabilities are a company's obligations – amounts the company owes. Examples of liabilities include loans (short-term debt, long-term debt), accounts payable, salaries and wages payable, interest payable, and income taxes payable. Liabilities can be viewed – along with stockholder equity – as a source of the company's assets.

Owner's equity is the amount left over after liabilities are deducted from assets:

$$Assets - Liabilities = Owner's\ Equity$$

Owner's equity also reports the amounts invested in the company by the owners plus the cumulative net income of the company that has not been withdrawn or distributed to the owners. The accounting equation should always be "in balance", meaning the left side should always equal the right side. The balance is maintained because every business transaction affects at least 2 of a company's accounts as we mentioned earlier.

EXHIBIT 2.3 General rules of debit and credit

A company keeps track of all of its transactions by recording them in accounts in the company's general ledger. Each account in the general ledger is designated as to its type: asset, liability, owner's equity, revenue, expense, gain, or loss account. The general debit and credit rules that apply to the aforementioned types of accounts are shown in Exhibits 2.3 and 2.4.

Debits are analogous to additions (+) in mathematics and likewise credits to subtractions (−). Thus, assets are increased by debiting them and are decreased by crediting them. For example, when we buy an asset we debit the relevant account and when we sell it we credit it. On the other hand, liabilities accounts are decreased by debiting them and increased by crediting them. So, when we buy something on credit from a supplier, our liability to him increases and thus we credit the relevant account. When we pay him, our liability decreases and thus we debit the account by the same amount.

The same applies to equity accounts. They are increased (credited) when capital, revenues, and gains (e.g. from a sale of an asset) are poured into the company. On the other hand, equity accounts are decreased (debited) when capital in the form of dividends to the owner, expenses (e.g. payroll), and losses (e.g. from sale of an investment) drain the company's resources.

The above transactions are recorded in the general ledger which in turn is used by accountants in order to prepare the financial statements. The most common financial statements are shown below:

- The balance sheet: provides a "snapshot" of the firm's financial condition, like a picture taken at a specific date.
- The income statement: reports on the "performance" of the firm like a movie for a period of time (monthly, quarterly, annual).
- The statement of cash flows: reports the cash receipts and cash outflows classified according to operating, investment, and financing activities.
- The statement of stockholder's equity: reports the amounts and sources of changes in equity from transactions with owners.
- The footnotes of the financial statements: allow users to improve assessment of the amount, timing, and uncertainty of the estimates reported in the financial statements.

EXHIBIT 2.4 Expanding the rules of debit and credit to owner's equity

Two of the principal financial statements, the income statement and the balance sheet, can be prepared directly from the accounts. Preparation of the statement of cash flows requires further analysis of the accounts. Let us now look in more detail at each of the above financial statements.

2.2 THE BALANCE SHEET

The balance sheet is a snapshot of a business's financial condition at a specific moment in time, usually at the close of an accounting period. A balance sheet comprises of assets, liabilities, and owner's equity and helps the reader quickly get a handle on the financial strength and capabilities of a business. For example is the business in a position to expand? Balance sheets can identify and analyze trends, particularly in the area of receivables and payables. Is the receivables cycle lengthening? Can receivables be collected more aggressively? Is some debt uncollectable? Has the business been slowing down payables to forestall an inevitable cash shortage? Exhibit 2.5 indicates the general format of a balance sheet presentation:

Assets	Liabilities & Owner's Equity
Non–Current Assets	Owner's Equity
Fixed assets	Capital stock
Intangible assets	Additional paid-in capital
Long-term investments	Retained earnings
Current Assets	Liabilities
Inventory	Long-term liabilities
Accounts receivable	Long-term debt
Cash	Current liabilities
Other Assets	Short-term debt
	Accounts payable
	Other liabilities

EXHIBIT 2.5   Balance sheet classifications

Let us describe below each of the above balance sheet accounts.

Non-current assets: Assets held for longer than a year. They include fixed assets, intangible assets, and long-term investments usually bought either because they are essential for the operations of a business or for the purpose of capital gains.

Fixed assets: Fixed assets include land, buildings, machinery, and vehicles that are used in connection with the business, i.e. properties of a durable nature used in the regular operations of the business.

- **Land:** Land is considered a fixed asset but, unlike other fixed assets, is not depreciated, because land is considered an asset that never wears out. We will explain later the concept of depreciation.
- **Buildings:** Buildings are depreciated over time.
- **Office equipment:** This includes office equipment such as copiers, fax machines, printers, and computers used in the business.

- **Machinery:** Machinery represents machines and equipment used to produce the product. Examples of machinery might include an oil rig, a food processing plant, or a baggage handling system.
- **Vehicles:** Include under this head any vehicles used in the business that have been bought and are not leased.

Intangible assets: They lack physical substance and usually have a high degree of uncertainty concerning their future benefits. They include patents, copyrights, franchises, goodwill, trademarks, trade names, secret processes, and organization costs. Generally, all of these intangibles are written off (amortized) to expense over 4 to 8 years. The concept of amortization is similar to that of depreciation that we will explain later.

Long-term investments: They are to be held for many years, and are not acquired with the intention of disposing of them in the near future. They can be:

- Investments in securities such as bonds or common stock that management does not intend to sell within 1 year.
- Investments in tangible fixed assets not currently used in operations of the business such as real estate held for speculation.
- Investments set aside in special funds such as a pension fund.
- Investments in subsidiaries or affiliated companies.

Current assets: These are cash and other assets expected to be converted into cash, sold, or consumed in the operating cycle. The operating cycle is the average time between the acquisition of materials and supplies and the realization of cash through sales of the product for which the materials and supplies were acquired. A complete operating cycle is shown in Exhibit 2.6.

The cycle operates from cash through inventory, production, and receivables back to cash. Where there are several operating cycles within 1 year, the 1-year period is used. If the operating cycle is more than 1 year, the longer period is used. Current assets are presented in the balance sheet in order of liquidity. The 4 major items found in the current asset section are:

- **Cash:** Include under this head cash in bank accounts and marketable securities, such as government bonds, commercial paper, and/or other money market instruments.
- **Accounts receivable:** Amounts owed to the firm by its customers for goods and services delivered.

EXHIBIT 2.6 The operating cycle

- **Inventories:** Products that will be sold in the normal course of business or existing stocks.
- **Prepaid expenses:** These are expenditures already made for services to be received within the operating cycle assuming it is no longer than a year. Typical examples are pre-paid rent, advertising, taxes, insurance policy, and office or operating supplies. They are reported at the amount of unexpired or unconsumed cost.

Other assets: These vary widely in practice. Examples include deferred charges (long-term prepaid expenses), non-current receivables, intangible assets, and advances to subsidiaries.

Liabilities and owner's equity: This includes all debts and obligations owed by the business to outside creditors, vendors, or banks plus the owner's equity. Often this side of the balance sheet is simply referred to as "liabilities".

Long-term liabilities: These are obligations that are not reasonably expected to be liqui-dated within the normal operating cycle but, instead, at some date beyond that time. Long-term debt, deferred income taxes, lease obligations, and pension obligations are the most common long-term liabilities.

Current liabilities: These are obligations that are reasonably expected to be liquidated within the operating cycle. They include accounts payable, accrued items (e.g. accrued pay-roll), income taxes payable, current maturities of long-term debt, etc.

- **Accounts payable:** This includes all short-term obligations owed by the business to creditors, suppliers, and other vendors. Accounts payable can include supplies and materials acquired on credit.
- **Accrued payroll:** This includes any earned wages that are owed to or for employees but have not yet been paid.

The excess of total current assets over total current liabilities is referred to as working capital. It represents the net amount of a company's relatively liquid resources; that is, it is the liquid buffer, or margin of safety, available to meet the financial demands of the operating cycle.

Owner's equity: Sometimes this is referred to as stockholders' equity. Owner's equity is made up of the initial investment in the business as well as any retained earnings that are reinvested in the business. The section is usually divided into 3 parts:

- **Capital stock:** The par or stated value of the shares issued.
- **Additional paid-in capital:** The excess of amounts paid in over the par or stated value.
- **Retained earnings:** The earnings reinvested in the business after the deduction of any distributions to shareholders, such as dividend payments.

A more managerial balance sheet view could be obtained by rewriting the accounting equation presented in the previous section as follows:

Fixed Assets + Commercial Current Assets + Cash + Other Long & Short-term Assets = Commercial Current Liabilities + Debt (Long & Short-term) + Grants + Owner's Equity,

or

Fixed Assets + Commercial Working Capital + Other Working Capital + Other Long/ Short-term Assets (net of liabilities) = Debt − Cash + Grants + Owner's Equity,

or

$$\boxed{\text{Capital Employed} = \text{Financing}}$$

where

Capital Employed = Fixed Assets + Commercial Working Capital + Other Working Capital +
Other Long/Short-term Assets (net of liabilities),
Financing = Net Debt + Grants + Owner's Equity, and Commercial Working Capital
= Accounts Receivable + Inventory − Accounts Payable

Finally the reader should be aware that many companies intentionally keep financing instruments off balance sheet in order to avoid affecting solvency ratios (see Section 2.6). These instruments are so-called "off balance sheet" items and are mainly liabilities that are not shown on a company's balance sheet although off balance sheet assets may also exist. By keeping them off the balance sheet, however, companies violate accounting standards in order to meet Wall Street's expectations and "fool" investors. Remember the case of Enron – one of the high-flying stocks on Wall Street throughout the 1990s – that deceived investors by keeping more than $13 billion of debt off balance sheet. Eventually Enron filed for bankruptcy on 2 December 2001. At the time, this bankruptcy was the largest in US history.

2.3 THE INCOME STATEMENT

An income statement shows what has happened in a business over a specific period of time, usually a year. As you can see in Exhibit 2.7, the income statement is the flow statement that links 2 balance sheets.

A **single-step income statement** groups revenues together and expenses together, without further classifying either of the groups. A **multi-step income statement** makes further classifications to provide additional important revenue and expense data. These classifications make the income statement more informative and useful. It is recommended because:

- it recognizes a separation of operating transactions from non-operating transactions;
- it matches costs and expenses with related revenues;
- it highlights certain intermediate components of income that are used for the computation of ratios used to assess the performance of the business.

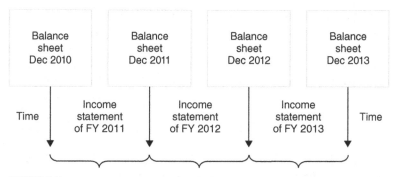

EXHIBIT 2.7   Relationship between balance sheet and income statement

The details of a multi-step income statement are broken down into the following major categories, as shown in Exhibit 2.8:

Sales
− Cost of Goods Sold
  ✓ Material
  ✓ Labour
  ✓ Fixed Costs of Goods Sold
= **Gross Profit**
+ Other Income from Operations
− Operating Expenses
  ✓ Sales and Marketing
  ✓ Research and Development
  ✓ General and Administrative
− Other Operating Expenses
= **Income from Operations (EBIT or EBITDA)**
+/−Interest Income / Interest Expense
− Depreciation
= **Income before Taxes**
− Income Taxes
= **Net Income after Taxes**

EXHIBIT 2.8   Breakdown of a multi-step income statement

Let us describe below each of the above income statement accounts.

Sales: These are the revenues generated from selling a company's products or services, and are generally recorded when a product is shipped or a service is provided. Sales are generally recorded by product lines that are appropriate for managerial purposes.

Cost of goods sold: This is recorded in the same time period (monthly or annually) as the sales revenue. In other words, we always record the sale and the costs associated with the products sold together. Cost of goods sold consists of material, labour and fixed cost of goods sold expenses.

- **Material:** This expense category is for materials purchased from other companies that are assembled or processed to become part of a company's product.
- **Labour:** This expense category is for the cost of the salaries for people directly involved with the assembly and manufacture of a company's products or the provision of its services. Labour consists of gross base salary plus overtime plus employer's social security contributions plus fringe benefits plus bonuses. Labour and material are considered variable costs, meaning that they vary directly with the volume of sales or production.
- **Fixed costs of goods sold:** Fixed costs of goods sold are the costs associated with producing products that tend to remain the same whether the sales volume increases or decreases. The following are some common fixed cost of goods sold expenses that could be included in a forecast:
  - **Production salaries:** These are salaries of personnel who hold "permanent" production management positions; in other words, positions that exist independent of sales volume, rather than positions that are regularly added or eliminated as sales volume fluctuates.
  - **Production facility expenses:** These are the costs to operate production-related facilities, including warehouse space and distribution centres.

- **Production equipment rental:** These are the costs for production equipment that is rented or leased rather than purchased.
- **Other production expenses:** Any other production-related expenses that were not covered by the previous categories could be summarized in a general category such as this.

All costs associated with producing products or providing services should be included in the "cost of goods sold" section of an income statement. Any significant cost that is variable in nature should be allocated on a percentage basis to material, labour, or both. Costs that are not significant may be allocated in the fixed cost section, even if they are variable in nature. A more detailed discussion of fixed and variable costs can be found in Section 4.4 of Chapter 4 (Forecasting Costs).

Gross profit: This is calculated as the total sales less the total cost of goods sold and is a measure of the efficiency of the management in controlling the costs (labour and materials) of the production process.

Operating expenses: They are commonly grouped into sales and marketing, research and development, and general and administrative categories. These categories represent all of the expenses involved in the day-to-day operations of a company other than what is included in the cost of goods sold paragraph described above:

- **Sales and marketing:** This expense category includes all the costs associated with marketing and selling products or services.
- **Research and development:** This expense category includes all the costs associated with the research and development of products or services.
- **General and administrative:** This expense category includes all the costs associated with the day-to-day operations (like lawyers' fees, maintenance, IT, office supplies, etc.).

Income from operations: This is calculated as the total gross profit less the total operating expenses. Finance professionals, when talking about the income from operations, sometimes refer to EBIT which is defined as the Earnings before Interest and Taxes or to EBITDA which is defined as the Earnings before Interest and Taxes Depreciation and Amortization. EBITDA is a measure of a company's ability to make money from its core business operations no matter how it is financed. For the depreciation and amortization descriptions see below.

Interest income/interest expense: This section includes non-operating costs such as interest income and expense. These items relate to the financing and not to the operations of a business. Separating these costs makes it easier to evaluate the fundamental profitability of a business without regard to whether the company is financed with debt, equity, or both.

Depreciation: Part of this is included in general and administrative and sales and marketing and part in cost of goods sold. Depreciation is the technique accountants use to apply the cost of fixed assets like buildings, equipment, furniture and fixtures, and cars and trucks to the sales they help generate. Unlike inventory, which is sold fairly quickly, these assets usually last for a number of years. Depreciation, therefore, is a method for expensing (prorating) the cost of the asset over its expected lifetime. Generally, straight-line depreciation is used for financial reporting. The price of the asset less its residual value (if any) is divided evenly over the estimated useful life. That constant amount is then recorded as depreciation expense for each period during the useful life (residual, or salvage, value is the value an asset has after its assigned useful life has elapsed).

There are other methods of depreciation, but in order to build our financial model we will use the most common method: the abovementioned straight-line depreciation.

Amortization: Similar to depreciation which refers to tangible assets, this refers to intangible assets.

Profit before taxes: This is calculated as the total income from operations less the net interest expense, that is, interest expense minus interest income.

Income taxes: These include all federal and state income taxes. Taxes are recorded based on when the income was earned, not when it is due to be paid. Assuming that the income tax expense will be positive for the year, it is traditional to calculate the effective average tax rate for the year and apply this rate to each month's income before taxes. This means that if there is a loss for an individual month, the income tax expense will be negative for that month, reflecting the tax savings that resulted from the loss. If there is no income tax expense for the full year, which is common for businesses that lose money, zero income tax expense should be estimated.

Net income after taxes: This is calculated as the total income before taxes less the total income taxes.

2.3.1 Cash Accounting Versus Accrual Accounting

The income statement is normally prepared by making use of the accrual principle of accounting. Under the *accrual principle*, revenue is considered earned and is recognized in statements for the period when the revenue transaction occurred, regardless of when the related cash is collected. For example, under the accrual method, a practice's earnings are posted at the time services are provided. Similarly, expenses are incurred at the moment the liability is incurred, regardless of payment terms. This principle is very different from the cash-basis accounting system. Under the cash-basis method of accounting, revenue is not recognized until it is received and expenses are not recognized until they are paid. The accrual principle of accounting is widely used and is the one that we will use for the projections we make in the rest of this book.

2.4 THE CASH FLOW STATEMENT

The primary purpose of the statement of cash flow is to provide information regarding a company's cash receipts and cash payments. The statement complements the income statement and balance sheet. Over the life of a company, total net income and net cash inflow will be equal. However, since income determination is based on accrual accounting, income and cash flow will rarely be equal in an annual accounting period.

The importance of cash flow is based on the simple fact that a company's obligations are satisfied with cash not profit. That is why cash is often referred to as "King". It is possible for a company to be very profitable and not be able to service its obligations. The cash flow statement is an important analytical tool used to determine whether a company is able to generate sufficient cash to meet its trade obligations. The ability of a company to adapt during a period of financial adversity, to obtain financing, and generate adequate amounts of cash for specific purposes are very important factors in order to evaluate its solvency, liquidity position, and financial flexibility.

Cash flow analysis provides valuable information about the quality of earnings. The higher the correlation between income and cash flow, the higher the earnings quality. The statement also provides insight into how effective the management team is at utilizing available resources and the company's ability to generate cash flows in the future. It provides a picture of where the cash comes from and where it goes. The Financial Accounting

Standards Board (FASB)[2] requires that a statement of cash flows accompany the income statement and the balance sheet. The FASB also requires that cash flows should be classified as operating, investing, and financing activities. The statement of cash flows must summarize the cash flows so that net cash provided or used by each of the 3 types of activities is reported.

2.4.1 Operating Activities

The statement provides information about the cash generated from a company's primary operating activities. Operating activities relate to a company's primary revenue-generating activities, and include customer collections from sales of products or services, receipts of interest and dividends, and other operating cash receipts. Operating activities that create cash outflows include payments to suppliers, payments to employees, interest payments, payment of income taxes, and other operating cash payments.

2.4.2 Investing Activities

Investing activities include lending money and collecting interest on those loans, buying and selling productive assets that are expected to generate revenues over long periods, and buying and selling securities not classified as cash equivalents. Cash inflows generated by investing activities include sales of assets such as property, plant, and equipment, sales of debt or equity instruments, and the collection of loans.

2.4.3 Financing Activities

Financing activities include borrowing and repaying money from creditors, obtaining resources from shareholders, for example through a share capital increase, and providing a return to shareholders in the form of dividends.

2.4.4 Income Flows and Cash Flows

As we mentioned earlier, the income statement and balance sheet are based on accrual accounting which was developed based on the concept of matching. The *matching principle* states that revenues generated and the expenses incurred to generate those revenues should be reported in the same income statement. This emphasizes the cause-and-effect association between revenue and expense. Many revenues and expenses result from accruals and allocations that do not affect cash. There are 2 classes of items that cause differences between income flows and cash flows: items that appear on the income statement that do not represent inflows and outflows of cash, such as depreciation, or items whose cash effects do not relate to operating activities, such as gains on the sale of fixed assets; and operating cash inflows and outflows that do not appear on the income statement, that must be reported on the statement of cash flows. For example a company may collect in the current period cash arising from credit sales made in a previous period. As a rule of thumb we can use the table in Exhibit 2.9 as a guide to determine the effect of balance changes. The table states that a decrease in an asset balance and an increase in a liability or equity account are cash inflows. The opposite holds true for increases in an asset balance or a decrease in a liability or equity account, which results in a cash outflow.

Cash Inflow	Cash Outflow
A Decrease in an Asset Account	An Increase in an Asset Account
An Increase in a Liability Account	A Decrease in a Liability Account
An Increase in an Equity Account	A Decrease in an Equity Account

EXHIBIT 2.9   Cash effects of balance sheet account changes

2.4.5 Preparing the Statement of Cash Flows

Information used to prepare this statement is obtained from the income statement for the year and comparative balance sheets for the last 2 years. Net income is adjusted in order to convert the accrual basis income statement to cash flows. As discussed earlier, the statement which follows is divided into operating, investing, and financing activities. There are 2 methods of calculating and reporting the net cash flow from operating activities. The *direct method* reports gross cash inflows and gross outflows from operating activities but is not as widely used as the indirect method as it is more complex to implement. The *indirect method* uses a format that differs from the direct method only in the section where net cash provided or used by operating activities is calculated. The investing and financing sections of the statement of cash flows are exactly the same under either method. When we use the indirect method to determine cash flows, we start with the net income figure from the income statement and adjust the net income amount to determine the net amount of cash provided or used in operating activities. In other words, we are reconciling the accrual method of accounting to the cash basis of accounting. We also examine the changes in current assets and current liabilities.

Below is a mathematical derivation of the cash flow statement under the indirect method. Let us use the accounting equation and modify it slightly by splitting cash from assets.

$$\text{Cash} + \text{Non-Cash Assets} = \text{Liabilities} + \text{Equity}$$

If we solve for Cash, we have:

$$\text{Cash} = \text{Liabilities} + \text{Equity} - \text{Non-Cash Assets}$$

We use the symbol Δ(delta) to define "change in" and apply it to the revised accounting equation:

$$\Delta\text{Cash} = \Delta\text{Liabilities} + \Delta\text{Equity} - \Delta\text{Non-Cash Assets}$$

This means that by examining the liabilities, equity, and non-cash asset accounts for changes from one period to another we are able to explain the change in the cash account.

If we split now:

Non-Cash Assets into Fixed Assets (FA) = CAPital EXpenditure (CAPEX) − Depreciation (Dep), Accounts Receivable (AR) and Inventory (INV),

Liabilities into Long-Term Debt (LTD), Short-Term Debt (STD) and Accounts Payable (AP), and

Equity into Share Capital (SC) and Retained Earnings (RE) = Net Income (NI) − Dividends (Div)

we may rewrite the above equation as follows:

$$\Delta Cash = \Delta(LTD + STD + AP) + \Delta(SC + RE) - \Delta(FA + AR + INV) \text{ or}$$

$$\Delta Cash = \Delta D + \Delta AP + \Delta SC + \Delta(NI - Div) - \Delta(CAPEX - Dep) - \Delta AR - \Delta INV, \text{ where}$$

$$D = Debt = LTD + STD, \text{ or}$$

$$\Delta Cash = \Delta D - \Delta WCR + \Delta SC + \Delta NI - \Delta Div - \Delta CAPEX + \Delta Dep,$$

where

$$WCR = \text{Working Capital Requirements} = AR + INV - AP, \text{ or}$$

$$\Delta Cash = (NI + Dep - \Delta WCR) - \Delta CAPEX + (\Delta SC + \Delta D - Div),$$

where

$$NI = \Delta NI, Div = \Delta Div \text{ and } Dep = \Delta Dep,$$

that is the net income difference between 2 balance sheet periods is the net income derived directly from the income statement and the same applies to the depreciation. Moreover dividends can be derived directly from a complementary financial statement, that of retained earnings, and this is the amount given back to shareholders within the reporting period.

What we see in the last equation is that the change in cash between 2 periods, $\Delta Cash$, equals, as shown in Exhibit 2.10:

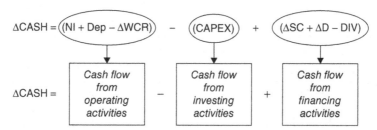

EXHIBIT 2.10 Mathematical derivation of the indirect method of the cash flow statement

Exhibits 2.11 and 2.12 present a sample statement of cash flows derived by both the direct method and the indirect method for the ABC Corporation for the fiscal year ended 20XX. A comparison of the direct method with the indirect method indicates that either method will generate the same results in terms of the operating activities of ABC for 20XX.

2.5 THE ARTICULATION OF INCOME STATEMENT, BALANCE SHEET, AND CASH FLOW STATEMENTS

When we record sales or expense entries using double entry accounting, we either increase an asset or decrease a liability in case of sales or we decrease an asset or increase a liability in case of an expense. Therefore, one side of every sales and expense entry is in the income statement, and the other side is in the balance sheet. We can't record a sale or an expense

ABC Corporation Statement of Cash Flows for the Year Ended
31 December 20XX

Cash Flows from Operating Activities (Indirect Method)	(€)	(€)
Net Income	65,000	
Adjustments to reconcile net income to net cash provided by operating activities		
Depreciation Expense	25,000	
Increase in Accounts Receivable	(10,000)	
Decrease in Inventories	25,000	
Increase in Accounts Payable	10,000	
Increase in Accrued Payroll	5,000	
Net Cash Provided by Operating Activities		**120,000**
Cash Flows from Investing Activities		
Sale of Equipment	30,000	
Purchase of Equipment	(40,000)	
Purchase of Land	(10,000)	
Net Cash Provided by Investing Activities		**(20,000)**
Cash Flows from Financing Activities		
Debt Repayment	(35,000)	
Payment of Dividends	(35,000)	
Net Cash Used by Financing Activities		**(70,000)**
Net Increase in Cash		**30,000**
Cash at Beginning of Year		**50,000**
Cash at End of Year		**80,000**

EXHIBIT 2.11　Sample statement of cash flows using the indirect method

without affecting the balance sheet. The income statement and balance sheet are inseparable, but they are reported in a different way. To interpret financial statements properly, we need to understand the links between the statements. Exhibit 2.13 shows the connection between income statement and balance sheet through the statement of retained earnings. Moreover we see the connection between the cash flow statement and the 2 recent balance sheets that we have described in detail in the previous section.

Below is a list of example transactions that affect both income statement (IS) and balance sheet (BS) accounts:

- Making sales on credit (IS) generates accounts receivable (BS).
- Selling products (IS) decreases the company's inventory (BS).
- Selling products or consuming raw materials (IS) involves prior purchases on credit that generate accounts payable and increases inventory (BS).
- Depreciation expense (IS) is recorded for the use of fixed assets. It is recorded in the accumulated depreciation contra account (BS).

ABC Corporation Statement of Cash Flows for the Year Ended
31 December 20XX

Cash Flows from Operating Activities (Direct Method)	(€)	(€)
Cash collections from Customers	250,000	
Cash payments to Suppliers	(85,000)	
Cash Payments for Salaries	(30,000)	
Cash Payments for Interest	(15,000)	
Net Cash Provided by Operating Activities		120,000
Cash Flows from Investing Activities		
Sale of Equipment	30,000	
Purchase of Equipment	(40,000)	
Purchase of Land	(10,000)	
Net Cash Provided by Investing Activities		**(20,000)**
Cash Flows from Financing Activities		
Debt Repayment	(35,000)	
Payment of Dividends	(35,000)	
Net Cash Used by Financing Activities		**(70,000)**
Net Increase in Cash		30,000
Cash at Beginning of Year		50,000
Cash at End of Year		80,000

EXHIBIT 2.12   Sample statement of cash flows using the direct method

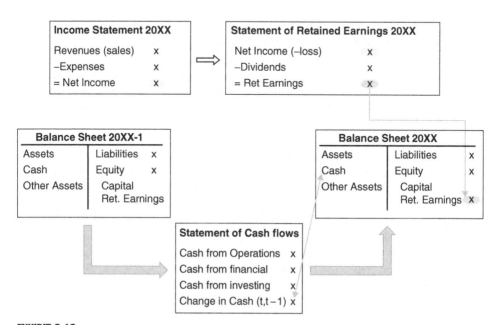

EXHIBIT 2.13   Connections between the 3 major financial statements

- Operating expenses (IS) is a broad category of costs encompassing selling, administrative, and general expenses:
  - Some of these operating costs are prepaid before the expense is recorded, and until the expense is recorded, the cost stays in the prepaid expenses asset account (BS).
  - Some of these operating costs involve purchases on credit that generate accounts payable (BS).
  - Some of these operating costs are from recording unpaid expenses in the accrued expenses payable liability (BS).
- Borrowing money increases liabilities (BS) and causes interest expense (IS).
- A portion of income tax expense (IS) for the year is unpaid at year-end, which is recorded as an accrued expenses payable liability (BS).
- Net income (IS) increases retained earnings and thus the shareholders' equity account (BS) whereas paying dividends decreases the aforementioned accounts.

Moreover, cash flow from operating activities starts with profit before tax from the income statement and then several adjustments are made in order to determine the final cash outcome. These adjustments have to do with the increases or decreases of the relevant balance sheet accounts. For example, the accounts receivable asset is increased (debited) when sales are made on credit. The inventory asset account is decreased (credited) when recording cost of goods sold expenses. The accounts payable account is increased (credited) when recording expenses that have not been paid. Cash flow adjustments to profit before tax are based on the 2 consecutive balance sheet changes and can be summarized as shown below:

- An asset increase during the period decreases cash flow from profit.
- A liability decrease during the period decreases cash flow from profit.
- An asset decrease during the period increases cash flow from profit.
- A liability increase during the period increases cash flow from profit.

2.6 FINANCIAL STATEMENT ANALYSIS: RATIO ANALYSIS

Financial analysis is part of a greater framework of business analysis that allows analysts to assess the performance of a company and identify in advance potential indicators of deterioration or even failure. Several factors can affect a company's performance as you can see in Exhibit 2.14.

The financial position is the most obvious one. Deteriorating profitability, liquidity, and solvency will lead to detrimental results for the company as we will see later on in this section. The financial position of a company is affected by the quality of the people that run it, that is, the quality of its management. A CEO that is also the chairperson, so that there is no segregation of duties, and a weak finance function with no strategic plans, inaccurate costing systems, poor cash flow forecasts and ineffective controls set in place are signs of poor management. Of course there is the case of management fraud. Frequent changes in accounting policies and the auditors of the company and ambiguous related party transactions are all signs of possible management fraud. The International Accounting Standards Board (IASB) has tried to regulate changes in accounting policies and related party transactions with the International Accounting Standards – IAS 8 and IAS 24 respectively. Operating/internal factors are company-related factors such as ineffective marketing and distribution network, non-competitive production costs, poor working capital management, and high turnover in key personnel that

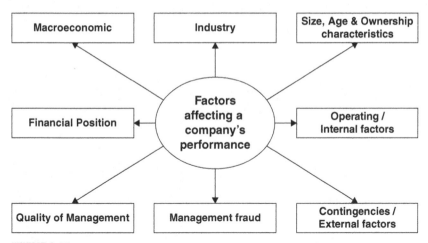

EXHIBIT 2.14   Factors affecting a company's performance

can cause structural problems in the long run. Size, age, and ownership characteristics are the last company-related factors than can make a difference in a company's performance. For example large companies have more controls in place than smaller ones and are less likely to become victims of internal fraud. Similarly public or listed companies are more transparent than private companies. Finally there is strong evidence that younger firms grow faster than older ones and thus incorporate higher risk and failure rates.

The other broad category of risk factors is industry related. For example, a high degree of competition or market saturation, accompanied by declining margins and rapid changes in the industry, such as significant declines in customer demand or rapid product obsolescence can lead to business failure. Similarly other contingencies and external factors like the loss of a major market or customer or supplier may have fatal results.

Finally macroeconomic environment is the last but not least significant reason for business failure. In most cases, an economic downturn only exposes entities which are over leveraged (i.e. have too much debt) or poorly managed. More businesses collapse during economic downturns and recessions.

Some of the above factors can be identified with quantitative analysis of the financial statements such as ratio analysis. Ratio analysis provides the analyst with information about the company relative to its peers. However, ratios do not inform the analyst as to why the observed results occurred – knowledge that is essential to the understanding of business risk and the probability that a company's estimated future economic benefits will be realized. This is where qualitative analysis that cannot be derived from the financial statements comes in. As a company operates on a day-to-day basis, it and its competitors are affected by external forces that require the analyst to conduct thorough risk analyses. The disciplines of strategic management and organizational theory provide useful tools such as the *business strategy* analysis of a firm's capability to create a sustainable competitive advantage. A more complete framework of risk analysis has been developed by credit rating agencies and credit professionals and consists of a hybrid approach that includes both quantitative and qualitative analysis as shown in Exhibit 2.15. The outcome of such an analysis is a score which usually falls within a rating scale and classifies the risk of a company from minimal (no risk, sound financials and

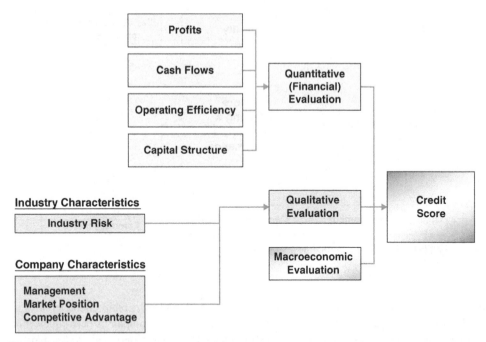

EXHIBIT 2.15 Company credit risk analysis framework

prospect) to loss (very high risk, high probability of default). However, such an analysis is outside the scope of this book.

Returning to quantitative analysis, ratio analysis is perhaps the most commonly used financial analysis tool. Financial ratios allow the analyst to assess and analyze the financial health of a company, its strengths and weaknesses, in terms of such measures as liquidity, performance, profitability, leverage, and growth, on an absolute basis and by comparison with other companies in its industry or the industry standard. The power of financial ratios comes from comparing them to relative ratios representing the general economy, the firm's industry, the firm's major competitors, and even the firm's own past performance record. The comparison of the firm's ratios to the aggregate economy is important because most firms are influenced by the general business cycle.

Two common types of ratio analyses exist: trend analysis (common-size analysis) and cross-sectional analysis. Trend analysis compares the company's ratios over a specified historical time period and identifies trends that might indicate financial performance improvement or deterioration. Common-size statements normalize balance sheet and income statements and allow the analyst to make easier comparisons of different sized firms. A common-size balance sheet expresses all balance sheet accounts as a percentage of total assets. A common-size income statement expresses all income statement items as a percentage of sales.

Common-size ratios convert the individual line items on the income statement to percentages. Raw numbers hide relevant information that percentages frequently unveil. Common-size income statement ratios are especially useful in studying trends in costs and profit margins.

$$\text{Common-size IS ratios} = \text{Income Statement Account} / \text{Sales}$$

Balance sheet accounts can also be converted to common-size ratios by dividing each balance sheet item by total assets.

Common-size BS ratios = Balance Sheet Account / Total Assets

Cross-sectional analysis compares a specified company's ratios to other companies or to industry standards/norms. It is most useful when the companies analyzed are reasonably comparable, e.g. business type, revenue size, product mix, degree of diversification, asset size, capital structure, markets served, geographic location, and the use of similar accounting methods. Moreover, in order to produce a meaningful analysis and compare like with like, financial statements need to be prepared in accordance with Generally Accepted Accounting Principles (GAAP) such as International Financial Reporting Standards (IFRS). The analyst performing ratio analysis is primarily interested that the company being analyzed will continue to operate in the foreseeable future or that the so-called "going concern" principle applies. Three main categories of financial ratios, when falling within industry norms, can ensure survival. These ratio categories represent the Holy Grail of corporate finance and are shown in Exhibit 2.16:

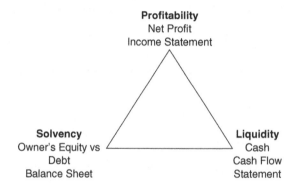

EXHIBIT 2.16   The Holy Grail of corporate finance: profitability, liquidity, and solvency

Profitability is examined because it is the primary goal of all business ventures. Without profitability the business will not survive in the long run. Liquidity is examined because every stakeholder is interested in the ability of the business to meet its short-term debt obligations. Finally Solvency is examined because it is a measure of the ability of the business to meet its long-term obligations. We will examine each of these 3 categories in turn and calculate the relevant ratios based on a year-end balance instead of the average beginning and ending year balances.

2.6.1 Profitability Ratios

The ratios in this section measure the ability of the business to make a profit which is the primary goal of every business, apart perhaps of the non-profit organizations.

We will examine the following ratios:

- Gross profit margin
- EBITDA margin

- EBIT margin or operating profit margin
- Net profit margin
- Return on equity – ROE
- Return on assets – ROA
- Return on invested capital – ROIC.

Gross profit margin: Is the indicator of how much profit is earned from selling a company's products without taking selling and administration costs into consideration. It is important that this ratio should always be positive and the higher it is the better. There is no norm about what is an accepted gross profit margin but a company should have enough gross profit to cover its operating and funding costs.

Gross Profit Margin = Gross Profit / Total Sales, where Gross Profit = Sales less Cost of Goods Sold

EBITDA margin: Determines how profitable a company is with regard to its operations. EBITDA margin is calculated by taking the company's earnings before interest, tax, amortization, and depreciation and dividing it by the company's total amount of sales.

EBITDA Margin = EBITDA / Total Sales

EBIT margin: Another ratio similar to the above that takes into account the depreciation expense of the period and compares earnings before interest and taxes (EBIT) to sales. Again this ratio shows how successful a company's management has been at generating income from the operation of the business.

Operating Profit (EBIT) Margin = Operating Profit (EBIT) / Sales

Net profit margin: Shows how much profit comes from each euro of sales.

Net Profit Margin = Net Profit / Total Sales

Return on Equity – ROE: determines the rate of return of the funds invested by the shareholders in the company. As an owner or shareholder this is one of the most important ratios as it shows the hard fact about the company – whether it is making enough of a profit to compensate for the risk of being a shareholder.

ROE = Net Profit / Equity

Return on Assets – ROA: is a measure of how effectively assets are used to generate a return. ROA shows the amount of income for each euro tied up in assets.

ROA = Net Profit / Total Assets

Return on Invested Capital – RoIC: is a measure of how effectively the capital invested in the company (as defined by owner's equity plus all kinds of debt) is used to generate a return. RoIC shows the amount of return for each euro invested in the company. Sometimes this ratio is referred as **Return on Capital Employed** or ROCE although you may find in the literature that these 2 ratios differ as well, as the numerator of RoIC can take various forms (profit before tax, profit after tax, net operating profit less adjusted taxes, and so on). For the purposes of this book RoIC is defined as:

RoIC = Net Profit / (Owner's Equity + Debt)

and is a very useful metric especially when compared with a company's Weighed Average Cost of Capital or WACC (see Chapter 5 for an analytic derivation of WACC). A RoIC greater than WACC shows that, as the company invests in its operations, it is adding value. On the other hand, a ROIC less than WACC shows the opposite: that the company destroys value as it invests more capital.

2.6.2 Liquidity Ratios

Financial ratios in this category measure the company's capacity to pay its debts as they fall due. The most important ratios in this category are the following:

- Current ratio
- Quick ratio
- Cash conversion cycle (net operating cycle).

Current ratio: This is the ratio between all current assets and all current liabilities or another way of expressing liquidity.

$$\text{Current Ratio} = \text{Current Assets / Current Liabilities}$$

A current ratio of 1:1 means that a company has €1.00 in current assets to cover each €1.00 in current liabilities. A current ratio as close to 2:1 as possible is a healthy indicator. One problem with the current ratio is that it ignores timing of cash received and paid out. For example, if all the bills are due this week, and inventory is the only current asset, but won't be sold until the end of the month, the current ratio tells us very little about the company's ability to survive.

Quick ratio: This is the ratio between all assets quickly convertible into cash and all current liabilities. It specifically excludes inventory.

$$\text{Quick Ratio} = \text{Cash} + \text{Accounts Receivable / Current Liabilities}$$

This ratio indicates the extent to which a company could pay current liabilities without relying on the sale of inventory – how quickly it can pay its bills. A ratio of 1:1 is considered good and indicates that it does not have to rely on the sale of inventory to pay its bills. Although a little better than the current ratio, the quick ratio still ignores timing of receipts and payments.

Cash conversion cycle: The time period that exists from when the firm pays out money for the purchase of raw materials to when it collects its money back from its customers.

$$\text{Cash conversion cycle} = \text{collection period} + \text{inventory period} - \text{payment period}$$

The collections period reveals the number of days it takes the company to collect its receivables and is determined by the following ratio:

$$\text{Days Sales Outstanding (DSO)} = \text{Accounts Receivable / Sales} \times 360\,\text{days}$$

The inventory period reveals the average number of days it will take the company to sell its inventory and is determined by the following ratio:

$$\text{Days Inventory Outstanding (DIO)} = \text{Inventory / Cost of Goods Sold} \times 360\,\text{days}$$

The above ratios, sometimes called asset management ratios, depend on the industry in which the company operates so they must always be compared to industry standards.

Finally the payment period shows the length of time trade payables are outstanding before they are paid and is determined by the following ratio:

$$\text{Days Payable Outstanding (DPO)} = \text{Accounts Payable} / \text{COGS} \times 360 \text{ days}$$

So the cash conversion cycle in days equals the DSO plus the DIO minus the DPO. The cash conversion cycle relates directly to the working capital of a company which is the part of the capital that is required to finance current assets such as accounts receivable and inventories. Working capital funds keep revolving fast and are constantly converted into cash and this cash flows out again in exchange for other current assets.

2.6.3 Solvency Ratios

Solvency is a measure of the long-term financial viability of a business which means its ability to pay off its long-term obligations such as bank loans and bonds payable. It can answer such questions as whether a company has the right amount of debt or if leveraging impacts its long-term viability. Information about solvency is critical for banks, employees, owners, bond holders, institutional investors, etc., as it shows the businesses' vulnerability to risk. These ratios are often used by creditors to determine the ability of the business to repay loans. The most common solvency ratios are the following:

- Total liabilities to equity ratio (financial leverage)
- Debt to equity ratio
- Debt to capital ratio
- Times interest earned ratio.

A business uses a combination of debt and equity to begin and maintain operations. Loans are often obtained to purchase equipment, fixtures, and inventory. Equity is contributed by owners or shareholders and builds with earnings that are retained for growth. Both types of capitalization are appropriate. But the degree to which a business uses debt to produce income, also known as leverage, impacts long-term solvency.

A business must be able to make principal and interest payments and continue profitable operations even through cyclical and economic downturns. A company that is too highly leveraged may become financially strained and end up bankrupt.

All categories of ratio analysis, including liquidity and profitability, provide information about financial viability. However, solvency ratio analysis provides a measure of whether a company is using a successful debt strategy and will likely remain solvent in the long run. As with all ratio analysis, the results provide early indicators of problems and suggest areas that require further investigation.

Total liabilities to equity ratio (financial leverage): Determines a company's use of financial leverage and is calculated as:

$$\text{Total Liabilities to Equity Ratio} = \text{Total Liabilities} / \text{Owner's Equity}$$

Total liabilities is a total on the balance sheet and includes all short- and long-term liabilities. The above ratio shows what percentage of a company's assets are financed by third parties including banks, suppliers, employees, the state, and any other stakeholder the company owes to. As a rule of thumb a ratio between 1:1 and 2:1 is acceptable but depends on the industry in which a company operates.

Debt to equity ratio: Shows the ratio between capital invested by the owners and the funds provided by lenders. One could argue that it is the most important measure of leverage and solvency.

$$\text{Debt to Equity Ratio} = \text{Total Debt} / \text{Owner's Equity}$$

The debt to equity ratio measures the balance between capitalizations provided by owners as compared to financing provided by creditors. An increasing amount of debt as a percentage of equity indicates that the company is funding operations and growth through creditors rather than through earnings. The higher this ratio the greater the risk present or future creditors face. Most lenders have credit guidelines and limits – the so-called covenants – for the debt to equity ratio (2:1 could be the highest acceptable value but again depends on the industry in which a company operates).

Too much debt can put a business at risk but too little debt may mean that management is not realizing the full potential of leveraging which in turn may hurt the overall returns to shareholders. This is particularly true for larger companies where shareholders want a higher reward (dividend rate) than lenders (interest rate).

Debt to capital ratio: similar to the debt to equity ratio, this is used to assess the debt structure of a company but is calculated as:

$$\text{Debt to Capital Ratio} = \text{Debt} / [\text{Debt} + \text{Owner's Equity}]$$

As a rule of thumb 40 to 60% of the company's assets could be financed through debt. A ratio that approaches 100% shows that a business is mostly financed by debt. Large interest payments can limit the amount of cash on hand and cut into profits.

Times interest earned ratio (interest coverage ratio): measures the company's ability to pay interest payments.

$$\text{Times Interest Earned} = \text{Earnings before Interest and Taxes} / \text{Interest Expense}$$

Earnings Before Interest and Taxes or EBIT as well as interest expense are both taken from the income statement. This ratio measures the number of times that operating income can cover interest expense. A number higher than 2.0 is generally a good indicator, although it may vary by industry. There are other forms of this ratio where, for example, one can take into account EBITDA instead of EBIT. Nevertheless the concept of the ratio remains the same.

2.6.4 Other Ratios

There are plenty of other ratios, for example the activity or efficiency ratios, measuring the efficiency with which a business uses its assets, such as inventories, accounts receivable, and fixed assets. Without going into detail the most common ratios of this category are the following:

- Inventory turnover – how many times inventory was turned over or sold in a year.
- Receivables turnover – how many times a period's revenue (sales) is recognized to the amount yet to be received.
- Payables turnover – how many times in a year the company pays off its creditors.
- Working capital turnover – how many sales are achieved with 1 unit of working capital.

- Working capital as a percentage of sales – what percentage of money needs to be invested in working capital for each euro of sales.
- Fixed asset turnover – how many sales are achieved with 1 unit of fixed assets.
- Total asset turnover – how many sales are achieved with 1 unit of total assets.
- Total assets to Owner's Equity – this is an indicator of the company's leverage used to finance its operations.

Another useful representation of ROE is the breakdown shown in Exhibit 2.17 into 3 components. This breakdown, originally developed by DuPont, is now in worldwide use. It's a fast and convenient financial measure that helps executives understand the relationships between profit, sales, total assets, and leverage. In particular, the model shows how a company generates profits (profit margin), how well it uses its assets to generate sales (asset turnover), and last but not least how it finances its assets. At its most basic level, as demonstrated by Exhibit 2.17, ROE can be broken down into:

$$ROE = \frac{Net\ Profit}{Sales} \times \frac{Sales}{Assets} \times \frac{Assets}{Owner's\ Equity}$$

profit margin   asset turnover   leverage ratio

EXHIBIT 2.17 DuPont's ROE breakdown into profit margin, asset turnover, and leverage ratio

Financial model and business case developers should craft plans that improve both turnover and profitability. A business plan that only increases profits and causes assets to swell is damaging to ROE and risky for the shareholder. Conversely, a plan to increase sales while decreasing total assets (say, by improving turnover) improves ROE and thus is desirable to shareholders.

All the ratios discussed previously are calculated in the "Ratios" worksheet provided in the website accompanying this book. The interested reader can access this particular worksheet and follow all the calculations that give rise to each ratio.

2.6.5 The Limitations of Financial Ratios

Although ratio analysis is widely used in practice, it is important for the user of this information to remember some of its limitations. Common ratio pitfalls result from the fact that a single financial ratio by itself is of little use. It is important to exercise professional judgment in determining which ratios to select in analyzing a given company. For example consider the following analysis: let us say that a company presents increasing revenues. Is that enough? It is certainly not. Somebody also has to examine the trend in profit margins. Even if margins are growing the return on equity needs to be examined to see if the company gives competitive returns compared to alternative investments. But, again, even if ROE is satisfactory and is growing, one needs to see what happens with the cost of funds. It may grow faster than ROE. Finally even if ROE presents double digit growth and the company's profits are growing one needs to ensure that the same happens with cash, in other words that earnings are converted to cash. A company can operate at a profit yet continually be short of cash and thus condemned to fail.

Some more limitations of financial ratio analysis include the following:

- Ratios deal mainly in numbers but they don't address qualitative issues such as product quality, customer service, and so on though these factors play an important role in financial performance.
- Ratios largely look at the past, not the future. However, during the modelling process we will examine later on we will use the ratio values as proxies for future performance.
- It is difficult to determine the appropriate industry to use in comparing firms. Many firms operate in several different lines of business, making it difficult to characterize the industry.
- There is always potential for earnings management or earnings manipulation. That is, financial information can be "massaged" in several ways to make the figures used for ratios more attractive. For example, many businesses delay payments to trade creditors at the end of the financial year to make the cash balance higher than normal and the creditor days will thus figure higher too.

In any case the modeller should always ask questions such as: Do the firms being compared have compatible accounting practices? Do the ratios being used give consistent readings? And finally, do the ratios yield a reasonable figure for the industry?

BIBLIOGRAPHY AND REFERENCES

1. Financial Accounting Standards Board, http://www.ifrs.org/Pages/default.aspx.
2. Financial Accounting Standards Board, http://www.fasb.org/home.

3

Financial Statement Modelling

Chapter 3 focuses on the process of financial statement modelling. The process is as much art as science. It starts with the collection and analysis of historical financial statements of SteelCo for 2011, 2012, and 2013 and explains how to forecast the future of the business up until 2017 putting special emphasis on the key forecast drivers (e.g. the change of rate of historical revenues or the operating expenses as a percentage of revenues). The income statement is forecast using these drivers, excluding the interest payments. Then historic working capital parameters are used to forecast some of the most important accounts on the balance sheet (e.g. receivables, inventory, and payables). After forecasting all other accounts on the balance sheet, it is balanced by using debt as a plug and the interest payment is calculated by making use of Excel's circular reference feature. Finally, the cash flow statement is modelled using 2 consecutive balance sheets and an income statement.

3.1 INTRODUCTION – HOW FINANCIAL MODELS WORK

In Chapter 1 we examined the financial modelling process in terms of the definition of the problem we are trying to solve and the specifications of the model under discussion. In this chapter we will apply the third step of the process described in Chapter 1, which is to build the model, and the 4th step of the process, that is checking that the model produces rational results. In order to build a real life model we need first to address a real-life problem that we will solve using the proposed model.

Let us describe the following situation. Steel Corporation SA, or SteelCo, is a long-established company in the steel sector but has been severely hit by the economic downturn which followed the 2008 financial crisis. The steel sector is a capital-intensive sector, both in terms of production facilities and working capital needs. The industry standard for *leverage*, as expressed by the total liabilities to equity ratio, is higher than 3. SteelCo expanded into new production facilities just before the onset of the crisis. The funding of the project was done by a syndication of banks and the following terms and conditions were agreed on the bond loan provided in June 2008 (see Exhibit 3.1):

BOND LOAN TERMSHEET	
Term	**Value**
Tenor (years)	9
Spread	2.50%
Repayment	61% at the Ninth year
Amount (€ mio)	€ 70 m
Covenants	Acceptable range
Current Assets / Current Liabilities	>1.0
Leverage (Total Liabilities/Shareholders Equity)	< 5
Interest cover (EBITDA / Interest Expense)	> 1.5

EXHIBIT 3.1   SteelCo's bond loan term sheet

The tenor of the loan represents the period for which the loan was granted and is usually expressed in years. The spread is used to calculate the amount of interest the borrower pays the bank for using the loan. The interest is calculated on a daily basis by applying the spread on the existing amount of the balance, divided by a 360-day year, and multiplied by the number of days being calculated from one due date to another. The repayment term refers to the amount of payment at the end of the term and anticipates that the loan will be refinanced in order to meet the payment obligation. Finally, before agreeing to a loan, lenders often require borrows to agree to abide by restrictive covenants. Covenants are the provisions banks attach to long-term debt that trigger technical default when violated by the borrowing company. For example, SteelCo's bank required that it keep its current ratio above 1.0, its leverage below 5 and its interest cover above 1.5. Breaking a covenant "triggers" a default and the lender's right to call the loan. Although banks pull the "trigger", they seldom call the loan. Doing so often results in bankruptcy for the company, bad publicity for the bank, and costly legal bills. However, the trigger forces the borrower to return to the bargaining table where the lender can demand a plan for corrective action, a higher interest rate, more collateral, and/or extra covenants. This is the case of SteelCo. The company breached the interest cover at the end of fiscal year 2013.

Unfortunately after the onset of the crisis, steel consumption plummeted and the company had to bear severe losses which in turn affected its equity adversely. Moreover, the cost of funding increased dramatically making things even worse. The company started funding its losses with debt and thus its liabilities started increasing year on year as well. The Chief Executive Officer of the company is worried about the fact that during the last quarter of fiscal year 2013 the third covenant of the loan was breached. The Financial Planning and Analysis manager (FP&A) of the company was assigned by the CEO the task of advising the Board of Directors about the possibility that SteelCo might breach the other covenants before the end of the loan should the economy remain stalled at current levels of consumption.

In seeking to respond to the CEO's request and to be able to monitor the possible range of the loan covenants, the FP&A needs to build a complete financial model of the company, forecast its future performance, and thus the values of the requested ratios. In other words he needs to create the so-called **Proforma Financial Statements**. Proforma balance sheets are created by forecasting individual account balances at a future date and then aggregating them into a financial statement format. Account balances are forecast by identifying the forces that influence them and projecting how the accounts will be influenced in the future by such forces. Sales, company credit and payments policy, and cost structure are often significant forces. Proforma financial statements are a forecasting method that uses sales figures and costs from the previous 2 to 3 years to create financial statements into the future.

At this point, somebody could ask why the FP&A needs a complete, fully operational financial model for just 3 ratios. Let us see why. Let us break down the problem as we said in Chapter 1. The first ratio is the *quick ratio* we referred to in Chapter 2 and it is a measure of liquidity. For this ratio the FP&A needs to forecast 2 balance sheet accounts, that is current assets and current liabilities. If we recall from Chapter 2 how these accounts are broken down then we see that for current assets we need to forecast trade receivables and inventory and for the current liabilities trade payables and short-term debt respectively. That is, in order to forecast just the first ratio, the FP&A needs to understand and model the whole operating cycle of the company. He needs to forecast the working capital needs and the funds required to support those needs.

The other 2 ratios are measures of solvency. Again let us break them down further. To forecast both total liabilities and equity requires a complete balance sheet plus an income statement. Remember that the equity at the year-end depends on the net income or net loss of the income statement. Total liabilities include, as well as the current liabilities, the long-term liabilities. Long-term liabilities normally include the portion of debt that has been used to finance long-lived assets such as heavy machinery and production machinery. So in order to forecast long-term liabilities the FP&A needs to understand the future strategic investment plan of the company. Moreover, the third ratio contains 2 income statement accounts, that is, EBITDA (operating profits) and interest expense. In turn, interest expense depends on the level of debt the company needs to operate. But the level of debt depends on the profits or losses of the year which, in turn, include interest expense. This is called a circular reference and we will deal with it in the last section of this chapter. Other information the FP&A needs to collect in order to complete the task includes the following:

- Projected sales growth rates for the period under analysis, i.e. up to 2017;
- Projected profit margins;
- Projected operating expenses;
- The breakdown of the company's debt and the cost of this debt;
- Any investment plans;
- Depreciation information.

The FP&A has now finished with the definition of the problem as described in Chapter 1. He has broken down the task into smaller parts and are ready to give the specifications of the model, i.e. its structure, before he starts forecasting. It is clear so far that he will have to model the standard financial statements, including the income statement (profit & loss), balance sheet, and statement of cash flow. The time frame of the forecast is dictated by the tenor (lifetime) of the long-term loan. The loan expires in 2017 so he will need to forecast up to 2017 on a yearly basis. Operating expenses will be grouped in one category, Selling General & Administrative (SG&A) as they do not need much detail about them. The Key Performance Indicators (KPI) that will be forecast in order to address the problem in question are the

3 covenants: the quick ratio, the leverage, and the interest cover. Neither sensitivity analysis nor a control panel was required for the time being.

Now that he has specified the structure of the model he is ready to proceed to step 3 of Chapter 1. He will build the model. What needs to be done is:

1. To collect 3 years' historical data of SteelCo.
2. To select the key forecast drivers that will help him to forecast future financial statement accounts.
3. To model the income statement.
4. To model and balance the balance sheet.
5. To model interest expense.

Please note that using historical information (2–3 years before the reference year) to estimate future performance has many pitfalls, mostly relating to the "anchoring" bias. In general a macroeconomic analysis coupled with company's strategic plans to navigate the macro environment would be more appropriate. Nevertheless for the scope of this modelling exercise we will assume that the analysis of historical data is appropriate.

Furthermore before we proceed further I should point out that, in principle, when doing financial/business modelling the approach is different, according to whether you are an external analyst having access only to published financial data or whether you are an insider having access to proprietary management information systems, exclusive data, and access to all of the executives/management team of the company. For the rest of this chapter we will take more of an external analyst's perspective only as far as the level of detail of the proforma financial statements is concerned. We want to model a complete set of financial statements with the right level of detail so that the whole process is comprehendible to the non-experienced reader. An insider could exploit the vast majority of data available in the company by using its enterprise resource planning (ERP) system, which is where it usually houses its general ledger. In doing so they could make a far more thorough analysis of the past by calculating specific KPIs and apply it to various types of budgets and forecasts. Typical KPIs include:

- Product (stock-keeping unit) SKU revenue
- Store Return on Investments – ROI
- Customer satisfaction
- Sales per square foot
- Payroll by store
- Margins by region/product SKU/business unit
- Year on year sales growth by product category/region/business unit, etc.
- ARPU – Average Revenue Per User
- Visiting customers per day
- Customer churn rate
- Yield
- Machine productivity
- Capacity utilization

depending on the company and the industry it operates.

Nevertheless since the FP&A is assigned to build a model for the company he works for he will use the insider perspective to gather and interpret information concerning various functions of the business, as we will see in the following sections of this chapter.

3.2 COLLECTING AND ANALYZING HISTORICAL DATA

There are a lot of sources from which someone can collect past financial information. To name a few: the Securities and Exchange Commission (SEC), Reuters Fundamentals database, S&P Capital IQ platform, and last but not least company websites are some useful sources of financial data. Moreover credit reports, company newsletters, press releases, and executive speeches are further secondary sources of information. A company that offers its common stock to the public typically needs to file periodic financial reports with the SEC. Various data providers collect these data, analyze company's financial performance, build valuations and transaction models, and create charts and reports that can be used by any analyst employing the proper application. For example Reuters Fundamentals database can be accessed by using the Thomson Reuters application. Moreover, these databases include a number of financial and non-financial data sets, such as company financials reported on the annual and interim financial statements (income statement, balance sheet, and statement of cash flow) as well as General Information. General Information includes company name, board of directors, industry and sector codes, contact details, web addresses, business and financial summaries, officer details, major customers, and competitors. The collection of the above information, which is previously published in any public platform or report, is called *Secondary research*. The biggest problem with collecting information through secondary research is that the information available could be outdated or old and hence could result in inaccurate outcomes. The alternative is to perform so-called *Primary research*. Primary research techniques mean collecting the information directly by speaking to several key participants and gathering the latest intelligence about the organization as well as the industry. Nevertheless primary research can be quite challenging as one needs first to identify the correct respondents they would want to interview, next, somehow persuade them to engage in a dialogue and then actually interview them in depth.

As far as SteelCo's case is concerned, the FP&A will have all this information available from his colleagues at the various company departments. He will have to cooperate closely with the accounting, commercial, procurement, technical, and HR departments in order to cross-check and validate model assumptions. The very first thing he has to do is to collect the proper raw data from the company's financial statements, footnotes, and external reports in one place. These raw data should include:

- The number of different product groups. SteelCo's revenues can be grouped into 2 product groups. The "long" products group and the "flat" products group.
- Unit volumes and prices per product group. Normally this kind of information is available in the notes of financial statements. Even if prices are not disclosed explicitly they can be derived easily by just dividing total revenues by unit volumes per product group.
- Information about SteelCo's profitability (gross profit margins, EBITDA margins, etc.).
- Information about SteelCo's operating cycle (credit terms, payment terms, etc.).
- Information about SteelCo's debt structure. That is the debt breakdown between short-term debt and long-term debt and the cost of each debt category respectively.
- Information about the depreciation that is charged in the income statement. The total amount and how it splits between production and selling/administrative costs. The amount of depreciation that results from the production facilities and machinery is charged in the Cost of Goods Sold (COGS) whereas the amount of depreciation that has to do with the warehouses of the distribution network as well as that which is related to office buildings is charged in the Selling General and Administrative (SG&A) expenses.

- Effective tax rate. Companies' income is subject to various taxes imposed by the government on their net profits. The effective tax rate is the net rate a company pays on its net income that includes all forms of taxes.
- Information about the investment plans, if any, of the company.
- Any macroeconomic indicators such as Gross Domestic Product (GDP) and inflation rate forecasts respectively.

In the specification part of the modelling process we discussed the single sheet on which we collect all the assumptions that we will use in the model. This sheet will resemble Exhibit 3.2 with the information the FP&A has gathered up to this point.

Note that there is a separate column presenting the Unit of Measure (UOM) of each relevant piece of information. Units are usually very obvious to the modeller, but this does not apply to everyone who sees the model over its lifetime. The model user should be able to understand the unit of measure for every input assumption.

Then the FP&A needs to transform the income statement, balance sheet, and statement of cash flows to the right level of detail. This level of detail will apply to both historical and forecast financial statements. While he needs to forecast many significant income statement, balance sheet, and cash flow statement accounts, as we discussed at the problem definition stage, to keep the model as simple as possible some other accounts need to be grouped together.

The first line of the income statement is the *revenue line*. Revenues are a product of units sold times price per unit. Since there are 2 product lines, flat and long products, the FP&A needs to monitor the units sold for both lines and their relevant prices. The rate of change for the revenue line is also calculated and will be used as a proxy of the evolution of sales in the forecast period. After the revenue line he monitors the *gross margin*. The gross margin percentage is calculated as a percentage of sales. Again this figure will be used to forecast the gross margin. Following this are the *other operating income*, the *operating expenses*, and the *other operating expenses*. Normally other operating expenses include a provision for bad debts. This provision refers to credit losses that pertain to the period of the income statement. A provision is a double entry that debits (increases) an expense account of the income statement and credits (decreases) a balance sheet asset account. The balance sheet account is the accounts receivable and is reduced by the amount about which there are doubts as to whether it will be collected (that is the allowance for bad debts).

Next come the *Earnings Before Interest Tax Depreciation and Amortization* or *EBITDA* figure. EBITDA is used to indicate the ability of a company to service its debt and allows us to analyze the performance of its operations while eliminating all non-operating and non-recurring items such as depreciation, interest, taxes, and one-time charges such as professional fees, or other non-recurring costs. Next is the *EBITDA margin* which is the EBITDA as a percentage of sales. The EBITDA margin is helpful when analyzing the growth of a company year over year because it reflects whether this growth was profitable and to what extent. Growth is good, provided that the new businesses added in are as profitable as the existing one.

Then the *net interest* is recorded. That is interest expense minus interest income. In case there is no explicit information about the cost of funds in the company financial statements, the FP&A can get an estimate of the average cost of debt by dividing interest expense by the average level of debt between 2 consecutive balance sheets. Then the *depreciation* is recorded and the *profits before tax* calculated after subtracting depreciation and interest expenses respectively from EBITDA. In case of profits the tax expense, let us say to the federal government, is reported and finally the *profits after taxes*. This final figure feeds directly into the balance sheet account of retained earnings if no dividends are given back to shareholders.

Assumptions				

Particulars	UOM	2011 A	2012 A	2013 A
Price				
Long Products	€/MT	700	670	650
Flat Products	€/MT	650	680	700
Volume				
Long Products	MT	200,000	170,000	150,000
Flat Products	MT	70,000	60,000	50,000
Total Sales MT	MT	**270,000**	**230,000**	**200,000**
Rate of change	%		−14.8%	−13.0%
Profitability				
% Gross Margin	%	8.2%	9.7%	9.5%
Financing				
Deposit rate	%	5.0%	3.0%	1.0%
Financing Cost - LT	%	−2.5%	−2.5%	−5.7%
Financing Cost - ST	%	−5.3%	−5.6%	−6.7%
Working Capital				
Stock Days - DIO	Days	86	91	95
Customer Days - DSO	Days	115	113	110
Supplier Days - DPO	Days	41	38	30
Effective Tax Rate	%	33.0%	33.0%	33.0%
Depreciation				
Depreciation rate	%	3.7%	3.4%	3.6%
Cost of sales	€' 000	995	945	1,028
Distribution/Selling	€' 000	1,200	1,122	1,207
Total	€' 000	**2,195**	**2,067**	**2,235**
% Cost of sales	%	45.3%	45.7%	46.0%
% in SG&A	%	54.7%	54.3%	54.0%
Investment	€' 000		2,590	400
Consumer Price Index	%	2.0%	1.8%	1.7%

EXHIBIT 3.2 "Assumptions" worksheet

It is considered best practice in financial modelling to record the income accounts in black and the expense accounts in red. Similarly, to record profits in black and losses in red. Exhibit 3.3 presents the historic income statement of SteelCo for the past 3 fiscal years 2011 to 2013 as they have been recorded by the FP&A.

	A	B	C	D	E	F
2	**SteelCo SA Historical Financial Statements 2011-2013**					
3						
4	Particulars		UOM	2011 A	2012 A	2013 A
5	**Income Statement**					
6	Long Products		MT	200,000	170,000	150,000
7	Flat Products		MT	70,000	60,000	50,000
8	**Total**			**270,000**	**230,000**	**200,000**
9	rate of change		%		-14.8%	-13.0%
13	Long Products @ €/MT		€/MT	700	670	650
14	Flat Products @ €/MT		€/MT	650	680	700
16	Turnover Long Products		€' 000	140,000	113,884	97,500
17	Turnover Flat Products		€' 000	45,500	40,800	35,000
18	**Total Turnover**		€' 000	**185,500**	**154,684**	**132,500**
19	rate of change		%		-16.6%	-14.3%
20						
21	Gross Margin W/O Depreciation		€' 000	15,211	15,004	12,588
22	% on Total Turnover		%	8.2%	9.7%	9.5%
23	Other Operating Income		€' 000	3,555	3,493	2,539
24	% on Total Turnover		%	1.9%	1.9%	1.9%
25	Operating Expenses		€' 000	-8,912	-8,516	-8,182
26	% on Total Turnover		%	-4.8%	-5.5%	-6.2%
27	Other Operating expenses		€' 000	-707	-985	-663
28	% on Total Turnover		%	-0.4%	-0.6%	-0.5%
29	**EBITDA**		€' 000	**9,147**	**8,997**	**6,282**
30	**EBITDA MARGIN**		%	6.5%	7.9%	6.4%
33	Net Interest Expenses		€' 000	-4,755	-4,470	-6,357
34	Depreciation		€' 000	-2,195	-2,067	-2,235
35	**Profit / Loss before tax**		€' 000	**2,197**	**2,459**	**-2,310**
36	Less: Income Tax Expense			-725	-812	-
37	% on Profit before tax		%	-33.0%	-33.0%	0.0%
38	**Profit/ Loss after tax**			**1,472**	**1,648**	**-2,310**

EXHIBIT 3.3   Historical income statements of SteelCo

Having finished with the Income statement, the FP&A reports the balance sheet in the following way.

Assets are broken down into *current assets* and *non-current assets*. Non-current assets are divided into net fixed assets, that is:

Fixed asset purchase price (*Gross Fixed Assets*) + Subsequent additions to existing assets – *Accumulated depreciation*

and *other non-current assets* which include intangible assets and investments in subsidiaries, joint ventures, and associates. Current assets include the *receivables* from the credit sales to customers, *inventory, cash* and *other assets*. The inventory is the value of materials and goods held by the company to support its sales and is divided into merchandise, finished goods, and spare parts. Inventory is a large item in the current assets and must be accurately counted and valued at the end of each accounting period in order to determine a company's profit or loss. Other assets include all the other categories of assets not described explicitly above. On the equity and liabilities side, owner's equity is grouped into *share capital* and *retained earnings or losses*, that is the accumulated earnings and losses over the years of operation of the company. Finally the liabilities part of the balance sheet is divided into *long-term debt, short-term debt, payable to suppliers*, and *other liabilities*. IASB dictates that we distinguish between short-term and long-term since only the short-term element participates in current liabilities which in turn participates in the current ratio. Other liabilities include all the other categories of liabilities not described explicitly above.

Exhibit 3.4 presents the historic balance sheets of SteelCo for the past 3 fiscal years 2011 to 2013 as they have been recorded by the FP&A.

Notice that at the end of the balance sheet there is a built-in check figure that should always equal zero. This figure simply entails a subtraction between total assets and owner's equity & liabilities and a result equal to zero ensures that the basic accounting equation holds.

	A	B	C	D	E	F
2	**SteelCo SA Historical Financial Statements 2011-2013**					
3						
4	**Particulars**		**UOM**	**2011 A**	**2012 A**	**2013 A**
45	**Balance Sheet**					
46	Gross Fixed Assets		€' 000	58,850	61,440	61,840
47	Accumulated Depreciation		€' 001	−15,000	−17,067	−19,302
48	Other Non Current Assets		€' 000	18,840	18,840	18,840
49	**Non Current Assets**		€' 000	**62,690**	**63,213**	**61,378**
50						
51	Account Receivables		€' 000	69,969	57,466	47,918
52	Inventory		€' 000	39,984	34,962	31,210
53	Cash		€' 000	15,579	12,290	7,000
54	Other Current Assets		€' 000	3,736	2,483	1,230
55	**Total Assets**		€' 000	**191,958**	**170,414**	**148,736**
56						
57	Share capital		€' 000	31,260	31,260	31,260
58	Retained earnings		€' 000	1,472	3,120	810
59	**Owners Equity**		€' 000	**32,732**	**34,380**	**32,070**
60						
61	Debt - Long Term		€' 000	59,383	56,350	53,317
62	Debt - Short Term		€' 000	76,167	61,795	51,347
63	Account Payables		€' 000	19,129	14,542	9,856
64	Other Liabilities		€' 000	4,546	3,346	2,147
65	**Total Liabilities**		€' 000	**159,225**	**136,034**	**116,666**
66	**Owners Equity & Liabilities**		€' 000	**191,958**	**170,414**	**148,736**
67	check			0	0	0

EXHIBIT 3.4   Historical balance sheets of SteelCo

Finally the statements of cash flow for the last 3 fiscal years is recorded at a certain level of detail. The adjustment for tax, depreciation, and the changes in working capital are recorded from the operating activities. The investing and financing activities are recorded at the minimum level of detail as shown in Exhibit 3.5.

	A	B	C	D	E	F
2	**SteelCo SA Historical Financial Statements 2011-2013**					
3						
4	**Particulars**		UOM	**2011 A**	**2012 A**	**2013 A**
70	**Cash Flow**					
71	**Operating Activities**					
72	Profit / Loss before taxation		€ '000	2,197	2,459	−2,310
73	**Adjustments for:**					
74	Depreciation & amortization		€ '000	2,195	2,067	2,235
75	**Adjustments for changes in working capital**					
76	Decrease/(increase) in receivables		€ '000	13,001	12,503	9,548
77	Decrease/(increase) in inventories		€ '000	3,842	5,022	3,752
78	(Decrease)/increase in payables		€ '000	−5,982	−4,587	−4,686
79	Decrease/(increase) in other receivables & payables		€ '000	173	54	54
80	**Total inflows / (outflows) from operating activities (a)**		€ '000	**15,426**	**17,517**	**8,592**
81	**Investing activities**					
82	Purchase or Disposals of assets		€ '000	−1,427	−2,590	−400
83	**Total inflows / (outflows) from investing activities (b)**		€ '000	−1,427	−2,590	−400
84	**Financing Activities**					
85	Share Capital Increase		€ '000			
86	New bank loans raised / Repayments of loans		€ '000	−16,274	−17,405	−13,482
87	**Total inflows / (outflows) from financing activities (c)**		€ '000	−16,274	−17,405	−13,482
88	**Net Increase/(Decrease) in cash and cash equivalents (a)+(b)+(c)**		€ '000	−2,274	−2,477	−5,290
89	**Cash and cash equivalents at the beginning of the period**		€ '000	**17,853**	**15,579**	**12,290**
90	**Cash and cash equivalents at the end of the period**		€ '000	**15,579**	**13,101**	**7,000**
91						

EXHIBIT 3.5   Historical statements of cash flow of SteelCo

Notice that in the cash flow statement the cash and cash equivalents at the beginning of a period should be equal to the cash and cash equivalents at the end of the previous period. Moreover the cash and cash equivalents at the end of a period should be the same as the cash account of the balance sheet of that period.

Now that the FP&A has collected the historical financial statement of the last 3 fiscal years, he needs to do some analysis and compute the key forecast drivers of interest. That is, for each line item in the financial statements, he will have to build historical ratios, as well as forecasts of future ratios. These ratios will form the basis for the forecast financial statements.

3.3 SELECTING THE KEY FORECAST DRIVERS

In order to forecast the financial statements up to 2017, the FP&A can make use of at least 2 classical forecasting methods and a variety of hybrids that use parts of each method. The 2 methods are the *T-account forecasting* and the *percent-of-sales forecasting*. The *T-account forecasting* method starts with a base year of financial statements (e.g. last year) and determines through double entries how each account will change and what the resulting balance will be. While more accurate than the alternative method it is cumbersome and may require a degree of forecast information about transactions unavailable to many analysts outside and even inside the company.

The *percent-of-sales forecasting* method starts with a forecast of sales and then estimates other income statement accounts based on some presumed relationship between sales and that account. For example operating expenses as a percentage of sales can be calculated for the 3 last available income statements accounts and an average percentage can be used as a proxy for the estimation of future operating expenses given the future sales forecasts. While simple to execute, this technique can lead to false conclusions which should always be cross checked for their reasonableness.

The most widely used approach is a mix of these two. T-account forecasting is mainly used to estimate balance sheet accounts like shareholders' equity, fixed assets, and the cash flow statement. Percent-of-sales is used to estimate mainly income statements accounts such as gross margin, operating expenses, other income, and other expenses, as these items usually vary with sales. Other items may vary as a percentage of accounts other than sales. For example, interest expense is a percentage of the average debt during the year. This percentage is the interest rate the banks charge the company for using their loans. Tax expense is usually a percentage of pretax income. This percentage is called the effective tax rate. Finally a dividend is usually a percentage of after-tax income, and depreciation usually varies with gross fixed assets.

As far as SteelCo's case is concerned, the FP&A will make use of both the approaches described above and they need to calculate the following drivers from each financial statement:

Income Statement

- Rate of change of sales
- Gross profit margin – gross profit as a percentage of sales (%)
- Other operating income as a percentage of sales (%)
- Operating expenses as a percentage of sales – OPEX (%)
- Other operating expenses as a percentage of sales (%)

- Income tax as a percentage of net income – effective tax rate (%)
- Dividends as a percentage of income after tax
- Depreciation as a percentage of gross fixed assets.

Balance Sheet

- Days sales outstanding – DSO
- Days inventory outstanding – DIO
- Days payable outstanding – DPO.

No drivers need to be calculated for the cash flow statement since it can be derived from 2 consecutive balance sheets and an income statement as we have seen in Chapter 2.

The first step in preparing the proforma financial statements is to forecast sales. Sales normally influence the current asset and current liability account balances. As sales increase or decrease, the company will generally need to carry more or less inventory and will have a higher or lower accounts receivable balance respectively. One simple way to forecast sales for the next 4 years is to extrapolate the current sales volume into the future. This is very easy to do in Excel. Excel can automatically generate future values based on existing data by making use of the linear trend function. By selecting the volume of long products for the last 3 years and then dragging into the next 4 cells to the right the FP&A can have an estimate for future sales, in terms of volume, based on past sales volume (See Exhibit 3.6).

To make the extrapolation described above work, the extrapolated cells need to contain values and not formulae. If the cells contain formulae then a simple dragging on the right will just copy the formulae on the right. If the cells contain formulae simply copy and paste them as numbers. If you do not want to destroy the formulae, copy them as numbers to a different part of the worksheet, do the extrapolation, and put the extrapolated numbers back into the model.

We can see that by applying the linear trend function to the sales volume of long products the FP&A ends up with 48,000 metric tons in 2017. As we said earlier, forecasts need to be cross checked for their reasonableness. Thus, a cross check with the Commercial Director reveals that this figure is extremely low and the decrease from the 2013 level of 150,000 Metric Tons is too much. These figures simply do not make sense. The FP&A has to figure out another way to forecast sales volumes. He decides to try to forecast the sales volumes

Particulars	UOM	2011 A	2012 A	2013 A
Income Statement				
Long Products	MT	200,000	170,000	150,000
Flat Products	MT	70,000	60,000	50,000
Total		**270,000**	**230,000**	**200,000**
rate of change	%		-14.8%	-13.0%

Particulars	UOM	2011 A	2012 A	2013 A	2014 F	2015 F	2016 F	2017 F
Income Statement								
Long Products	MT	200,000	170,000	150,000	123,333	98,333	73,333	48,333
Flat Products	MT	70,000	60,000	50,000				
Total		**270,000**	**230,000**	**200,000**				
rate of change	%		-14.8%	-13.0%				

EXHIBIT 3.6   Application of Excel's linear trend feature of forecast long products volume

rate of change instead of the volumes themselves, using the same approach (see Exhibit 3.7). They now select the rate of change of the total product volume for the last 2 years and drag it into the next 4 cells to the right. As you can see the forecast rate of change in 2014 is -11.3%, in 2015 it is -9.5%, in 2016 -7.7%, and in 2017 -6%. By working in reverse order he applies this rate of change to the total product volume. That is the total volume in 2014 is the volume of 2013 multiplied by $(1 - 11.3\%)$ or

$$177,456 = 200,000 *(1 - 11.3\%)$$

Then by applying to the total 2014 figure the actual proportion between long and flat products from 2013 they have the breakdown of 2014 into long and flat products. That is, flat products represent the $50/200 = 25\%$ of 2013 total volume and long products represent the other 75%. Then 2014 flat products and long products will be respectively:

$$44,364 = 25\%*177,456 \text{ and } 133,092 = 75\% * 177,456$$

By applying the same methodology, the total sales volume for 2015, 2016, and 2017 is forecast and then broken down between long and flat products. Again sales forecasts need to be cross checked with commercial people. The commercial manager now believes that, although this is a bad scenario, it is a plausible one.

The FP&A then proceeds with the next key driver which is the Gross Margin (GM). The historical GMs have already been calculated for the last 3 actual fiscal years. The question he now faces is what GM to use for the forthcoming years. He can use the average GM of the last 3 years or alternatively take the most recent one. Again, since this is a commercial issue,

Particulars	UOM	2011 A	2012 A	2013 A				
Income Statement								
Long Products	MT	200,000	170,000	150,000				
Flat Products	MT	70,000	60,000	50,000				
Total		**270,000**	**230,000**	**200,000**				
rate of change	%		-14.8%	-13.0%				

Particulars	UOM	2011 A	2012 A	2013 A	2014 F	2015 F	2016 F	2017 F
Income Statement								
Long Products	MT	200,000	170,000	150,000				
Flat Products	MT	70,000	60,000	50,000				
Total		**270,000**	**230,000**	**200,000**				
rate of change	%		-14.8%	-13.0%	-11.3%	-9.5%	-7.7%	-6.0%

Particulars	UOM	2011 A	2012 A	2013 A	2014 F	2015 F	2016 F	2017 F
Income Statement								
Long Products	MT	200,000	170,000	150,000				
Flat Products	MT	70,000	60,000	50,000				
Total		**270,000**	**230,000**	**200,000**	**177,456**	**160,596**	**148,183**	**139,354**
rate of change	%		-14.8%	-13.0%	-11.3%	-9.5%	-7.7%	-6.0%

Particulars	UOM	2011 A	2012 A	2013 A	2014 F	2015 F	2016 F	2017 F
Income Statement								
Long Products	MT	200,000	170,000	150,000	133,092	120,447	111,137	104,515
Flat Products	MT	70,000	60,000	50,000	44,364	40,149	37,046	34,838
Total		**270,000**	**230,000**	**200,000**	**177,456**	**160,596**	**148,183**	**139,354**
rate of change	%		-14.8%	-13.0%	-11.3%	-9.5%	-7.7%	-6.0%

EXHIBIT 3.7 Forecasting sales volumes using the linear trend function

after consulting with the commercial people he chooses the GM of 2013 as the one for the forecast years of 2014, 2015, 2016, and 2017. This is 9.5%.

The next key driver is the other operating income as a percentage of sales. This percentage is constant at 1.9% and the FP&A decides to keep it the same in the forecast period.

OPerating EXpenses (OPEX) as a percentage of sales is the next driver. The FP&A has noticed that this ratio is deteriorating over the years. In 2011 operating expenses represented 4.8% of turnover. Two years later it was 6.2%. Although expenses are declining, turnover is declining at a much faster rate. He is puzzled about how to forecast this ratio in the future. One way is to extrapolate it as he did above over the next 4 years. Would such a scenario be probable? Another way is to take the average of the last 3 years and keep it constant for the next 4 years. The FP&A finally chooses to do some more digging in the expense accounts and examine their relationship with sales volume. He concludes that a good approximation would be to consider 70% of operating expenses as fixed, which are increased in line with the annual inflation rate, and 30% of them as variable, which vary along with the sales volume. The operating expenses then, as a percentage of 2014 sales, would be:

$$OPEX_{2014} = 30\%*OPEX_{2013}*SalesVolume_{2014}/SalesVolume_{2013}+70\%*OPEX_{2013}*(1+inflation\ rate)$$

As a proxy for the inflation rate the FP&A uses the Consumer Price Index (CPI) that forms part of the principal European economic indicators that can be found at European Commission Eurostat website (http://ec.europa.eu/eurostat/euroindicators). Using the above formula he can forecast the OPEX of years 2015, 2016, and 2017. So starting with OPEX equal to €8,182k in 2013 and assuming constant inflation over the years equal to 2%, by using the above formula he gets:

$$OPEX\ 2014 = -€8,020k,$$
$$OPEX\ 2015 = -€7,904k,$$
$$OPEX\ 2016 = -€7,831k,\ and$$
$$OPEX\ 2017 = -€7,801k.$$

Notice that in this case the FP&A does not forecast OPEX using OPEX% but the other way round. He forecasts next year's OPEX and will then calculate the OPEX% as we will see in the following paragraph. Moreover an external analyst would not have access to this kind of information and would have to model OPEX by using past years' OPEX as a percentage of sales driver instead.

The next key driver is the other operating expenses as a percentage of sales. This percentage varies very little with the annual turnover, from 0.4% in 2011 to 0.6% in 2012. So he decides to keep this percentage constant at 0.5% of the annual turnover, that is, the average of the last 3 years, for the forecast period.

Regarding the other drivers, the effective tax rate remains constant over the years at 33% when there are profits to be taxed. Moreover the company has not distributed any dividends since the onset of the crisis. This is easy to verify since:

Equity of Year 2013 = Equity of Year 2012 + Net Profits after Tax

and the same applies for Equity 2012. If the company had distributed any dividends then the above equation should have been short of the distributed dividends. There are 2 more accounts that the FP&A needs to figure out how to forecast, in order to have everything required for the proforma income statement: interest expense and depreciation. In the next 2 sections we will see how he handled these accounts and estimated the depreciation as a percentage of gross fixed assets.

The FP&A now proceeds with the balance sheet drivers. The Days Sales Outstanding (DSO) for 2013 and likewise for the previous 2 years are calculated as follows:

$$\text{DSO } 2013 = \text{Account Receivables } 2013 \text{ / Annual Turnover } 2013 * 365 \text{ / VAT}$$

If you recall the definition of DSO from Chapter 2 and you compare it with the above formula, you will see that, in addition, the FP&A has divided the DSO with the Value Added Tax figure. He does so because revenues as recorded in the income statement do not include VAT, unlike accounts receivable which do include it. Thus the DSO for 2013, taking into account VAT at 20%, is:

$$\text{DSO } 2013 = 110 = 47{,}918 \text{ / } 132{,}500 \times 365 \text{ /} 1.2$$

Likewise, based on a similar calculation, the DSOs for 2011 and 2012 are 115 and 113 days respectively. Regarding the Days Inventory Outstanding (DPO), the calculation for a typical year is as follows (as we discussed in Chapter 2):

$$\text{DPO } 2013 = \text{Accounts Payables } 2013 \text{/ Cost of Goods Sold } 2013 * 365 \text{ / VAT}$$

Note here that if accounts payable includes VAT then it should be removed since COGS does not include VAT. In the case of SteelCo, the majority of its suppliers are foreign but within the European Union, so VAT should be removed only from local suppliers (foreign transactions between Member States of the European Union do not incorporate VAT). For reasons of simplicity, the FP&A has decided not to include VAT at all in the above calculation since only a small part of the supplies carry VAT. So the DPO for 2013 equals 30:

$$\text{DPO } 2013 = 30 = 9{,}856 \text{ / } (132{,}500 - 12{,}588) \times 365$$

Note that COGS equals turnover minus gross margin, which is why the FP&A subtracted from the total turnover of 2013, amounting to €132,500k, the gross margin which was €12,588k. Likewise, based on a similar calculation, the DPOs for 2011 and 2012 are 38 and 41 days respectively.

Finally the days inventory outstanding (DIO) for a typical year is calculated using the following formula, as described in Chapter 2:

$$\text{DIO } 2013 = \text{Inventory } 2013 \text{/ Cost of Goods Sold } 2013 * 365$$

So based on the above formula the DIO for 2013 is equal to 95:

$$\text{DIO } 2013 = 95 = 31{,}210 \text{ / } (€132{,}500k - €12{,}588k) \times 365$$

Likewise, the DIO for 2011 and 2012 are 86 and 91 days respectively.

Exhibit 3.8 shows the calculation of the key forecast drivers of the working capital for the past 3 years, 2011 to 2013. The FP&A has noticed that while stock days or DIOs are deteriorating, customer days or DSOs are improving and supplier days or DPOs are also deteriorating. The higher the stock days and the customer days, the more funds are required to support the operating cycle of the business. On the other hand, the higher the supplier days the better in terms of liquidity.

Particulars	UOM	2011 A	2012 A	2013 A
Assumptions				
Stock Days	Days	86	91	95
Customer Days	Days	115	113	110
Supplier Days	Days	41	38	30

EXHIBIT 3.8 Balance sheet key drivers

The FP&A needs to project these working capital parameters into the future and then, based on the forecast turnover and cost of goods sold, to estimate the proforma accounts receivable, accounts payable, and inventory. The easiest way is to select them and then extrapolate them linearly in the way he did above with the rate of change of sales volume. Such a method would give the results shown in Exhibit 3.9a. However, 114 days of inventory in 2017 is almost a month more than the days of 2011. Such an increase would be disastrous for the liquidity of the company. The same applies for the 9 supplier days. Nine days means almost cash purchases. Thus the FP&A has decided to cross check the above parameters, if they are reasonable, with the appropriate managers in charge, i.e. the commercial and the purchasing managers respectively. What he ends up with are the parameters of Exhibit 3.9b which are based on the targeted inventory management, credit, and purchasing policy of the company. The FP&A was informed that the company intends to decrease its inventory by 15 days in the following 4 years. Moreover the company intends to collect money from its clients sooner and pay its suppliers later with the sole purpose of improving its liquidity.

The FP&A, as an insider, could have analyzed the working capital parameters into more categories instead of a single number for DSO, DIO, and DPO respectively. For example different product categories or customer mix may have different paying patterns. That is, domestic, European, and Rest of World customers may have different paying patterns (e.g. DSOs). Similarly different suppliers may request different payment terms. Finally inventory could have been broken down into raw materials, Work in Progress (WIP), and finished products and thus DIOs too. Nevertheless, this is a modelling exercise and we will try to keep it as simple as possible.

Thus, the complete "Assumptions" worksheet of SteelCo's model for the years 2014 to 2017 will resemble the one in Exhibit 3.10.

Particulars	UOM	2011 A	2012 A	2013 A	2014 F	2015 F	2016 F	2017 F
Assumptions								
Stock Days	Days	86	91	95	100	105	109	114
Customer Days	Days	115	113	110	108	105	103	101
Supplier Days	Days	41	38	30	25	20	14	9

(a)

Particulars	UOM	2011 A	2012 A	2013 A	2014 F	2015 F	2016 F	2017 F
Assumptions								
Stock Days	Days	86	91	95	85	80	80	80
Customer Days	Days	115	113	110	85	80	75	75
Supplier Days	Days	41	38	30	50	50	55	55

(b)

EXHIBIT 3.9 Forecast working capital parameters by linear extrapolation (a) and (b) based on the targeted inventory management, credit, and purchasing policy of the company

Assumptions								
Particulars	**UOM**	**2011 A**	**2012 A**	**2013 A**	**2014 F**	**2015 F**	**2016 F**	**2017 F**
Price								
Long Products	€/MT	700	670	650	650	650	650	650
Flat Products	€/MT	650	680	700	700	700	700	700
Volume								
Long Products	MT	200,000	170,000	150,000	133,092	120,447	111,137	104,515
Flat Products	MT	70,000	60,000	50,000	44,364	40,149	37,046	34,838
Total Sales MT	MT	**270,000**	**230,000**	**200,000**	**177,456**	**160,596**	**148,183**	**139,354**
Rate of change	%		−14.8%	−13.0%	−11.3%	−9.5%	−7.7%	−6.0%
Profitability								
% Gross Margin	%	8.2%	9.7%	9.5%	9.5%	9.5%	9.5%	9.5%
Financing								
Deposit rate	%	5.0%	3.0%	1.0%	1.0%	1.0%	1.0%	1.0%
Financing Cost - LT	%	−2.5%	−2.5%	−5.7%	−5.7%	−5.7%	−5.7%	−5.7%
Financing Cost - ST	%	−5.3%	−5.6%	−6.7%	−6.7%	−6.7%	−6.7%	−6.7%
Working Capital								
Stock Days - DIO	Days	86	91	95	85	80	80	80
Customer Days - DSO	Days	115	113	110	85	80	75	75
Supplier Days - DPO	Days	41	38	30	50	50	55	55
Effective Tax Rate	%	33.0%	33.0%	33.0%	33.0%	33.0%	33.0%	33.0%
Depreciation								
Depreciation rate	%	3.7%	3.4%	3.6%	3.6%	3.6%	3.6%	3.6%
Cost of sales	€' 000	995	945	1,028	1,029	1,034	1,039	1,044
Distribution/Selling	€' 000	1,200	1,122	1,207	1,208	1,214	1,220	1,225
Total	€' 000	**2,195**	**2,067**	**2,235**	**2,237**	**2,248**	**2,259**	**2,269**
% Cost of sales	%	45.3%	45.7%	46.0%	46.0%	46.0%	46.0%	46.0%
% in SG&A	%	54.7%	54.3%	54.0%	54.0%	54.0%	54.0%	54.0%
Investment	€' 000		2,590	400	300	300	300	300
Consumer Price Index	%	2.0%	1.8%	1.7%	2.0%	2.0%	2.0%	2.0%

EXHIBIT 3.10 "Assumptions" worksheet of SteelCo's model

The FP&A is now ready to create the proforma financial statements for the years 2014 to 2017.

3.4 MODELLING THE INCOME STATEMENT

As we have seen previously, the first step in preparing the proforma income statement is to forecast sales. The 2 main variables in sales are unit prices and volumes. These 2 variables usually have a reciprocal relationship. Forecasting sales is a demanding approach that has little to do with the linear extrapolation we saw in the previous section. A more scientific approach will follow in the next chapter. In general, sales forecasters need to identify important trends and quantify their impact on the company's business. But let us accept for the time being that the sales volume the FP&A forecast is correct. In order to calculate sales revenues, i.e. the turnover of the company, he needs to forecast unit prices for the years 2014 to 2017. He decides for the sake of urgency to keep unit prices constant rather than using a more scientific approach such as regression analysis or elasticity curves. In doing so, he has the very first

SteelCo SA Proforma Financial Statements 2014-2017

Particulars	UOM	2011 A	2012 A	2013 A	2014 F	2015 F	2016 F	2017 F
Income Statement								
Long Products	MT	200,000	170,000	150,000	133,092	120,447	111,137	104,515
Flat Products	MT	70,000	60,000	50,000	44,364	40,149	37,046	34,838
Total		**270,000**	**230,000**	**200,000**	**177,456**	**160,596**	**148,183**	**139,354**
rate of change	%		-14.8%	-13.0%	-11.3%	-9.5%	-7.7%	-6.0%
Long Products MT/month	MT	16,667	14,167	12,500	11,091	10,037	9,261	8,710
Flat Products MT/month	MT	5,833	5,000	4,167	3,697	3,346	3,087	2,903
Long Products @ €/MT	€/MT	700	670	650	650	650	650	650
Flat Products @ €/MT	€/MT	650	680	700	700	700	700	700
Turnover Long Products	€' 000	140,000	113,884	97,500	86,510	78,291	72,239	67,935
Turnover Flat Products	€' 000	45,500	40,800	35,000	31,055	28,104	25,932	24,387
Total Turnover	€' 000	**185,500**	**154,684**	**132,500**	**117,564**	**106,395**	**98,171**	**92,322**
rate of change	%		-16.6%	-14.3%	-11.3%	-9.5%	-7.7%	-6.0%

EXHIBIT 3.11   Building the first line of the proforma income statement of SteelCo

line of the income statement, the total turnover, which is a simple multiplication of volume in Metric Tons (MT) x unit prices in € as shown in Exhibit 3.11.

Note that since the unit prices are constant over the forecasting period, the rate of change of turnover is the same as that of the total volume.

The next income statement account is the gross margin excluding depreciation. We talked about depreciation in Chapter 2. Remember that depreciation is an accounting method of spreading out the cost of fixed assets over the period in which these assets are used. The part of depreciation that represents use of machinery for the purposes of production goes into cost of goods sold and it is frequently included in gross margin. For practical reasons it is a good idea to keep all the depreciation expenses in a single account and present them after EBITDA (Earnings Before Interest Tax Depreciation and Amortization). The 9.5% gross margin chosen for the forecasting period 2014 to 2017, if applied to the total turnover, gives the gross margin of the proforma income statements as shown in Exhibit 3.12:

SteelCo SA Proforma Financial Statements 2014-2017

Particulars	UOM	2011 A	2012 A	2013 A	2014 F	2015 F	2016 F	2017 F	
Income Statement									
Long Products	MT	200,000	170,000	150,000	133,092	120,447	111,137	104,515	
Flat Products	MT	70,000	60,000	50,000	44,364	40,149	37,046	34,838	
Total		**270,000**	**230,000**	**200,000**	**177,456**	**160,596**	**148,183**	**139,354**	
rate of change	%		-14.8%	-13.0%	-11.3%	-9.5%	-7.7%	-6.0%	
Long Products MT/month	MT	16,667	14,167	12,500	11,091	10,037	9,261	8,710	
Flat Products MT/month	MT	5,833	5,000	4,167	3,697	3,346	3,087	2,903	
Long Products @ €/MT	€/MT	700	670	650	650	650	650	650	
Flat Products @ €/MT	€/MT	650	680	700	700	700	700	700	
Turnover Long Products	€' 000	140,000	113,884	97,500	86,510	78,291	72,239	67,935	
Turnover Flat Products	€' 000	45,500	40,800	35,000	31,055	28,104	25,932	24,387	
Total Turnover	€' 000	**185,500**	**154,684**	**132,500**	**117,564**	**106,395**	**98,171**	**92,322**	
rate of change	%		-16.6%	-14.3%	-11.3%	-9.5%	-7.7%	-6.0%	
Gross Margin W/O Depreciation	€' 000	15,211	14,386	12,588	11,169	10,108	9,326	8,771	⇐ Result
% on Total Turnover	%	8.2%	9.3%	9.5%	9.5%	9.5%	9.5%	9.5%	⇐ Driver

EXHIBIT 3.12   Forecasting the gross margin account

SteelCo SA Proforma Financial Statements 2014-2017

Particulars	UOM	2011 A	2012 A	2013 A	2014 F	2015 F	2016 F	2017 F
Income Statement								
Long Products	MT	200,000	170,000	150,000	133,092	120,447	111,137	104,515
Flat Products	MT	70,000	60,000	50,000	44,364	40,149	37,046	34,838
Total		**270,000**	**230,000**	**200,000**	**177,456**	**160,596**	**148,183**	**139,354**
rate of change	%		−14.8%	−13.0%	−11.3%	−9.5%	−7.7%	−6.0%
Long Products MT/month	MT	16,667	14,167	12,500	11,091	10,037	9,261	8,710
Flat Products MT/month	MT	5,833	5,000	4,167	3,697	3,346	3,087	2,903
Long Products @ €/MT	€/MT	700	670	650	650	650	650	650
Flat Products @ €/MT	€/MT	650	680	700	700	700	700	700
Turnover Long Products	€' 000	140,000	113,884	97,500	86,510	78,291	72,239	67,935
Turnover Flat Products	€' 000	45,500	40,800	35,000	31,055	28,104	25,932	24,387
Total Turnover	€' 000	**185,500**	**154,684**	**132,500**	**117,564**	**106,395**	**98,171**	**92,322**
rate of change	%		−16.6%	−14.3%	−11.3%	−9.5%	−7.7%	−6.0%
Gross Margin W/O Depreciation	€' 000	15,211	14,386	12,588	11,169	10,108	9,326	8,771
% on Total Turnover	%	8.2%	9.3%	9.5%	9.5%	9.5%	9.5%	9.5%
Other Operating Income	€' 000	3,555	3,493	2,539	2,234	2,022	1,865	1,754
% on Total Turnover	%	1.9%	1.9%	1.9%	1.9%	1.9%	1.9%	1.9%
Operating Expenses	€' 000	−8,912	−8,516	−8,182	−8,020	−7,904	−7,831	−7,801
% on Total Turnover	%	−4.8%	−5.5%	−6.2%	−6.8%	−7.4%	−8.0%	−8.4%
Other Operating expenses	€' 000	−707	−985	−663	−588	−532	−491	−462
% on Total Turnover	%	−0.4%	−0.6%	−0.5%	−0.5%	−0.5%	−0.5%	−0.5%
EBITDA	€' 000	**9,147**	**8,378**	**6,282**	**4,794**	**3,693**	**2,869**	**2,262**
EBITDA MARGIN	%		6.5%	7.4%	6.4%	5.5%	4.7%	4.0%	3.3%

EXHIBIT 3.13   Forecasting the income statement accounts up to EBITDA

Following are the accounts Other Operating Income, Operating Expenses, and Other Operating Expenses respectively. OPEX has already been calculated in the previous paragraph and it is €8,020k, €7,904k, €7,831k, and €7,801k for the years 2014 to 2017 respectively. Moreover, other operating income and other operating expenses as a percentage of sales have been chosen to keep constant during the forecasting period at 1.9% and 0.5% respectively. So far the FP&A has forecast all the income statement accounts up to EBITDA and can derive EBITDA and EBITDA margin (EBITDA as a percentage of sales) as shown in Exhibit 3.13.

Next is the net interest expense account, that is, the interest expense minus the interest income gained from the cash deposits of the company. The interest expense is comprised of the interest that the company pays for its short-term debt plus the interest that it pays for its long-term debt. Usually the cost of these 2 kinds of debt differs. In the preliminary analysis of the historical financial statements the FP&A found out that these costs are 5.7% and 6.7% respectively. Moreover the average income from the cash deposits of the firm is 1%. Then the net interest expense will be derived from the following equation:

Net Interest Expense = 5.7% × Long-term Debt + 6.7% × Short-term Debt − 1% × Cash Deposits

The balance of the long-term debt until its refinancing is known and thus the interest expense can be calculated explicitly. Moreover, the minimum amount of cash required by the company to operate smoothly can also be found from SteelCo's treasury department. What is not known is the amount of funds required in the form of short-term debt during the forecast period. So the FP&A leaves the calculation of this account for the time being and will come back to it later on.

Finally he needs to forecast depreciation expense. To do so he needs to forecast, in turn, the gross fixed assets which is a balance sheet account.

The relationship between 2 consecutive years' fixed assets is as follows:

$$\text{Fixed Assets 20XX} = \text{Fixed Assets 20XX}-1 + \text{Investments in Fixed Assets 20XX}$$

The investments in fixed assets or CAPital EXpenditure (CAPEX) made by the company in years 2011 to 2013 have been recorded in the assumption sheet during the collection phase of raw data (see Exhibit 3.2). For example, in 2013 the company's CAPEX was €400k and thus the gross fixed assets for 2013 are €61,440k (gross fixed assets of 2012) plus €400k or €61,840k in total. Dividing the gross fixed assets for 2013 by the depreciation expense for 2013, which is €2,235k, the FP&A gets:

$$3.6\% = \text{Depreciation 2013} / \text{Gross Fixed Assets 2013} = €2,235 / €61,840k$$

He decides to keep this rate constant during the forecast period. What he now needs to do is to forecast the gross fixed assets for this period and then apply to them the depreciation rate derived earlier. As a rule of thumb, future CAPEX should be more or less equal to annual depreciation. This is almost true of the CAPEX for fiscal years 2011 and 2012 with minor deviations. But during 2013 the company invested in fixed assets well below that level. Since sales volume is declining, only the CAPEX which is strictly necessary for the smooth operation of the company has been implemented. The FP&A decides to consult the Technical Director regarding any planned investments in the following years. The Technical Director, in turn, requests the forecast sales plan and the FP&A gives him or her the volumes presented in Exhibit 3.7. The Technical Director notices that sales volumes will continue to decline and thus informs the FP&A that the CAPEX will be kept to a minimal €300k in each of the years 2014 to 2017. This is the information the FP&A needed in order to model the gross fixed assets and thus the depreciation. The following are thus obtained:

$$\text{Gross Fixed Assets 2014} = \text{Gross Fixed Assets 2013} + \text{CAPEX 2013, or}$$

$$\text{Gross Fixed Assets 2014} = €61,840k + €300k = €62,140k.$$

In the same way, gross fixed assets for 2015 = €62,440k, gross fixed assets for 2016 = €62,740k and, and gross fixed assets for 2017 = €63,040k. Depreciation is now easy to derive:

$$\text{Depreciation 2014} = \text{Gross Fixed Assets 2014} \times \text{Depreciation Rate, or}$$

$$\text{Depreciation 2014} = €62,140k \times 3.6\% = €2,237k.$$

In the same way, depreciation for 2015 = €2,248k, depreciation for 2016 = €2,259k, and depreciation for 2017 = €2,269k. The proforma income statement now looks like the one in Exhibit 3.14:

Note that the FP&A could have forecast depreciation simply by selecting the actual depreciation for years 2011 to 2013 and then using the linear trend function of Excel to drag these cells to the left as shown in Exhibits 3.6 and 3.7. Had he done so, the depreciation forecast would have been €2,206k, €2,226k, €2,246k, and €2,266k for the years 2014, 2015, 2016, and 2017 respectively. You can see that the results would be quite similar.

SteelCo SA Proforma Financial Statements 2014-2017								

Particulars	UOM	2011 A	2012 A	2013 A	2014 F	2015 F	2016 F	2017 F
Income Statement								
Long Products	MT	200,000	170,000	150,000	133,092	120,447	111,137	104,515
Flat Products	MT	70,000	60,000	50,000	44,364	40,149	37,046	34,838
Total		**270,000**	**230,000**	**200,000**	**177,456**	**160,596**	**148,183**	**139,354**
rate of change	%		−14.8%	−13.0%	−11.3%	−9.5%	−7.7%	−6.0%
Long Products MT/month	MT	16,667	14,167	12,500	11,091	10,037	9,261	8,710
Flat Products MT/month	MT	5,833	5,000	4,167	3,697	3,346	3,087	2,903
Long Products @ €/MT	€/MT	700	670	650	650	650	650	650
Flat Products @ €/MT	€/MT	650	680	700	700	700	700	700
Turnover Long Products	€' 000	140,000	113,884	97,500	86,510	78,291	72,239	67,935
Turnover Flat Products	€' 000	45,500	40,800	35,000	31,055	28,104	25,932	24,387
Total Turnover	€' 000	**185,500**	**154,684**	**132,500**	**117,564**	**106,395**	**98,171**	**92,322**
rate of change	%		−16.6%	−14.3%	−11.3%	−9.5%	−7.7%	−6.0%
Gross Margin W/O Depreciation	€' 000	15,211	15,004	12,588	11,169	10,108	9,326	8,771
% on Total Turnover	%	8.2%	9.7%	9.5%	9.5%	9.5%	9.5%	9.5%
Other Operating Income	€' 000	3,555	3,493	2,539	2,234	2,022	1,865	1,754
% on Total Turnover	%	1.9%	1.9%	1.9%	1.9%	1.9%	1.9%	1.9%
Operating Expenses	€' 000	−8,912	−8,516	−8,182	−8,020	−7,904	−7,831	−7,801
% on Total Turnover	%	−4.8%	−5.5%	−6.2%	−6.8%	−7.4%	−8.0%	−8.4%
Other Operating expenses	€' 000	−707	−985	−663	−588	−532	−491	−462
% on Total Turnover	%	−0.4%	−0.6%	−0.5%	−0.5%	−0.5%	−0.5%	−0.5%
EBITDA	€' 000	**9,147**	**8,997**	**6,282**	**4,794**	**3,693**	**2,869**	**2,262**
EBITDA MARGIN	%	6.5%	7.9%	6.4%	5.5%	4.7%	4.0%	3.3%
Net Interest Expenses	€' 000	−4,755	−4,470	−6,329				
Depreciation	€' 000	−1,756	−2,447	−2,235	−2,237	−2 248	−2,259	−2,269

EXHIBIT 3.14 Proforma income statement

Only the net interest expense is missing from the income statement and the tax expense if there are going to be profits. The FP&A will come back to these figures later on. He is now ready to model the balance sheet.

3.5 MODELLING THE BALANCE SHEET

As we saw in Chapter 2, the balance sheet consists of 3 main categories – assets, liabilities, and owner's equity – and must comply with the basic accounting equation that total assets equal total liabilities and total owner's equity. The very first account of the proforma balance sheet, gross fixed assets, has already been created in the previous section when the FP&A tried to model the depreciation expense for the income statement. If you recall Exhibit 3.4, the next account is the accumulated depreciation. But the depreciation expense has already been forecast for the years 2014 to 2017. So the accumulated depreciation for 2014 would be:

Accumulated Depreciation 2014 = Accumulated Depreciation 2013 + Depreciation 2014, or

Accumulated Depreciation 2014 = €19,302k + €2,237k = €21,539.

In the same way the accumulated depreciation of years 2015 to 2017 is €23,787k, €26,045k, and €28,315k respectively. Notice that the accumulated depreciation is a contra balance sheet account or a credit account and is always subtracted from gross fixed assets in order to give the net fixed assets. Remember that the net fixed assets are part of the non-current assets. The level of detail that the FP&A chose for the balance sheet includes one more account in the non-current assets subcategory. This is the other non-current assets. The other non-current assets

	A	B	C	D	E	F	G	H	I	J
					SteelCo SA Proforma Financial Statements					
2					**2014-2017**					
3										
4	Particulars		UOM	2011 A	2012 A	2013 A	2014 F	2015 F	2016 F	2017 F
45	Balance Sheet									
46	Gross Fixed Assets		€ 000	58,850	61,440	61,840	62,140	62,440	62,740	63,040
47	Accumulated Depreciation		€ 000	−15,000	−17,067	−19,302	−21,539	−23,787	−26,045	−28,315
48	Other Non Current Assets		€ 000	18,840	18,840	18,840	18,840	18,840	18,840	18,840
49	**Non Current Assets**		€ 000	**62,690**	**63,213**	**61,378**	**59,441**	**57,493**	**55,534**	**53,565**

EXHIBIT 3.15   Proforma balance sheet non-current accounts

include long-term investments of SteelCo and the FP&A decides to leave this account intact for the next 4 years. Exhibit 3.15 shows the proforma balance sheet up to now.

Next the FP&A needs to forecast the current assets accounts. Recalling Exhibit 3.4, the current accounts include the accounts receivable, inventory, cash and the other current assets.

In order to forecast accounts receivable, the FP&A needs the forecast sales for the years 2014 to 2017 and the days sales outstanding or DSO for the same period. He has both of the above (see Exhibits 3.10 and 3.11). So the accounts receivable for 2014 will be:

Accounts Receivable 2014 = Sales 2014 × DSO 2014 / 365 * 1.2, or
Accounts Receivable 2014 = €117,564k × 85 / 365 * 1.2 = €32,854k.

Following a similar rationale he calculates the accounts receivable for 2015, 2016, and 2017 which are €27,983k, €24,207k, and €22,764k respectively. Remember here that the VAT charge of 20% is added to accounts receivable to denote that a customer owes the company not only the sale price but also the VAT on the sale.

Moving on, inventory needs to be forecast. Again the FP&A needs an income statement account which is the cost of goods sold and the Days Inventory Outstanding or DIO. The DIO has already been forecast for the years 2014 to 2017 (see Exhibit 3.10) and the cost of goods sold can be derived indirectly from Exhibit 3.12 where both the sales and the gross margin have been calculated. Thus the inventory for 2014 will be:

Inventory 2014 = Cost of Goods Sold 2014 * DIO 2014 / 365, where
Cost of Goods Sold 2014 = Sales 2014 − Gross Margin 2014, or
Inventory 2014 = (€117,564k − €11,169k) * 85 / 365 = €24,777k.

In a similar way the inventory for 2015, 2016, and 2017 is forecast as €21,104k, €19,473k, and €18,313k respectively. Cash deposits is the next current assets account that needs to be modelled. This is a fairly easy task. Historic financial statements have shown that the company has never operated with cash deposits below €3,500k and the treasury department has verified that. Because cash plays such a vital role in the smooth operation of businesses, some companies maintain a minimum cash balance that ensures that they have sufficient funds to pay their suppliers when needed. The minimum cash balance for SteelCo is set at €3,500k. Finally, the other current assets, although they have been declining year on year, probably due to the decline in SteelCo's activity, are set constant at the last actual year amount, that is €1,230k. The FP&A could model them as a percentage of sales or as a percentage of total assets although the latter would result in a circular reference. Since this amount is fairly small compared to the total assets (less than 1% in the balance sheet for 2013) he does not bother with it any more. The balance sheet so far looks like the one shown in Exhibit 3.16.

	A	B	C	D	E	F	G	H	I	J
				SteelCo SA Proforma Financial Statements						
2				**2014-2017**						
3										
4	Particulars		UOM	2011 A	2012 A	2013 A	2014 F	2015 F	2016 F	2017 F
45	**Balance Sheet**									
46	Gross Fixed Assets		€' 000	58,850	61,440	61,840	62,140	62,440	62,740	63,040
47	Accumulated Depreciation		€' 001	−15,000	−17,067	−19,302	−21,539	−23,787	−26,045	−28,315
48	Other Non Current Assets		€' 000	18,840	18,840	18,840	18,840	18,840	18,840	18,840
49	**Non Current Assets**		€' 000	**62,690**	**63,213**	**61,378**	**59,441**	**57,493**	**55,534**	**53,565**
50										
51	Account Receivables		€' 000	69,969	57,466	47,918	32,854	27,983	24,207	22,764
52	Inventory		€' 000	39,984	34,962	31,210	24,777	21,104	19,473	18,313
53	Cash		€' 000	15,579	12,290	7,000	3,500	3,500	3,500	3,500
54	Other Current Assets		€' 000	3,736	2,483	1,230	1,230	1,230	1,230	1,230
55	**Total Assets**		€' 000	**191,958**	**170,414**	**148,736**	**121,802**	**111,310**	**103,944**	**99,372**

EXHIBIT 3.16   Forecast balance sheet assets accounts

Next the FP&A needs to model the owner's equity and liabilities accounts. If you recall Exhibit 3.4, owner's equity is broken down into the share capital and retained earnings accounts. The share capital account remains fairly stable unless there is a share capital increase. For the time being such information is not available so it will be left intact.

Period profits after tax and after dividends, if any, affect the retained earnings account (see Exhibit 2.13). So, assuming that the share capital will not change in the next 4 years, the FP&A has to forecast only retained earnings. Since the income statement is not yet ready, he leaves this account for later and proceed with the liability accounts. The balance of long-term debt is easy to forecast since he knows the repayment schedule of the loan. The company has to repay the 39% by June of 2017 in 2 instalments per year. The duration of the loan is 9 years and its initial amount was €70 million. So by applying some simple maths each year the company will have to repay:

$$€70,000k \times 39\%/9 \text{ years} = €3,033k$$

During the last year of the loan the company will have to repay half of this amount in June 2017 since in the first year they paid half of this amount in December 2008. Thus:

Long-term Debt 2014 = Long-term Debt 2013 − Debt Repayment 2013, or
Long-term Debt 2014 = €53,317k − €3,033k = €50,283k.

Similarly, long-term debt for years 2015 to 2017 is calculated at €47,250k, €44,217k, and €42,700k respectively.

The next account is short-term debt. This account is used to balance the balance sheet as we will see in the next paragraph. So for the time being it will remain empty. Then there follows the accounts payable account. As with accounts receivable and inventory, the FP&A needs the income statement account of COGS and DPO. The DPO has already been forecast for the years 2014 to 2017 (see Exhibit 3.10) and the COGS has been derived above. Thus the accounts payable for 2014 will be:

Accounts Payable 2014 = Cost of Goods Sold 2014 * DPO 2014 / 365, or
Accounts Payable 2014 = (€117,564k − €11,169k) * 50 / 365 = €14,575k.

In a similar way, accounts payable for the years 2015 to 2018 are forecast at €13,190k, €13,388k, and €12,590k respectively. Finally, the other liabilities account is the last one

	A	B	C	D	E	F	G	H	I	J
				SteelCo SA Proforma Financial Statements						
2				**2014-2017**						
3										
4	Particulars		UOM	2011 A	2012 A	2013 A	2014 F	2015 F	2016 F	2017 F
45	Balance Sheet									
46	Gross Fixed Assets		€ 000	58,850	61,440	61,840	62,140	62,440	62,740	63,040
47	Accumulated Depreciation		€ 001	−15,000	−17,067	−19,302	−21,539	−23,787	−26,045	−28,315
48	Other Non Current Assets		€ 000	18,840	18,840	18,840	18,840	18,840	18,840	18,840
49	**Non Current Assets**		€ 000	**62,690**	**63,213**	**61,378**	**59,441**	**57,493**	**55,534**	**53,565**
50										
51	Account Receivables		€ 000	69,969	57,466	47,918	32,854	27,983	24,207	22,764
52	Inventory		€ 000	39,984	34,962	31,210	24,777	21,104	19,473	18,313
53	Cash		€ 000	15,579	12,290	7,000	3,500	3,500	3,500	3,500
54	Other Current Assets		€ 000	3,736	2,483	1,230	1,230	1,230	1,230	1,230
55	**Total Assets**		€ 000	**191,958**	**170,414**	**148,736**	**121,802**	**111,310**	**103,944**	**99,372**
56										
57	Share capital		€ 000	31,260	31,260	31,260	31,260	31,260	31,260	31,260
58	Retained earnings		€ 000	1,472	3,120	810	810	810	810	810
59	**Owners Equity**		€ 000	**32,732**	**34,380**	**32,070**	**32,070**	**32,070**	**32,070**	**32,070**
60										
61	Debt - Long Term		€ 000	59,383	56,350	53,317	50,283	47,250	44,217	42,700
62	Debt - Short Term		€ 000	76,167	61,795	51,347	-	-	-	-
63	Account Payables		€ 000	19,129	14,542	9,856	14,575	13,190	13,388	12,590
64	Other Liabilities		€ 000	4,546	3,346	2,147	2,147	2,147	2,147	2,147
65	**Total Liabilities**		€ 000	**159,225**	**136,034**	**116,666**	**67,005**	**62,587**	**59,751**	**57,437**
66	**Owners Equity & Liabilities**		€ 000	**191,958**	**170,414**	**148,736**	**99,075**	**94,657**	**91,821**	**89,507**
67	check			0	0	0	22,726,745	16,653,629	12,122,839	9,865,254

EXHIBIT 3.17   The complete structure of the balance sheet (not yet balanced)

missing from a complete balance sheet. Like the other current assets account, other liabilities has a declining trend year over year, probably due to the decline of SteelCo's activity, and is set constant at the last actual year's amount which is €2,147k.

Exhibit 3.17 shows the balance sheet with all the forecast accounts up to 2017 except the retained earnings and short-term debt accounts. Note that the FP&A has made use of an in-built error check that raises the alert that the balance sheet does not balance (last line of the balance sheet of Exhibit 3.17). This issue will be resolved in the next section. Moreover, given the way the balance sheet has been modelled, all the line items are either linked to the income statement directly, or determined through the creation of an assumption that is held to a different area of the model (e.g. the "Assumptions" worksheet). Tempting as it was, no hard-coded numbers have been entered! For example, CAPEX, Depreciation, DSO, DIO, and DPO are recorded elsewhere and pulled through to the balance sheet.

The FP&A is now approaching the end of the modelling process. The structure of the balance sheet has been built and in the next section they will attempt to balance it.

3.6 MODELLING INTEREST AND CIRCULAR REFERENCES

What the FP&A has left so far is to forecast interest expense in the proforma income statement and Short-Term Debt (STD) in the proforma balance sheet. These 2 accounts are interlinked. Debt is used to *close* and *match* the balance sheet and this is the reason why it is sometimes known as a plug. A plug is a formula to match the balance sheet using differences in some of the items listed in it in such a way that the accounting equation holds. In our case:

STD = Total Assets − Owners Equity − Long-Term Debt − Account Payables − Other Liabilities,

Owner's Equity = Share Capital + Retained Earnings + Profit / (Loss) after Tax,
Profit / (Loss) after Tax = f(Interest Expense) and
Interest Expense = f(Short-term Debt) = Interest Rate × Short-term Debt,

where f() is a symbol that means *a function of.*

It is easy to understand that something is peculiar in the relationships above. The FP&A, in order to calculate interest expense, needs to know the actual amount of short-term debt and, in order to calculate short-term debt, needs to know the actual amount of interest expense. This is a problem and is called *Circular Reference* in excel.

Thank goodness Excel has a solution to this problem! To resolve this issue the FP&A will make use of the *iterative calculations* feature of Excel (see Exhibit 3.18). He sets the recalculation mode to MANUAL so that the model will iterate only when CALC (F9) is pressed. He chooses the **Files** menu, then the **Options** menu, then the **Formulas** menu, and then selects the button to **Manual** in the **Calculations Options**. He also selects the **Enable Iterative Calculations** and sets the number of iterations to 1 (simply by entering 1 in **Maximum Iterations**). The FP&A will now be able to see Excel re-estimate the plug figure and interest expense at each iteration. He could set the number of iterations higher (Excel's default is 100), but Excel will converge on a solution after 5 or 6 iterations, so a setting of 1 is best to see the iterations in action. Every time he presses the F9 key he should see the worksheet change. After pressing

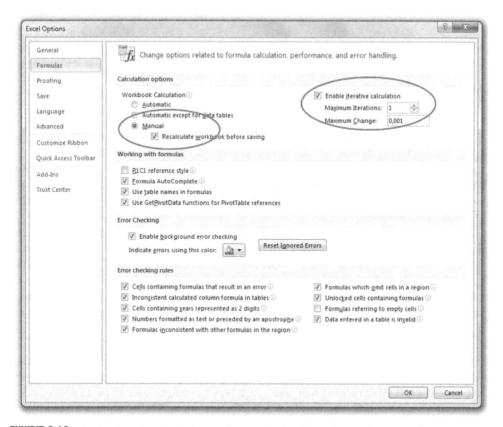

EXHIBIT 3.18 Setting Excel recalculation mode to manual and iterations to 1

the F9 key several more times the numbers stop changing, which means that the model has converged to a solution. Net interest expense for year 20XX is exactly:

Net Interest Year 20XX = 5.7 % × Long-term Debt + 6.7% of Short-term Debt − 1% of Cash Deposits,

Retained Earnings Year 20XX = Retained Earnings Year 20XX − 1 + Net Income Year 20XX,

and the balance sheet balances which means that the short-term debt has converged to a single number. Once the FP&A has seen how this works, they decide to have the model converge without having to press CALC (F9) several times. In order to do this, they set the number of iterations they want Excel to perform. They set the number of iterations back to 100, Excel's default, and allow its computer to recalculate automatically.

The next figure shows the complete proforma income statement and balance sheet statements. Once again, the 3 formulae that enabled the financial statements to balance are as follows:

Net Interest for Year 2014 = Cell G33 = 5.7% × Cell G61 + 6.7% × Cell G62 − 1% × Cell G53, or

Reads from the assumption sheet

Cell G33 = 5.7% × €50,283k + 6.7% × €24,612k − 1% × €3,500k = €4,443k,

Retained Earnings Year 2014 = Cell G58 = Cell F58 (Ret. Earn. 2013) + Cell G38 (Net Inc. 2014), or

Cell G58 = €810k + (− €1,885)k = − €1,076k, and

Short-term Debt for Year 2014 = Cell G62 = Cell G55 − Cell G59 − Cell G61 − Cell G63 − Cell G64, or

Cell G62 = €121,802k − €30,184k − €20,283k − €14,575k − €2,147k = €24,612k.

By selecting the above cells G33, G58, and G62 and dragging them to the left the FP&A can forecast quite easily the net interest expense, retained earnings, and short-term debt for years 2015, 2016, and 2017 respectively (see Exhibit 3.19). It should be obvious by now how the 2 statements are interlinked.

Please always remember to verify that the check figure which has been implemented at the bottom of the balance sheet is zero. The zero check figure confirms that the balance sheet balances.

As a final note to this section I would like to stress that for many financial modelling organizations, circular references must be avoided as they have many drawbacks. The major problem with using circular references is that once you have one it is very difficult to distinguish between mistakes that have created inadvertent circular references and the intentional circular reference. Although I try to avoid circular references whenever possible there are some cases where a circular reference gives a shorter solution than a non-circular variation of it. This is the case we described above. The interested reader can visit various financial modelling websites (e.g. corality.com[1] or chandoo.org[2]) and find alternatives on how to overcome circular references. Meanwhile I will give you a workaround in case you face a #Value error. In this case Excel may be unable to find an acceptable answer due to another error in some of the cells of your workbook (e.g. due to a #DIV/0 error). First make sure you make all the required changes so that you avoid that particular error (i.e. the #DIV/0 error). Then, if the #Value error persists to the cells with the iteration, you have to break the circular reference and jump start the model. For example you will have to go to cells G62 to J62 and delete the formulae that created the circular reference in the first instance (or copy them to an adjacent empty cell). Replace them with a hard-coded number, say 10. You will see immediately that now the balance sheet does not balance. Also at the same time the #Value error will disappear. Now you may rewrite the circular reference equation described above (or paste it back) so that the balance sheet balances again. Everything will now be just fine.

3.7 MODELLING THE CASH FLOW STATEMENT

The cash flow statement is the last statement the FP&A will model. It is not needed for the monitoring of the 3 covenants of the long-term loan but should be done for the sake of completing the forecasting exercise. If you recall in Chapter 2 we proved that a cash flow statement needs 2 balance sheets and 1 income statement to complete. The FPA will model the proforma cash flow statement using the indirect method as described in Chapter 2.

The indirect method starts with the profit/loss before tax and then makes various adjustments to non-cash items. The first adjustment is the corresponding tax in case the company had profits. In SteelCo's case the forecast income statements up to 2017 presented losses so there is no tax adjustment. Then the depreciation is added back to the profit or loss figure since it does not have a cash impact. Then he follows the adjustments that have to do with the increase or decrease of working capital accounts of the balance sheet. For example the FP&A will have to record the differences of the accounts receivable, inventory, and accounts payable between 2012 and 2013 in order to derive the 2013 figures. What is important to keep in mind that an increase in accounts receivable, inventory, and/or other current assets is a cash outflow whereas a decrease in accounts receivable, inventory, and/or other current assets is a cash inflow. You have to spend money to buy inventory (and thus increase it) and you make money when you sell inventory (and thus decrease it).

On the other hand an increase in accounts payable and/or other liabilities is a cash inflow whereas a decrease in accounts payable and/or other liabilities is a cash outflow. When you pay a supplier you spend money (cash outflow) in order to decrease your obligation to that supplier. In the same way when you buy on credit (cash inflow) you increase your obligation to the supplier.

Exhibit 3.20 shows the cash flows from operating activities for SteelCo for the years 2014 to 2017.

Let us verify the figures the FP&A recorded as the 2014 cash flow from operating activities. €1,885k is the net income before tax which is the same as the net income after tax since there are no taxes (see the complete income statement at Exhibit 3.19). The figure of €2,237 is the depreciation for year 2014 as shown in the income statement. €15,064k is the difference between €47,918k and €32,854k which are the accounts receivable for 2013 and 2014 respectively (see balance sheet at Exhibit 3.19). The €6,433k is the difference between €31,210k and €24,777k which are the inventories for 2013 and 2014 respectively. Finally the €4,719k is the difference between €14,575k and €9,856k which are the accounts payable for 2014 and 2013 respectively.

In the case of an asset account, we subtract the asset of the most recent year from the asset of the oldest year. In the case of a liability account, we subtract the liability of the oldest year from the liability of the most recent year.

	A	B	C	D	E	F	G	H	I	J
1										
2				**SteelCo SA Proforma Financial Statements**						
				2014-2017						
3										
4	Particulars		UOM	2011 A	2012 A	2013 A	2014 F	2015 F	2016 F	2017 F
5	**Income Statement**									
6	Long Products		MT	200,000	170,000	150,000	133,092	120,447	111,137	104,515
7	Flat Products		MT	70,000	60,000	50,000	44,364	40,149	37,046	34,838
8	**Total**			**270,000**	**230,000**	**200,000**	**177,456**	**160,596**	**148,183**	**139,354**
9	rate of change		%		-14.8%	-13.0%	-11.3%	-9.5%	-7.7%	-6.0%
13	Long Products @ €/MT		€/MT	700	670	650	650	650	650	650
14	Flat Products @ €/MT		€/MT	650	680	700	700	700	700	700
16	Turnover Long Products		€' 000	140,000	113,884	97,500	86,510	78,291	72,239	67,935
17	Turnover Flat Products		€' 000	45,500	40,800	35,000	31,055	28,104	25,932	24,387
18	**Total Turnover**		€' 000	**185,500**	**154,684**	**132,500**	**117,564**	**106,395**	**98,171**	**92,322**
19	rate of change		%		-16.6%	-14.3%	-11.3%	-9.5%	-7.7%	-6.0%
20										
21	Gross Margin W/O Depreciation		€' 000	15,211	15,004	12,588	11,169	10,108	9,326	8,771
22	% on Total Turnover		%	8.2%	9.7%	9.5%	9.5%	9.5%	9.5%	9.5%
23	Other Operating Income		€' 000	3,555	3,493	2,539	2,234	2,022	1,865	1,754
24	% on Total Turnover		%	1.9%	1.9%	1.9%	1.9%	1.9%	1.9%	1.9%
25	Operating Expenses		€' 000	-8,912	-8,516	-8,182	-8,020	-7,904	-7,831	-7,801
26	% on Total Turnover		%	-4.8%	-5.5%	-6.2%	-6.8%	-7.4%	-8.0%	-8.4%
27	Other Operating expenses		€' 000	-707	-985	-663	-588	-532	-491	-462
28	% on Total Turnover		%	-0.4%	-0.6%	-0.5%	-0.5%	-0.5%	-0.5%	-0.5%
29	**EBITDA**		€' 000	**9,147**	**8,997**	**6,282**	**4,794**	**3,693**	**2,869**	**2,262**
30	**EBITDA MARGIN**		%	6.5%	7.9%	6.4%	5.5%	4.7%	4.0%	3.3%
33	Net Interest Expenses		€' 000	-4,755	-4,470	-6,357	-4,443	-4,040	-3,778	-3,795
34	Depreciation		€' 000	-2,195	-2,067	-2,235	-2,237	-2,248	-2,259	-2,269
35	**Profit / Loss before tax**		€' 000	**2,197**	**2,459**	**-2,310**	**-1,885**	**-2,595**	**-3,167**	**-3,802**
36	Less: Income Tax Expense			-725	-812	-	-	-	-	-
37	% on Profit before tax		%	-33.0%	-33.0%	0.0%	0.0%	0.0%	0.0%	0.0%
38	**Profit/ Loss after tax**			**1,472**	**1,648**	**-2,310**	**-1,885**	**-2,595**	**-3,167**	**-3,802**
45	**Balance Sheet**									
46	Gross Fixed Assets		€' 000	58,850	61,440	61,840	62,140	62,440	62,740	63,040
47	Accumulated Depreciation		€' 001	-15,000	-17,067	-19,302	-21,539	-23,787	-26,045	-28,315
48	Other Non Current Assets		€' 000	18,840	18,840	18,840	18,840	18,840	18,840	18,840
49	**Non Current Assets**		€' 000	**62,690**	**63,213**	**61,378**	**59,441**	**57,493**	**55,534**	**53,565**
50										
51	Account Receivables		€' 000	69,969	57,466	47,918	32,854	27,983	24,207	22,764
52	Inventory		€' 000	39,984	34,962	31,210	24,777	21,104	19,473	18,313
53	Cash		€' 000	15,579	12,290	7,000	3,500	3,500	3,500	3,500
54	Other Current Assets		€' 000	3,736	2,483	1,230	1,230	1,230	1,230	1,230
55	**Total Assets**		€' 000	**191,958**	**170,414**	**148,736**	**121,802**	**111,310**	**103,944**	**99,372**
56										
57	Share capital		€' 000	31,260	31,260	31,260	31,260	31,260	31,260	31,260
58	Retained earnings		€' 000	1,472	3,120	810	-1,076	-3,670	-6,837	-10,640
59	**Owners Equity**		€' 000	**32,732**	**34,380**	**32,070**	**30,184**	**27,590**	**24,423**	**20,620**
60										
61	Debt - Long Term		€' 000	59,383	56,350	53,317	50,283	47,250	44,217	42,700
62	Debt - Short Term		€' 000	76,167	61,795	51,347	24,612	21,134	19,770	21,315
63	Account Payables		€' 000	19,129	14,542	9,856	14,575	13,190	13,388	12,590
64	Other Liabilities		€' 000	4,546	3,346	2,147	2,147	2,147	2,147	2,147
65	**Total Liabilities**		€' 000	**159,225**	**136,034**	**116,666**	**91,617**	**83,721**	**79,521**	**78,752**
66	**Owners Equity & Liabilities**		€' 000	**191,958**	**170,414**	**148,736**	**121,802**	**111,310**	**103,944**	**99,372**
67	check			0	0	0	0	0	0	0

EXHIBIT 3.19 Complete proforma income statement and balance sheet

Next are the cash flows from investing activities. In the "Assumptions" worksheet the FP&A has recorded that the CAPEX for each year of the forecast period will be €300k. This is an investment in non-current assets and thus a cash outflow. So the flows from investing activities would be €300k negative (outflow).

Finally, the cash flows from financing activities are derived by considering the differences in short-term debt and long-term debt between 2013 and 2014. Since the debt is a liability

	A	B	C	D	E	F	G	H	I	J
1										
2			**SteelCo SA Proforma Financial Statements**							
			2014-2017							
3										
4	Particulars		UOM	2011 A	2012 A	2013 A	2014 F	2015 F	2016 F	2017 F
70	Cash Flow									
71	**Operating Activities**									
72	Profit / Loss before taxation		€' 000	2,197	2,459	−2,310	−1,885	−2,595	−3,167	−3,802
73	**Adjustments for:**									
74	Depreciation & amortization		€' 000	2,195	2,067	2,235	2,237	2,248	2,259	2,269
75	**Adjustments for changes in working capital** Decrease/(increase) in									
76	receivables		€' 000	13,001	12,503	9,548	15,064	4,870	3,777	1,442
77	Decrease/(increase) in inventories		€' 000	3,842	5,022	3,752	6,433	3,673	1,631	1,160
78	(Decrease)/increase in payables		€' 000	−5,982	−4,587	−4,686	4,719	−1,385	198	−798
79	Decrease/(increase) in other receivables & payables		€' 000	173	54	54	-	-	-	-
80	**Total inflows / (outflows) from operating activities (a)**		€' 000	**15,426**	**17,517**	**8,592**	**26,568**	**6,812**	**4,697**	**272**

EXHIBIT 3.20 Cash flow from operating activities

the FP&A would subtract the debt of 2013 from the debt of 2014. So the cash flows from financing activities (CFFA) would be:

CFFA 2014 = LTD 2014 − LTD 2013 + STD 2014 − STD 2013, or
CFFA 2014 = €50,283k − €53,317k + €24,612k − €51,347k = −€29,768k, or
€29,768k repayment of loans.

The algebraic addition of the 3 cash flow activities – operating, investing, and financing – results in a cash reduction of €3,500k:

Cash decrease in 2013 = €26,568k − €300k − €29,768k = −€3,500k.

As an *error checking practice* we should cross check with the cash account balances of the 2013 and 2014 balance sheets and verify that this is the exact decrease between the 2 years, or

Cash 2014 = Cash 2013 − €3,500k = €7,000k − €3,500k = €3,500k.

Using the same methodology and dragging each cell's formula to the next 3 cells to the right, the FP&A has created the proforma cash flow for the years 2015 to 2017 as shown in Exhibit 3.21.

You do not need to be a financial expert to understand that the company will make losses in the next 4 years but will cash in a lot of money during the same period. For example in 2014 SteelCo is forecast to lose €1,885k accounting-wise but will cash in €26,568k from its operations. You can see that the income statement gives completely different information from the cash flow statement. Where will all this cash come from? A closer look at the operating activities reveals that this cash is fed in from working capital due to:

1. Decreasing sales activity which leads to fewer working capital needs, and
2. Improving working capital parameters in terms of DSO, DPO, and DIO as a reaction of SteelCo's management to improve its liquidity.

	B	C	D	E	F	G	H	I	J
1									
2			**SteelCo SA Proforma Financial Statements** **2014-2017**						
3									
4 Particulars		UOM	2011 A	2012 A	2013 A	2014 F	2015 F	2016 F	2017 F
70 Cash Flow									
71 **Operating Activities**									
72 Profit / Loss before taxation		€' 000	2,197	2,459	-2,310	-1,885	-2,595	-3,167	-3,802
73 **Adjustments for:**									
74 Depreciation & amortization		€' 000	2,195	2,067	2,235	2,237	2,248	2,259	2,269
75 **Adjustments for changes in working capital**									
76 Decrease/(increase) in receivables		€' 000	13,001	12,503	9,548	15,064	4,870	3,777	1,442
77 Decrease/(increase) in inventories		€' 000	3,842	5,022	3,752	6,433	3,673	1,631	1,160
78 (Decrease)/increase in payables		€' 000	-5,982	-4,587	-4,686	4,719	-1,385	198	-798
79 Decrease/(increase) in other receivables & payables		€' 000	173	54	54	-	-	-	-
80 **Total inflows / (outflows) from operating activities (a)**		€' 000	**15,426**	**17,517**	**8,592**	**26,568**	**6,812**	**4,697**	**272**
81 **Investing activities**									
82 Purchase or Disposals of assets		€' 000	-1,427	-2,590	-400	-300	-300	-300	-300
83 **Total inflows / (outflows) from investing activities (b)**		€' 000	-1,427	-2,590	-400	-300	-300	-300	-300
84 **Financing Activities**									
85 Share Capital Increase		€' 000							
86 New bank loans raised / Repayments of loans		€' 000	-16,274	-17,405	-13,482	-29,768	-6,512	-4,397	28
87 **Total inflows / (outflows) from financing activities (c)**		€' 000	-16,274	-17,405	-13,482	-29,768	-6,512	-4,397	28
88 **Net Increase/(Decrease) in cash and cash equivalents (a)+(b)+(c)**		€' 000	-2,274	-2,477	-5,290	-3,500	-	0	0
89 Cash and cash equivalents at the beginning of the period		€' 000	17,853	15,579	12,290	7,000	3,500	3,500	3,500
90 Cash and cash equivalents at the end of the period		€' 000	15,579	13,101	7,000	3,500	3,500	3,500	3,500
91									

EXHIBIT 3.21   Complete proforma cash flow statement for 2014 to 2017

In the next chapter we will see how much of the above cash results from the first reason above and how much from the second.

As a final note to the cash flow statement, please note that, in practice, its preparation for statutory purposes is a much more complicated procedure than the plain recording of the account differences between 2 consecutive balance sheets. Let us illustrate this through an example. Imagine that SteelCo took a provision of €500k in 2013 for bad debts, that is, clients that are doubtful payers. This accounting entry would be to debit an expense account of the income statement (thus increasing it) and to credit a liability (provision) account of the balance sheet (thus increasing it). By subtracting from the later balance sheet account the relevant account of last year's balance sheet we would record a cash inflow which is false. The proper adjustment to the cash flow statement would be to add back to the operating activities the amount of bad debt provision – since it is not a cash expense – and remove it from the difference of the liability accounts. Nothing is going to change in the bottom line but the presentation of cash flows from various sources would be more realistic. Nevertheless, for the purposes of this book and the modelling techniques it presents, a bare difference between 2 consecutive balance sheet accounts will denote the cash inflow or outflow.

Having finished with the modelling of the 3 basic financial statements of SteelCo, the presentation of the 3 covenants – which is the main reason the FP&A built the whole model above – is still pending. It is best practice in financial modelling to put the results or the outcome of the model onto a different page from the workings. In our case the workings are the 3 financial statements and that is why they are all included on a single sheet as you will see in the Excel file that accompanies the book.

The next chapter starts by describing how the FP&A treats the presentation of his findings. He will build a summary page giving an overview of the answer to the main problem the model was addressed to solve and will focus on the parameters that influence these results the most.

BIBLIOGRAPHY AND REFERENCES

1. http://www.corality.com/tutorials/circular-interest-interest-average-balances.
2. http://chandoo.org/wp/2010/09/16/excel-circular-references/.

4

Forecasting Performance

Chapter 4 deals with the mechanics of forecasting and specifically the methods behind the development of an integrated set of financial forecasts that reflect the company's expected performance.

Firstly, a dashboard-like control panel is designed with the proper financial indicators that need to be monitored according to the specific problem the model is required to solve. For example, in order to deal with liquidity issues one needs to focus on working capital parameters. Secondly, the basic statistical methods used to forecast sales are examined. Almost all financial statement models are sales driven, in that they assume that many of the balance sheet and income statement items are directly or indirectly related to sales. So forecasting sales is one of the greatest challenges for the business modeller. Regression analysis (a statistical method that enables one to fit a straight line that on average represents the best possible graphical relationship between sales and time) is used in order to extrapolate future sales based on the past sales trend. Moreover regression analysis is used to look at the relationship between any 2 measures, say, sales and CAPital EXpenditures (CAPEX), sales and costs, and so on. These relationships can be the best possible proxies for many P&L and balance sheet figures when combined with sales, especially in the absence of any analytical working about these figures.

4.1 INTRODUCTION: DESIGNING A DASHBOARD-LIKE CONTROL PANEL

In this section, we will see why a dashboard-like control panel is an exceptionally useful interface for measuring and visualizing key performance indicators. There is little point in building a complex model in order to communicate its output results poorly to the people to whom it really matters. With the rapid rise of information technology, there is an increased demand for high-quality visualization of information. The difficulty comes in finding a means of presenting this information to the proposed audience in a way that is quick and easy to interpret – and here is where dashboards come in.

Based on SteelCo's case described in Chapter 3 we will build a control panel where the user will be able to monitor all the relevant information of interest. We will consider the control panel as the user interface to our model. The control panel will be the size of an A4 report. Since the space available is limited, the most important decision is what kind of information we will present in the control panel. This decision is ultimately dictated by the problem the model is required to solve (model output) and the key performance indicators that drive this output. Information visualization expert Stefen Few highlights some common metrics that can be found on a business dashboard, categorized by individual business areas (e.g. in the sales area, sales volume and selling prices; in the finance area, revenues and profits, etc.).[1] As far as SteelCo's case is concerned, we will try to monitor on the one hand the assumptions with the greatest impact on the evolution of the 3 covenants (which are the output of the model) and on the other hand the covenants themselves. We could argue about which are the most important Key Performance Indicators (KPIs) driving the values of covenants but for the sake of this exercise we will monitor the values of the working capital parameters, that is, the Days Sales Outstanding (DSO), the Days Inventory Outstanding (DIO), and the Days Payable Outstanding (DPO), the growth rate of the sales volume of the long and flat products, and finally the gross margin assuming constant sales prices. We will embed buttons in our control panel so that it is easy to change the values of the above parameters without having to input a hard coded number each time. Moreover, we will add graphs in order to see the relevant balance sheet and income statement accounts. For example, when we change the working capital parameters, the funding needs of SteelCo change and so does the debt of the company.

Before we start to build the control panel it is essential to sit down with pencil and paper and plan the design and structure of it. A typical structure will look like the one in Exhibit 4.1. The blank area of a worksheet will be divided into 3 parts: one for the main inputs of the model, another for the main outputs, and the third part will include some of Excel's charting facilities in order to improve the understanding of the output. Please note that in the upper left corner of the inputs we have embedded form controls by making use of Excel's developer module.

We split the input area into 2 subparts: one that accommodates the working capital parameters which are the most important ones and the other the operational parameters, such as the growth of sales volume and the gross margin. Then we insert 3 form controls from the developer module of Excel. If you do not have the developer module in the Excel ribbon go to Excel options and choose the **Popular** tab (default tab) and tick the third button as shown in Exhibit 4.2. To insert a form control, just go to the developer module, turn on the **Design mode**, and then insert a **scroll bar** (see Exhibit 4.3). Once you insert a scroll bar (form control), while staying in the design mode, place it close to the legend of the variable which the control will change. To connect the control with the variable, say the DSO, you have to **link** the control with a specific cell that will form the input of the variable. To do so turn on the **Design mode**, then select the control, right click on it, and select the **Properties** tab (see Exhibit 4.4). You see 3 arrows pointing:

1. at the linked cell where I have manually inputted cell D6,
2. at the maximum value where I have chosen 150 days, and
3. at the minimum value where I have chosen 0 days, that is cash sales (Exhibit 4.4a).

Note that the value of a scroll bar can only be an integer between 0 and 65,535. Now, if you leave (exit) the **Design mode** you will be able to increase or decrease the value of the cell linked by the scroll bar by clicking the scroll arrows. In a similar way, we can insert a scroll

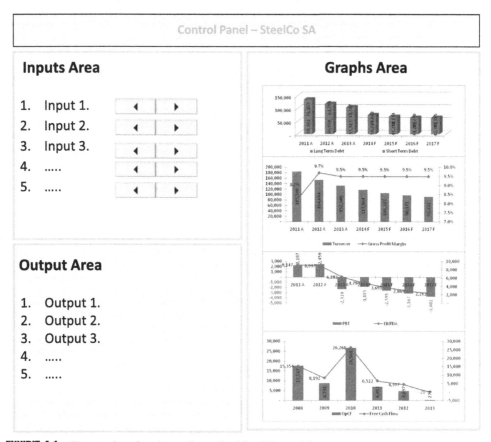

EXHIBIT 4.1 The user interface (control panel) of SteelCo model

bar for the DIO and another one for the DPO. We need 2 more scroll bars to link them with the input of the growth rate of the sales volume of the long and flat products and the gross margin.

We face 2 problems with the above inputs:

1. The growth rate and the gross margin should be in decimal values, e.g. 5%, and
2. The growth rate should be able to take negative values. Remember in Chapter 3 that the sales volume for both the long and the flat products was decreasing year after year.

As we said before, scroll bars can only be set to positive integers in Excel. Hence to get decimal values and negative numbers we need to use formulae in a separate cell from the one the scroll bar is linked with.

For example to get decimal values for the gross margin from 0 to 15% we set the maximum value of the scroll bar to 15 and the minimum to 0. When an amount is selected, the value is divided by 100 to give the desired value. In this way we can increase the value of the growth rate by 1 percentage point. We can go from 8% (8/100) to 9% (9/100) but not to 8.5%. If we want more granularity then we have to set the maximum to 150 and divide the amount of the scroll bar by 1000 to give the desired value. For example, 150/1000 is 15%, 145/1000 is 14.5%, and so on.

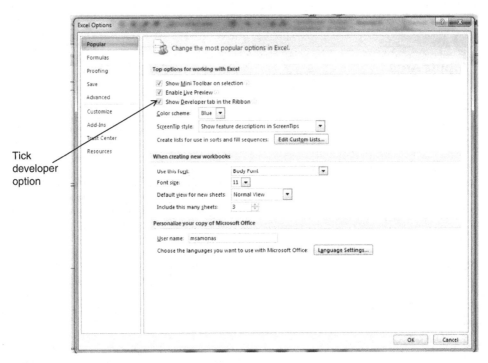

Tick developer option

EXHIBIT 4.2 Installing the developer module in Excel 2007

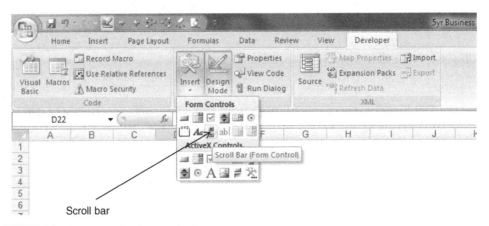

Scroll bar

EXHIBIT 4.3 Inserting a scroll bar

Finally, to get negative numbers, e.g. so that the growth rate moves between −15% and 15% to precision of 1 decimal place, we will set the maximum value, at the properties window, to 300 and the minimum to 0 and we will use the following formula in a separate cell:

$$\text{Growth rate} = \frac{(D15 - 150)}{1000}$$

where D15 is the cell linked to the scroll bar and takes values between 0 and 300 (Exhibit 4.4b).

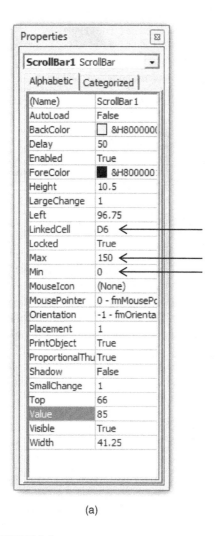

(a)

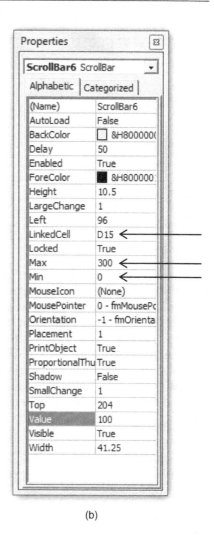

(b)

EXHIBIT 4.4   Scroll bars properties

Exhibit 4.5 presents the input area of the control panel that is dedicated to the operational parameters and especially the sales volume increase (growth rate) and the gross margin. You can see here what we have discussed previously. That is, the cells that are linked to the scroll bars and the formulae that use these cells in order to obtain decimal and negative values.

Now that everything is in place we can format cells D15 and D17 (the cells linked with the scroll bars) to the background colour (e.g. white) so that they do not appear in the control panel. In doing so the control panel user sees that by clicking the scroll arrows they can choose a new sales volume increase and a new gross margin in percentage form.

Note that the input parameters that participate in the control panel should feed directly into the assumptions page with the desired values. That is, for 2014 the values of the DSO, DIO, DPO, the percentage of sales volume increase, and the percentage of gross margin will be dictated from the control panel whereas the same parameters for the rest of the years in

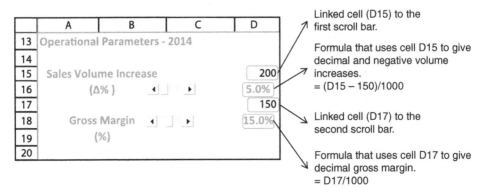

EXHIBIT 4.5 Formulae used with scroll bars in order to obtain decimal and negative values

the explicit forecast period up to 2017 will take values from the "Assumptions" worksheet or other worksheets, as we will see later in the book. Or we could choose to use the same percentage of sales volume increase and percentage of gross margin across the years from 2014 up to 2017, equal to the desired values set from the control panel. For the specific case of SteelCo we will choose to change, from the control panel, only the input parameters of 2014, in order to see their immediate impact on the covenants of interest.

Now we have finished with the inputs area (see Exhibit 4.1) we can proceed to the outputs. We will definitely include monitoring of the 3 covenants of interest. Moreover, other financial indicators, in order of their importance, include the following:

1. Annual Turnover
2. EBITDA
3. Profit/(Loss) Before Tax
4. Free Cash Flow
5. Net Debt.

The above outputs will read directly from the workings page of the model where we have modelled the income statement, the balance sheet, and the cash flow. The 3 covenants for 2014 will read directly from the "Ratio" worksheet. The "Ratio" worksheet computes all the ratios described in Chapter 2 based on the actual and the proforma financial statements covered in Chapter 3. The "Ratio" worksheet is part of the complete model described in the Appendix and can be found in the website which accompanies the book.

Finally, we need to define which charts to include in the graphs area of the control panel. As far as SteelCo's case is concerned we have included a chart that shows the evolution of both the short- and the long-term debt (see Exhibit 4.6). A further chart with 2 axes presents the evolution of annual turnover on the first axis (left hand axis) and the gross margin percentage on the other (right hand axis).

The third chart we will incorporate is one which shows, again on a double axis, the evolution of profits/(losses) before tax (LHA) and EBITDA (RHA). Finally, the fourth chart is a double-axis one presenting the Operating Cash Flow (OpCF) (LHA) and the Free Cash Flow (FCF) (RHA). Exhibit 4.6 shows what the control panel will look like when it is ready.

Although this is not a book on how to exploit Excel's capabilities for graphical applications we will describe briefly how to create a double-axis chart in the control panel.

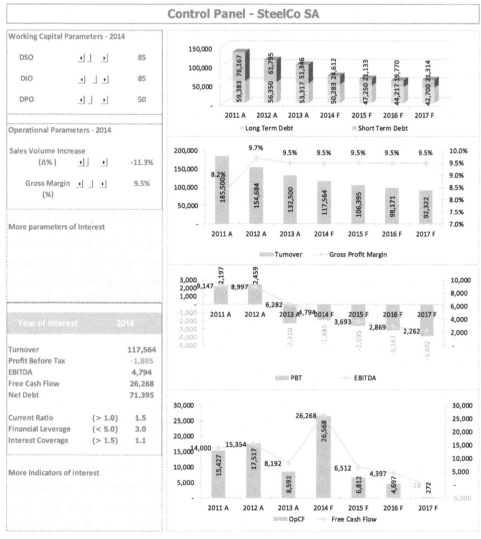

All Figures are in € '000 unless otherwise stated

EXHIBIT 4.6 Complete control panel of SteelCo for year 2014

First of all let's consider why we use double-axis charts. The idea is that instead of having a single chart for each variable we want to monitor, it is more efficient to see both on the same chart, so that we can better evaluate their trend over time and simultaneously save space. Then let's describe how to construct such a chart. It's very simple. Go to the **Insert tab** from the toolbar at the top of the screen. In the **Charts group**, click on the **Column button** and select the first chart under **2-D Column**. A blank chart object should appear in your spreadsheet. Next right click on this chart object and choose **Select Data** from the popup menu. In the Select Data window you need to enter the data that you want to plot. Let us plot Profit Before Tax (PBT) on our primary Y-axis (left side) first. To do so click the **Chart data range button**

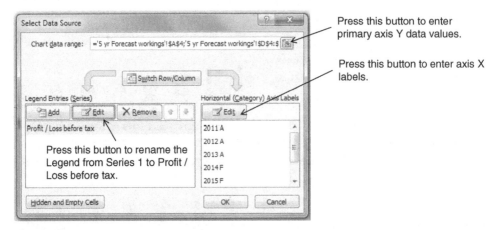

EXHIBIT 4.7   Adding data to a blank chart

and select the row with the data to be plotted from the "Workings" worksheet. Next click the
Edit button of the Horizontal (category) Axis Labels in order to select the row with the name
of the years from the "Workings" worksheet. Finally click the **Edit button** of the Legend
Entries (Series) to select the name (Legend) of the plotted data (see Exhibit 4.7).

By clicking the **OK button** of the above Select data source window you will see the chart
with the profit (loss) before tax data plotted in a bar (columns) format. By default the legend
of the chart appears on the right of it. It is better for practical reasons to have it at the bottom.
To do so, right click the chart, go to the **Layout tab** of the **Chart tools**, click **Legend**, and
select **Show Legend at Bottom**.

Now let us add the second axis. To do so first you need to add the second data series (the
EBITDA) as a column chart. Click on the chart and choose **Select data** from the **Design tab**
of the **Chart Tools**. Then click the **Add button** of the Legend Entries (Series) to select the
data to be plotted (see Exhibit 4.7 and Exhibit 4.8). Now the chart has 2 series of data, PBT
and EBITDA, both in columnar format.

We do not want both data sets to be in columnar format. It is better to present the second
one as a line chart. To do so select the EBITDA data series by clicking on the Columns of
the chart, right click on them and from the **Design tab** of the **Chart Tools** select the **Change
Chart Type** (see Exhibit 4.9).

EXHIBIT 4.8   Adding a second data set (EBITDA) to the chart

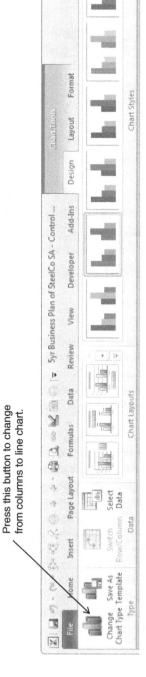

EXHIBIT 4.9 Adding a send data set (EBITDA) to the chart

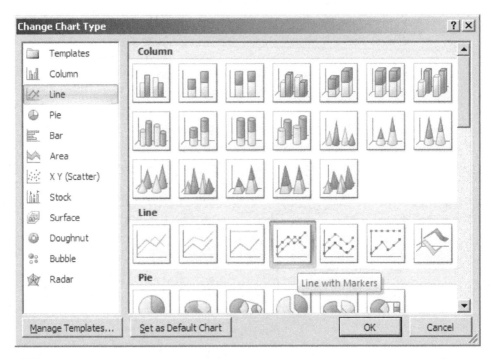

EXHIBIT 4.10   Adding a send data set (EBITDA) to the chart

When the **Change Chart Type** window appears, select the fourth chart under the **Line Chart** section and click on the **OK button** (Exhibit 4.10). The 2 data sets now appear in the chart, the first in columnar format and the second in line format. Nevertheless both data sets are plotted on the same axis. To plot the EBITDA data set on a different axis go back to the chart, right click on the data points of the line, and select **Format Data Series** from the popup menu to add the additional Y axis (see Exhibit 4.11).

The chart is finally ready and is the same as the third chart of the control panel shown in Exhibit 4.6. To adjust the size of the chart so that it fits exactly on the designated area of the control panel, click on the chart and from the **Format tab** of the **Chart Tools** go to the **Size** option and change the dimensions of the chart as required (see Exhibit 4.12).

Now that we have briefly covered chart construction, let us come back to the original reason we designed the control panel: to help us decide what should be the input parameters of the model so that the covenants for 2014 meet the criteria required by the banks. As we see in the output area of the control panel, the interest coverage covenant is breached with the current input assumptions. The interest coverage ratio is defined as the EBITDA over the net interest expense. So in order to improve this ratio we have either to improve EBITDA or to reduce interest expense or do both at the same time. Let us assume that we are trying to improve EBITDA since it is at the discretion of the management of the company. To improve EBITDA we can either increase the turnover of the company or increase its profitability (gross

EXHIBIT 4.11   Adding a send data set (EBITDA) to the chart

margin) or both. The current situation for 2014 is that the sales volume will be reduced by 11.3% and the gross profit margin will be 9.5%, the same levels as in 2013. The user of the model can easily forecast, by using the scroll bars, a smaller reduction in sales volume and a higher gross profit margin and see the immediate effect on the interest coverage covenant. As we change the reduction in sales volume and increase profitability the interest coverage improves. If we set sales volume reduction at 5% and gross profit margin at 10.5%, interest coverage of 1.51 results and the covenant is not breached. So the user of this model should inform the management of SteelCo that it is imperative to stem the decline in sales volume

EXHIBIT 4.12   Adjusting the size of the chart as required

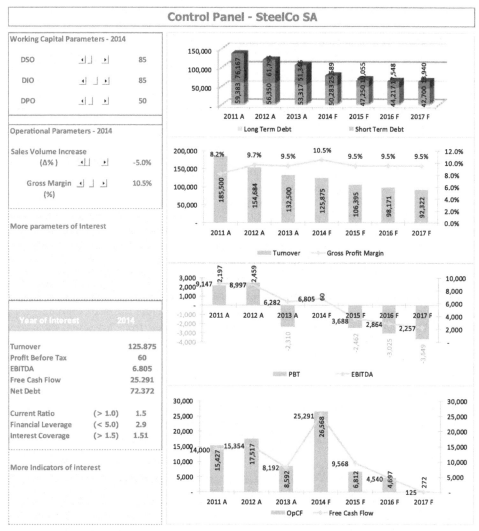

All Figures are in € '000 unless otherwise stated

EXHIBIT 4.13 The control panel after the adjustment of the operational parameters of 2014 so that the interest coverage ratio is higher than 1.5 and is not breached

and to increase profitability if the covenants are not to be breached. Exhibit 4.13 shows the aforementioned adjustments in the operational parameters of 2014 and the new output of the key financial values.

Needless to say we could achieve an interest coverage ratio higher than 1.5 by adopting various combinations of the assumptions of the model for 2014. But for the purpose of understanding the use of the control panel the way we did it is adequate.

4.2 BASIC STATISTICAL METHODS USED FOR FORECASTING

As the world becomes more and more unpredictable, forecasting practice is one of the priorities for a financial modeller. Accurate forecasts play an important role in helping businesses operate in an efficient and effective manner. In this section we will try to describe some basic statistical methods frequently used in financial statement forecasting. The objective of a forecast is to predict or estimate a future activity level such as demand, sales volume, capital expenditure, inventory levels, and so on based on the analysis of historical data.

John Tennent and Graham Friend, in their book *Guide to Business Modelling*[2], describe 3 different approaches to forecasting which can be classified as follows:

- Extrapolation techniques, such as time series analysis, implicitly assume that the past will be a reasonable predictor of the future. This assumption may be valid for mature and stable businesses, such as water and gas utilities. However, many industry sectors are experiencing increasing levels of structural change. The use of extrapolative techniques for these sectors may generate poor results.
- Causative techniques, such as regression analysis, attempt to understand the fundamental relationships that determine the dynamics of a market. This understanding, combined with a set of assumptions about the future, provides the basis for the forecast. Because the underlying relationships are often estimated from historical data, these techniques are useful when only small, incremental changes in assumptions are expected in the future.
- Judgemental techniques: modellers may often be asked to produce a forecast for a new product or market where there is no available historic data. In these cases, forecasting can become judgemental and highly subjective. Although the forecasts can be refined through studying the results of market research and by examining the experiences of similar or related products in other markets and countries, the task of forecasting becomes more like an art than a science.

In practice, most modellers rely on a mixture of all 3 techniques. They may establish the current market trends through time series analysis, and attempt to understand market dynamics through regression techniques. We will give a short description of time series analysis and its various forms (e.g. exponential smoothing and moving averages – simple and weighted) and we will then elaborate on linear regression as a tool to derive forecasts based on historical data.

A time series is a set of data observed over equally spaced time intervals like the monthly sales volume of SteelCo. Time series analysis seeks to discern whether there is some pattern in the data collected to date and assumes that this pattern will continue in the future. A time series can be broken down into 4 components: the trend (long-term direction), the seasonality (related movements over the year), the cyclical (changes due to cyclical movements – recession or expansion – of the economy), and the irregular (unsystematic short-term fluctuations). The development of a time series model requires a moderate amount of statistical knowledge that is beyond the scope of this book. Nevertheless the moving average and weighted moving average smoothing methods that are used to average out the irregular component of the time series are relatively simple, especially when a trend is present and there is no clear evidence of seasonality or cycles. The moving average method consists of computing an average of the most recent *n* data values for the series and using this average to forecast the value of the time series for the next period. Moving averages are useful if one can assume that the item to be forecast will stay fairly steady over time. In the weighted moving averages, older data are usually less important and the more recent observations are typically given more weight than older observations. In any case the weights are based on intuition. Moving averages and weighted moving averages are effective in smoothing out sudden fluctuations in a trend pattern in order to provide stable estimates but require maintaining extensive records of past data. On the other hand exponential smoothing requires little record keeping of past data. It is a form of weighted moving average where the weights decline exponentially as we move from the most recent data. That is, the most recent data have the most weight. A brief presentation on the various forms of time series analysis, entitled "Time Series: The Art of Forecasting", can be found on the website of Sacramento University provided by Professor Emeritus Bob Hopfe.[3]

For the rest of this section we will elaborate on regression analysis. We have already used a linear trend function in Chapter 3 to forecast the growth rate in sales volume based on historic data. The function we used in Chapter 3 is the simplest form of regression analysis. Regression analysis is a statistical technique that finds a mathematical expression that best describes a set of historic data set (X, Y). Then this expression may be used to forecast future data values of Ys given future data values of Xs. The latter is called extrapolation and is the process by which we use the regression line to predict a value of the Y variable for a value of the X variable that is *outside* the range of the data set. The opposite is called interpolation and is the process by which we use the regression line to predict a value of the Y variable for a value of the X variable that is not one of the data points but is *within* the range of the data set.

Let us see how we forecast in Excel the growth rate of 2014 equal to -11.3% based on the growth rates of 2012 and 2013 which were -14.8% and -13.0% respectively. The linear trend function fits a straight line to an array of known Ys and known Xs and then returns the y-values along that line for any new x's that you specify. How does it do this? You will recall from your introductory maths class that you can always draw a straight line between any 2 points. If these 2 points are (Y_1, X_1) and (Y_2, X_2) then the straight line is defined as:

$$y = m x + b,$$

where *m* is the so-called slope of the line or gradient and equals to:

$$m = \frac{(Y_2 - Y_1)}{(X_2 - X_1)}$$

and *b* is the intercept, determines the point at which the line crosses the *y*-axis, and equals to:

$$b = y - m x = Y_1 - \frac{(Y_2 - Y_1)}{(X_2 - X_1)} * X_1 = Y_2 - \frac{(Y_2 - Y_1)}{(X_2 - X_1)} * X_2$$

As far as SteelCo's case is concerned, if $(Y_1, X_1) = (-14.8, 1)$ and $(Y_2, X_2) = (-13.0, 2)$ and we want to find (Y_3, X_3) where $X_3 = 3$ then:

$$m = \frac{(-13.0-(-14.8))}{(2-1)} = 1.77\% \text{ and}$$

$$b = -14.8\% - 1.77\%*1 = -16.59\%$$

Thus

$$Y_3 = 1.77\% *x - 16.59\% = 1.77\%*3 - 16.59\% = -11.27\% \text{ (see Exhibit 3.7).}$$

Instead of doing all the above calculations back in Chapter 3, we simply selected the 2 cells containing the values of 14.8% and -13.0% respectively and we dragged them to the right.

Now imagine we have a set of data which consists of the N observed data points (x_1, y_1), (x_2, y_2), ..., (x_N, y_N) and we want to fit a straight line in the form $y = m x + b$ described above. This straight line, or *best-fitting line as it is called,* can be obtained by using the method of least squares. The idea behind the least squares method is that we can find m and b by minimizing the sum of the squares of the deviations *(least square error)* of the actual values of y_i from the line's calculated value of y. The formulae for m and b are:

$$m = \frac{\Sigma xy - \dfrac{(\Sigma x)(\Sigma y)}{n}}{\Sigma x^2 - \dfrac{(\Sigma x)^2}{n}}$$

and

$$b = \bar{Y} - m\,\bar{X},$$

where

$$\bar{Y} = \frac{\Sigma Y}{n}$$

and

$$\bar{X} = \frac{\Sigma X}{n}$$

In all equations, the summation sign is assumed to be from 1 to n.

The easiest way to get the best fit of a data set is to plot it in Excel and add a linear trendline. Let us take the 7 data points of the annual revenues of SteelCo for the years 2011 to 2017 as presented in Exhibit 3.11 and plot them using a line chart (see Exhibit 4.14). By right clicking on the line and selecting the **Add Trendline** at the window that pops up you get another window like the one in Exhibit 4.15.

Please note that the window popup of the **Trendline** has by default ticked the **Linear trendline button**. Please also note that at the bottom of this window we have ticked the **Display Equation on chart** and **Display R-square value on chart** boxes respectively.

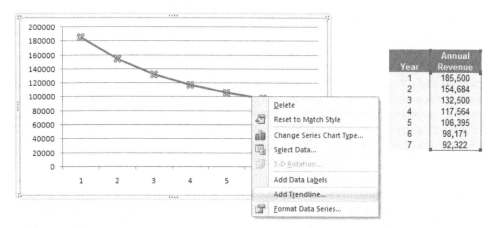

EXHIBIT 4.14   Plotting and adding a trendline to SteelCo's revenues

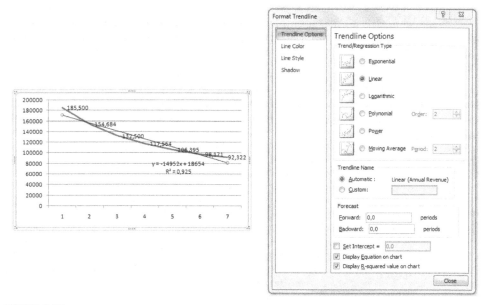

EXHIBIT 4.15   Using a linear trendline to model SteelCo's revenues

On the left hand side of Exhibit 4.15 we see the line chart with the best fit (least squares equation):

$$y = -14952x + 18654$$

and another value, that of R^2 which equals $R^2 = 0.925$. R^2 is a statistic that gives information about the goodness of fit of a linear trendline. In regression, the R^2 coefficient is a statistical measure of how well the regression line approximates the real data points. An R^2 of 1 indicates that the regression line perfectly fits the data whereas an R^2 of 0 indicates that there is no fit between the regression line and the data points.

Apart from the linear trendline you see in Exhibit 4.15 many other options (e.g. nonlinear trendlines) that can also be inserted if appropriate. Describing these options is definitely outside the scope of this book but we will make another attempt and try to fit a nonlinear trendline in order to get a better R^2 than the 0.925 of the linear trendline. If we choose the polynomial trendline with order 2 then we get the graph shown in Exhibit 4.16. You see that now $R^2 = 0.997$ this is an almost perfect fit. Even without the R^2 statistic you can assess visually that this is a much better fit than that of the linear trendline.

Polynomial trendlines are useful when there is reason to believe that the relationship between the Y (dependent) and the X (independent) variables is curvilinear. Curvilinear relationships are presented either by a maximum or a minimum in the (X, Y) curve. In a polynomial regression model of order n the relationship between the dependent and independent variables is modelled as a nth order polynomial function:

$$y = a_n x^n + a_{n-1} x^{n-1} + \ldots + a_2 x^2 + a_1 x + a_0$$

Polynomial models are also useful in approximating functions to unknown and possibly very complex nonlinear relationships. The most frequently used polynomial model is the quadratic one (second-order model) like the one we have used to model SteelCo's revenues in Exhibit 4.16.

The interested reader can add other regression trendlines to the chart with the revenue data of SteelCo and see how well they fit. This example, as well as the whole model we are building, is provided in an Excel spreadsheet so that the user can experiment him- or herself with various regression options.

Now it is time to use the analysis provided above in order to forecast the sales revenues of SteelCo for 2018.

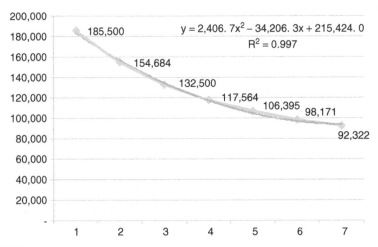

EXHIBIT 4.16   Using a quadratic polynomial trendline to model SteelCo's revenues

4.3 FORECASTING SALES

When a company employs statistical sales forecasting techniques, it uses its historical sales data in order to predict future sales. Because of the complex mathematical formulae used to create sales forecasts, most companies rely on advanced software to accomplish this task. In case of an existing business things are a little easier since there is a sales history. Sales are trending up or down and the forecast reflects the company's business strategy. Sales revenues are forecast using the unit method:

Sales Revenues = Number of Units Sold × Price per Unit

Using the above method we forecast the sales revenues of SteelCo for years 2014 to 2017. Forecasting sales is more difficult for a start-up business. Sometimes, the *break-even point* can provide a starting point for creating the sales forecast. The break-even point determines the sales volume at which a company's total sales equal its total expenses, that is, it neither makes any profit nor incurs any loss. In this case the sales forecast is not something we are trying to estimate but rather a definite goal we need to achieve.

The forecast break-even sales are given by the following formula:

$$X = F / (P - V)$$

where

X: Volume of output (in units)

F: Total fixed costs

V: Variable costs per unit

P: Price per unit.

For example, a start-up coffee shop with total fixed costs equal to €100k, variable cost per coffee of €0.4, and selling price per coffee equal to €2 needs to sell 62,500 coffees in the first year of operation if it wants to break even:

No. of coffees = X = €100,000 / (€2 − €0.4) = 62,500 per year

The above figure could be used as the sales forecast for the first year the coffee shop would operate.

Another approach to forecasting the number of units sold, especially for a start-up high tech business, is to use a "technology adoption" or diffusion curve. The process of adopting new innovations has been studied for over 30 years, and one of the most popular adoption models is described by Everett Rogers in his book *Diffusion of Innovations*, first published in 1962.[4] The idea of diffusion or adoption of new innovations has been derived from the "contagion" models developed in the biological literature to model the spread of contagious diseases.[5] Models describing the adoption process have been applied to a wide range of new products and technologies,[6] and have been used by many companies[7] to predict sales of major new technologies.

Rogers[4] explained that the probability that a consumer adopts a new technology was expected to increase with the proportion of people who have already adopted it (adopters). He categorizes adopters as: innovators, early adopters, early majority, late majority, and laggards, as shown in Exhibit 4.17 taken from the 2003 edition of *Diffusion of Innovations*.[4] We can see that new adopters are presented in a bell-shaped curve whereas the rate of adoption (market share) takes the form of a so-called S-shaped diffusion curve. *Innovators* are people that are willing to trial new products/services. Typically, the excitement and personal satisfaction of being one of the few to be actually using the product/service are the main reasons for take-up. For example, when technology-based companies release early versions of software, innovators are the target market and the catalyst for penetration. *Early adopters* are closely tied to Innovators and are strong opinion formers within their social networks. They typically give advice and recommendations to their friends and colleagues and when they have found something they think is of value they often become brand advocates. The *early majority* are pragmatists, comfortable with moderately progressive ideas, but unwilling to act without solid proof of benefits. They are followers who are influenced by mainstream fashions. The *late majority* are conservative pragmatists who hate risk and are uncomfortable with new ideas. Practically their only driver is the fear of not fitting in. Finally, *laggards* are people who see a high risk in adopting a particular product or service and are the last individuals of a social network to try it.

Among the various types of S-shaped diffusion curves we could use, we will elaborate on the Gompertz Curve named after Benjamin Gompertz, who derived it back in 1825 in order to estimate human mortality. The formula of the Gompertz Curve is the following:

$$F(t) = S \ e^{(-K \ e^{(-qt)})}$$

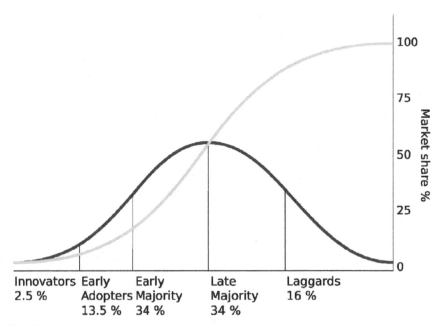

EXHIBIT 4.17 The diffusion of innovations adapted from Rogers
    With successive groups of consumers adopting the new technology (bell-shaped curve shown in dark line), its market share (S-shaped curve shown in gray line) will eventually reach saturation level[4]

where

> *F(t)*: the number of people who have already adopted the technology,
> *S*: the number of people who will eventually adopt the technology (potential market),
> *K*: a change in *K* shifts the diffusion curve horizontally without changing the speed of the diffusion process,
> *q*: a decrease/increase in parameter *q* slows down/accelerates the diffusion process, and
> *T*: time (e.g. in years).

Let us use the Gompertz Curve to verify the curves of Exhibit 4.17. If we set the following values – *S* equals 1, *K* equals 15, *q* equals 0.5 – and plot the formula below for 18 periods (let us say quarters) then we get the curve of Exhibit 4.18 (dark line; refers to left hand axis).

$$F\left(t=1..18\right)=1*e^{\left(-15\ *\ e^{(-0.5*t)}\right)}$$

A detailed description of how the coefficients *K* and *q* can be derived according to the maximum penetration and the number of periods (*t*) can be found in [2]. The gray line of Exhibit 4.18 (refers to the right hand axis) represents the number of new adopters at any point in time (*t*) which can be calculated by subtracting from the number of adopters who have already taken up the new product or service at point (*t*) the number of adopters who had taken up the new product or service at point (*t-1*). That is, the new adopters of the period (*t*) are derived from the following equation:

$$\text{New adopters } (t) = F(t) - F(t-1)$$

For example for t=3 (i.e. the third quarter from the launch of the product or service), the diffusion is:

$$F\left(3\right)=e^{\left(-15\ *\ e^{(-0.5*3)}\right)}=3.5\%$$

of the potential market, and the new adopters for the third quarter are:

$$\text{New adopters } (t=3) = F(3) - F(2) = 3.5\% - 0.4\% = 3.1\%$$

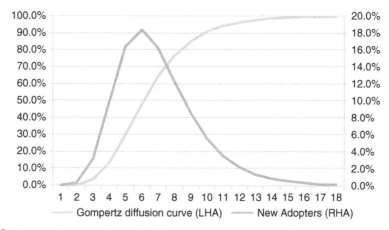

EXHIBIT 4.18 Plotting Gompertz Curve (dark line) and new adopters (gray line) for 18 periods

Now it is time to determine the number S of people who will eventually adopt the new product or service. New adopters (potential market) are always a subset of the addressable market of the new product or service as shown in Exhibit 4.19. For example, if the total market is 100% and (a) only 50% of the market has sufficient income to consume our product or service and (b) 60% of the market is in the age range 18–45 that will most probably adopt our product or service, then the addressable market is 50%*60% = 30%. To forecast the potential demand over the years we will multiply the adoption rate from the Gompertz Curve by the addressable market. So for a country with population of 50 million, and an addressable market of 30%, the number S of people who will eventually adopt the new product or service are:

$$50m \times 30\% = 15 \text{ million people}$$

Then the potential demand at the 10th quarter of the forecast will be 91% and the number of potential customers will be:

Potential Market = Market Size (population) × Addressable Market (%) × Adoption Rate (%), or

Potential Market = 50m × 30% × 91% = 13.6 million customers

If we want to forecast sales revenues for the 10th quarter of the forecast then we should multiply:

Potential Market (Potential Customers) × Sales/Customer/Quarter (units) × Unit Price

Following the above method we have broken down sales revenues into the following components:

Sales Revenues = Market Size (population) × Addressable Market (%) × Adoption Rate (%) × X Sales/Customer/Quarter (units) × Unit Price

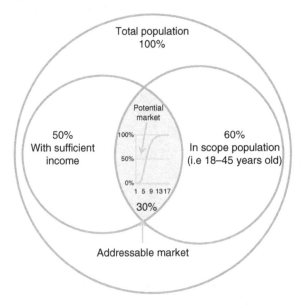

EXHIBIT 4.19 Deriving the potential market of a new product or service

4.3.1 Bottom-up Versus Top-down Forecasting

The revenue forecasts described so far are the so-called "bottom-up" forecasts since they include the units that will be sold at some point in time.

An alternative to bottom-up models is to forecast total revenue directly, without examining the individual elements that comprise total revenue. A forecast based on this approach is sometimes referred to as a "top-down" forecast [2]. In practice, many modellers adopt both top-down and bottom-up approaches when faced with an uncertain future market. To add confidence to a forecast, it is often advisable to use a number of different approaches. For example, when we want to forecast the revenues of a start-up business that offers new technology products or services, we may be forced to adopt both approaches. Imagine the uncertainties associated with the new product or service adoption and the difficulty we will face if we try to forecast revenues on a long-term horizon of more than 7 years. Bottom-up models are useless in this case. Consequently, the forecasts have to be derived from an analysis of customers' disposable income and the percentage of it that could be allocated to the product or service of interest. For example, if we want to model the revenue of a new mobile entertainment application, we will have to make assumptions concerning the level of current entertainment expenditure on other similar applications and then multiply this figure by the potential market as we did above. Thus, if we know that 5% of the disposable income of a customer between 18 and 45 years old goes on mobile entertainment and his or her disposable income is €200 per month, then the potential market for 15 million people, described in terms of value, would be:

$$€200 \times 5\% \times 15 \text{ million} = €150 \text{ million}$$

A top-down approach would consider that the revenue of the new mobile entertainment application will be a tiny percentage, e.g. 4% at the first year of the launch followed by a higher percentage year on year of the total pie of €150 million.

4.3.2 Forecasting Sales of Existing Products or Services

If we come back to SteelCo's case, since it is an existing company with a certain history of sales data, we will use regression analysis as described in Chapter 3 to forecast revenues. We have already applied regression analysis to forecast the growth rate of SteelCo's sales volume for years 2014 to 2017. We then estimated sales revenues indirectly. We could forecast sales revenues for 2018 using the same technique we did for 2014–2017. Nevertheless SteelCo already faces 2 years of reduced sales (2012–2013) and we have forecast another 4 recessionary years (2014–2017). As we will see in Chapter 5, recent research has shown that the average duration of a downturn is between 5 and 6 years. So in our view we should use a different forecasting technique that will assume that 2017 will be the last year of the downturn and from 2018 SteelCo will return to growth. As we mentioned previously, polynomial trendlines assume a curvilinear relationship between variables that shows a minimum in the curve. If we examine carefully the curve of Exhibit 4.16 we can see that the minimum could be at the 7th period (year 2017) and if we had a function that described the relationship of the data point plotted on the chart we could easily forecast the value of Y for the 8th period (year 2018). But this function is presented in the right top corner of Exhibit 4.16 and is as follows:

$$Y = 2,406.8 * x^2 - 34,206*x + 215,424$$

where x equals the period under forecast and ranges from 1 to 7. So if we want to forecast (extrapolate) sales for 2018 then we should use the above formula for $x = 8$ (Exhibit 4.17):

$$\text{Sales}_{2018} = 2{,}406.8 * 8^2 - 34{,}206 * 8 + 215{,}424 = €95{,}811\text{k}$$

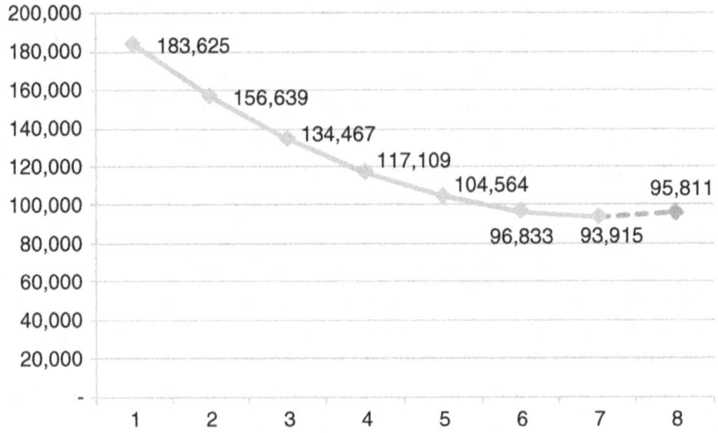

EXHIBIT 4.20   Forecasting sales for 2018 based on a polynomial quadratic function

It is clear from the curve shown in Exhibit 4.20 that the sales of the 7th period (year 2017) are the curve's minimum point.

An alternative approach would be to use a "*top-down*" model as described in the previous section, to try and forecast the evolution in the size of the steel market up to 2018 and then estimate SteelCo's share of that market. Multiplying the addressable steel market by SteelCo's market share we could arrive at a sales estimate for a certain year. For example, assuming that the addressable steel market in the country in which SteelCo operates will be 1,750,000 Metric Tons (MTs) in 2014 and SteelCo's market share will be 10%, then SteelCo's sales in 2014 would be the following:

$$1{,}750{,}000 \text{ MTs} \times 10\% = 175{,}000 \text{ MTs}$$

a figure that is close enough to the one derived in Chapter 3 through a different logic. To forecast activity in the steel market for the years to come, we could find correlations between it and some macroeconomic indices (such as GDP growth, private consumption, consumer confidence, home sales, industrial production, unemployment rate, etc.) that are published and forecast by official bureaux (IMF, World Bank, Central Banks, etc.). This kind of forecast is called a macroeconomic or econometric forecast and could be derived from an equation of the following form:

$$S_t = a + b\, GDP_{t-1} + c\, P_t + d\, H_t + e_t$$

where

S_t is the steel market in year t,
GDP_{t-1} is the Gross Domestic Product during the previous year,
P_t is the industrial production forecast for the year t,

H_t is the home sales forecast of the year t, and

e_t is an error term measuring the extent to which the model cannot fully explain the steel market.

Then the objective of the macroeconomist or the econometrician would be to obtain estimates of the parameters a, b, c, and d; these estimated parameter values, when used in the model's equation, should enable predictions for future values of the steel market to be made contingent upon the prior year's GDP and future year's production and home sales. I would like to stress here that the construction and preparation of macroeconomic forecasts is one of the most publicly visible activities of professional economists as they concern many aspects of economic life including financial planning, state budgeting, and monetary and fiscal policy. The production of these kinds of forecasts requires a clear understanding of the associated econometric tools even though it results in forecasts which tend to be little better than intelligent guesswork – and that is a fact. During the years before the Great Recession of 1929 forecasts might have appeared to improve, but that was only because most economies became less volatile. As is well known, the Great Recession was completely missed, not to mention the 2007 financial crisis which started as an asset bubble. In any case macroeconomic or econometric forecasting is far beyond the scope of this book.

We have now adequately covered the topic of forecasting sales for both new and existing businesses, products, and services and it is time to move on to forecasting costs.

4.4 FORECASTING COSTS

The first cost item of the income statement is the Cost of Goods Sold (COGS). The COGS forecast relates directly to the sales forecast. The cost of producing goods varies directly with the level of sales. To calculate the cost of goods forecast, either we may use the unit costing method or we can work indirectly (as we did in Chapter 3) and estimate the gross profit by forecasting the gross profit margin percentage, as shown below:

$$COGS = Sales - Gross\ Profit = Sales - Sales \times Gross\ Profit\ Margin$$
$$(\%) = Sales \times (1 - \%\ GPM)$$

The alternative method, that is the unit costing method (direct method), is exactly like the unit sales forecast, except that instead of using price, we use cost per unit. Just as in the revenue forecast, we must do this for each unit sold:

$$Cost\ of\ Goods\ Sold = Number\ of\ Units\ Sold \times Cost\ per\ Unit$$

The cost per unit is sometimes referred to as a standard cost. A standard cost in a manufacturing company consists of per unit costs for direct materials, direct labour, and overheads as we mentioned in Chapter 2. Although standard costing is an important subtopic of cost accounting, a description of it is beyond the scope of this book.

Next come the Selling General and Administrative (SG&A) costs or, to use the terminology of Chapters 2 and 3, the OPerating EXpenses (OPEX). These costs typically include the following cost categories:

OPEX Cost Categories	
Payroll	Cleaning
Transport (e.g. fuel, car rentals, tolls, etc.)	Printing, photocopies, stationery
Electricity and utilities	Insurances
Office supplies	Telecoms
Indirect materials (e.g. packaging)	Training and development
Rent	Professional fees
Dues and subscriptions	Travel and accommodation
Marketing, advertising, and promotion	Distribution
Contract services	

and are spread between different functions or departments according to the type of industry in which the company operates:

OPEX Functional Categories	
Finance	Human Resources
Sales and Marketing	Corporate Services
Information Technology	Legal
Production	Operations.

For a new business the above costs have to be estimated from scratch (from a zero base) or to be approximated based on industry averages. For example, you may use Aswath Damodaran's web page from the Stern School of Business at New York University to download the following data set which lists the SG&A cost as a percentage of sales for more than 20 industries (http://people.stern.nyu.edu/adamodar/pc/datasets/uValuedata.xls).[8] For an existing business several approaches can be used ranging from the *percent-of-sales* to full *regression analysis* between SG&A costs and sales. In Chapter 3 we broke down costs between fixed and variable. The fixed costs remained relatively constant and increased in line with the inflation rate whereas the variable costs increased according to the sales volume increases. The breakdown between fixed and variable costs was based on the actual cost analysis of past years' cost data of SteelCo. The approximation was made that 30% of SG&A was fixed and the other 70% was variable.

Fixed costs are the costs that a company has to pay regardless of the level of sales activity. Typical fixed costs include rent, utilities (e.g. electricity consumed in the offices and not during the production), insurance, service costs (e.g. accountancy costs), and salaries of the full time personnel.

Variable costs, on the other hand, depend on production volumes. They are lower when there is less production or lower sales and higher when there is more production or higher sales. They include raw materials, labour (mainly in terms of hourly wages), utilities (e.g. electricity that relates to the operation of machinery for production purposes), packaging, and delivery costs.

In practice very few costs are totally fixed or vary directly with production volume. The majority of the costs are either step fixed or step variable. An example of a step fixed cost is the rent the company pays for its offices or the salaries of full-time administration personnel. As the company grows, more and more administrative staff need to be added to accomplish its operations. After a certain increase in the activity of the company more personnel and greater office space will be needed to accommodate it so those costs that were considered fixed will be increased. That is, these costs are more or less constant over a low level shift in activity, but increase incrementally when activity shifts substantially. Similarly, an example of a step variable cost is the hiring of additional workers to produce a certain amount of products (units). If, for example, each worker is capable of producing 100 units per day and the company plans to produce 150 units per day then 2 extra workers are needed. As long as the number of units remains under 200 no other worker is needed. When the level of activity shifts above 200 units per day an extra worker needs to be hired.

Let us now return to the SteelCo case and try to forecast the operating expenses (SG&A costs) with (a) the percent-of-sales method and (b) by using regression analysis. Exhibit 4.21 shows the operating expenses already forecast in Chapter 3 using the approach of fixed and variable costs described above. We see that OPEX as a percentage of sales change from 6.8% in 2014 to 8.4% in 2017. That is, we see an increasing trend.

We could take the average OPEX as a percentage of sales for years 2011 to 2013 (5.5%) or that of 2013 (6.2%) and use it as a proxy for the forecast years 2014 to 2017. If we choose 6.2%, then the OPEX for 2014 would be (see Exhibit 4.23):

$$\text{OPEX}_{2014} = 6.2\% \times \text{Sales}_{2014} = 6.2\% \times €117,546k = €7,260k$$

Following the same approach we get the following OPEX figures:

$$\text{OPEX}_{2015} = 6.2\% \times \text{Sales}_{2015} = €6.570k$$

$$\text{OPEX}_{2016} = 6.2\% \times \text{Sales}_{2016} = €6.062k$$

$$\text{OPEX}_{2017} = 6.2\% \times \text{Sales}_{2017} = €5.701k$$

We see that with this approach OPEX in 2017 is substantially lower than the one we forecast in Chapter 3. Let us now try the regression approach. First we have to plot using an XY (Scatter) graph the actual data of sales (Annual Revenue) – X-axis versus OPEX – Y-axis. This is the dark line of the graph in Exhibit 4.22. Then we add a linear trendline in the way we demonstrated in Section 4.2. We see that the trendline, which is the gray line overlapping the dark one, fits almost perfectly ($R^2 = 0.99$).

	A	B	C	D	E	F	G	H	I	J
				SteelCo SA Proforma Financial Statements						
2				2014-2017						
3										
4	Particulars		UOM	2011 A	2012 A	2013 A	2014 F	2015 F	2016 F	2017 F
5	Income Statement									
16	Turnover Long Products		€' 000	140,000	113,884	97,500	86,510	78,291	72,239	67,935
17	Turnover Flat Products		€' 000	45,500	40,800	35,000	31,055	28,104	25,932	24,387
18	**Total Turnover**		€' 000	**185,500**	**154,684**	**132,500**	**117,564**	**106,395**	**98,171**	**92,322**
19	rate of change		%		−16.6%	−14.3%	−11.3%	−9.5%	−7.7%	−6.0%
20										
25	Operating Expenses		€' 000	−8,912	−8,516	−8,182	−8,020	−7,904	−7,831	−7,801
26	% on Total Turnover		%	−4.8%	−5.5%	−6.2%	−6.8%	−7.4%	−8.0%	−8.4%

EXHIBIT 4.21   OPerating EXpenses estimation as a percentage of sales

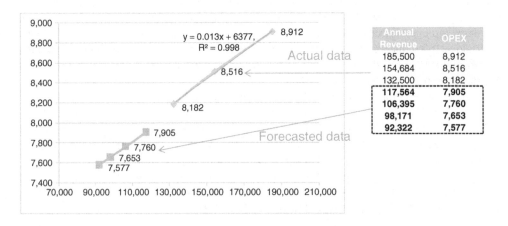

EXHIBIT 4.22   Using regression analysis to forecast OPEX (SG&A costs)

We then use the trendline of the top right corner of Exhibit 4.22 in order to forecast OPEX for 2014 based on annual revenue of 2014:

$$\text{OPEX}_{2014} = 0.013 \times \text{Sales}_{2014} + 6,377 = 0.013 \times 117,564 + 6,377 = €7,905\text{k}$$

Similarly OPEX for 2015, 2016, and 2017 equals:

$$\text{OPEX}_{2015} = €7,760\text{k}$$
$$\text{OPEX}_{2016} = €7,653\text{k}$$
$$\text{OPEX}_{2017} = €7,577\text{k}$$

Exhibit 4.23 presents OPEX (the SG&A costs) following the 3 different approaches we have already discussed. We see that the first one (breakdown of costs between fixed and variable) and the third one (linear regression between sales and OPEX) give similar results.

We could simply have selected cells D26:F26 of Exhibit 4.21, that is the actual figures of OPEX as a percentage of sales, and dragged them to the right to cells G26:J26. In this way

	A	B	C	D	E	F	G	H	I	J
				SteelCo SA Proforma Financial Statements						
2					2014-2017					
3										
4	Particulars		UOM	2011 A	2012 A	2013 A	2014 F	2015 F	2016 F	2017 F
5	Income Statement									
16	Turnover Long Products		€ 000	140,000	113,884	97,500	86,510	78,291	72,239	67,935
17	Turnover Flat Products		€ 000	45,500	40,800	35,000	31,055	28,104	25,932	24,387
18	**Total Turnover**		**€ 000**	**185,500**	**154,684**	**132,500**	**117,564**	**106,395**	**98,171**	**92,322**
19	rate of change		%		−16.6%	−14.3%	−11.3%	−9.5%	−7.7%	−6.0%
20										
25	Operating Expenses		€ 000	−8,912	−8,516	−8,182	−8,020	−7,904	−7,831	−7,801
26	% on Total Turnover		%	−4.8%	−5.5%	−6.2%	−6.8%	−7.4%	−8.0%	−8.4%
101										
102	Operating Expenses		€ 000	−8,912	−8,516	−8,182	−7,260	−6,570	−6,062	−5,701
103	% on Total Turnover		%	−4.8%	−5.5%	−6.2%	−6.2%	−6.2%	−6.2%	−6.2%
104										
105	Operating Expenses		€ 000	−8,912	−8,516	−8,182	−7,905	−7,760	−7,653	−7,577
106	% on Total Turnover		%	−4.8%	−5.5%	−6.2%	−6.7%	−7.3%	−7.8%	−8.2%

Approach

Fixed & variable costs

Percentage of sales

Regression analysis

EXHIBIT 4.23   Forecasting SG&A costs (OPEX) with 3 different approaches

the forecast OPEX as a percentage of sales would be: 6.9%, 7.6%, 8.2%, and 8.9% for years 2014, 2015, 2016, and 2017 respectively. This would give the highest increase in OPEX as a percentage of sales.

So far we have covered the Selling, General, and Administrative costs (SG&A) which are classified as periodic expenses. In the next section we will cover another cost category, Capital Expenditure (CAPEX), which gives rise to the fixed assets of a company. Only a portion of CAPEX and fixed asset costs, in contrast to SG&A costs, are classified through depreciation as periodic expenses.

4.5 FORECASTING CAPEX AND DEPRECIATION

Capital Expenditures (CAPEX) refers to the buying of fixed assets related to buildings, office equipment, furniture and fittings, computers, motor vehicles, etc. You will recall from Chapter 2 that fixed assets are items which are not for resale and have an economic life which is greater than 1 year. CAPEX is a cash flow item (cash flow from investing activities); it affects the balance sheet (fixed assets) but also the income statement through depreciation. So understanding the relationship between CAPEX, depreciation, and the financial statements is important for the financial modeller.

If we are forecasting the CAPEX of a new business, then we must decide what fixed asset we need to have in place. Different fixed asset categories have different depreciation rates. Under International Financial Reporting Standards (IFRS), the period over which an asset is depreciated is its expected useful life. The expected useful life is the time an asset is used in order to generate income for the business. Depreciation rates under IFRS are different compared to those for income tax purposes which depend on the country in which the company operates. That is, the useful life allowed for income tax purposes is different from that which might be acceptable under IFRS but for the purposes of this book we will not deal with the former. Typical depreciation rates for some common asset classes are shown below:

- Office furniture, fixtures, and equipment have a 5-year useful life.
- Cars, taxis, and trucks have a 6-year useful life.
- Information systems including hardware and software have a 6-year useful life.

■ Land improvements (e.g. fences) have a 15-year useful life; however land is not depreciated.

■ Assets used in construction have a 5-year useful life.

■ Nonresidential real estate, including offices and warehouses, has a useful life of between 20 and 33 years.

Let us assume now that we have to prepare a CAPEX and depreciation plan for a new company (NewCo). This company plans to have in place the following fixed assets during its first year of operation:

■ Land
■ Building (for office purposes)
■ Building (warehouse for production purposes)
■ Transportation (5 company cars and a truck)
■ Equipment (machinery for production purposes)
■ Office equipment (furniture, fixtures, and fittings)
■ IT equipment (hardware and software).

The founders of the company have agreed to buy a piece of land for €400k in order to build the company's offices and the warehouse. The main office building is estimated to cost around €480k and will be ready in May whereas the warehouse will cost approximately €500k and will be ready in August. They also plan to buy various office fixtures and fittings in May and a welding machine in August when the office building and the warehouse respectively will be ready. Finally, they plan to buy 5 company cars and a truck for distribution purposes and some IT infrastructure in order to equip both their offices and the warehouse.

Exhibit 4.24 shows the CAPEX plan of NewCo during its first year of operation. Next we need to define the useful lives of the different asset classes presented in NewCo's CAPEX plan and derive the depreciation rate. The land is assumed to be freehold (as opposed to leasehold) and is not depreciated as we mention previously, that is, it has an infinite useful life. Buildings have a useful life of 20 years in the case of the offices and 33 in the case of the warehouse. For the cars and tracks we will use a 6-year useful life and for the equipment a 10-year useful life. Finally, for the office equipment and the IT infrastructure we will use a 7-year and a 5-year useful life respectively. The depreciation rate is the inverse of the useful life and is given by the following equation:

$$\text{Depreciation Rate} = \frac{1}{\text{Estimated Useful Life}}$$

The depreciation using the straight-line method is derived as follows:

$$\text{Depreciation} = \frac{\text{Cost of Asset} - \text{Estimated Residual Value}}{\text{Estimated Useful Life}}$$

$$= (\text{Cost of Asset} - \text{Estimated Residual Value}) \times \text{Depreciation Rate},$$

where the *useful life* is the period over which the company intends to use the asset and is not necessarily equal to the physical life of the asset, and the *residual value* is the amount received after disposal of the asset. That is, depreciation is computed by dividing

CAPEX (€' 000)	JAN	FEB	MAR	APR	MAY	JUNE	JULY	AUG	SEP	OCT	NOV	DEC	TOTAL
					CAPEX - DEPRECIATION SCHEDULE FOR YEAR 1								
Cash Outflow													
Land													
Land plot		400											**400**
Buildings													
Main office building					480								**480**
Warehouse								500					**500**
Cars - Trucks													
Corporate vehicles		44		22		22			22				**110**
Truck										68			**68**
Equipment													
Welding machine								124					**124**
Office Fixtures and Fittings													
Various					60								**60**
IT infrastructure													
Software					15	20	25						**60**
Hardware					50				10				**60**
Total CAPEX	**0**	**444**	**0**	**22**	**605**	**42**	**25**	**624**	**32**	**68**	**0**	**0**	**1,862**

EXHIBIT 4.24   Timing plan of the CAPital EXpenditures (CAPEX) of NewCo

the depreciable amount of the asset by the expected number of the accounting periods of its useful life.

There are also other methods that could be used to calculate the depreciable cost of an asset over its life. The most commonly used depreciation methods are the following although a detailed description will not detain us here:

- Straight-line method
- Reducing balance method
- Revaluation method
- Sum of digits method
- Units of production method.

Based on the useful life of the various asset categories the depreciation rate for the main office building is $1/20 = 5\%$, the rate for the warehouse is $1/33 = 3\%$ and so on. Exhibit 4.25 shows a similar table to that of Exhibit 4.24 but with the depreciation schedule attached. This file in Excel can be found on the website accompanying the book. We can see the depreciation rates in the depreciation schedule in the column next to the description of the assets.

We see that for reasons of simplicity the depreciation starts in the month the expense is incurred. For example, the company plans to buy 2 cars costing €22k each in February. The depreciation that corresponds to this purchase for the month of February is $2 \times 22*17\%/12 = €0.6k$ assuming that the residual value of the cars is nil. The depreciation for March (cell E28) will be the same as for February since there are neither acquisitions nor disposals of any cars. That is, the depreciation expense in any given month is made up of 2 components, the depreciation on the existing assets and the depreciation on any new asset. For example, the depreciation in April equals the depreciation which arises from February's purchase plus the depreciation of the new purchase in April $(2 \times 22*17\%/12 + 22*17\%/12 = €0.9k)$.

From the above schedule we have both the gross value of the fixed assets that will form the first account of the balance sheet and the depreciation that will be subtracted from the

	A	B	C	D	E	F	G	H	I	J	K	L	M	N	O
1							CAPEX - DEPRECIATION SCHEDULE FOR YEAR 1								
2	CAPEX (€' 000)		JAN	FEB	MAR	APR	MAY	JUNE	JULY	AUG	SEP	OCT	NOV	DEC	TOTAL
3	Cash Outflow														
4	Land														
5	Land plot			400											400
6	Buildings														
7	Main office building						480								480
8	Warehouse									500					500
9	Cars - Trucks														
10	Corporate vehicles			44		22		22			22				110
11	Truck											68			68
12	Equipment														
13	Welding machine									124					124
14	Office Fixtures and Fittings														
15	Various						60								60
16	IT infrastructure														
17	Software						15	20	25						60
18	Hardware						50					10			60
19	Total CAPEX		0	444	0	22	605	42	25	624	32	68	0	0	1.862
20															
21			JAN	FEB	MAR	APR	MAY	JUNE	JULY	AUG	SEP	OCT	NOV	DEC	TOTAL
22	Depreciation	Rate													
23	Buildings	5%													
24	Main office building	-	-	-	-	-	2.0	2.0	2.0	2.0	2.0	2.0	2.0	2.0	16.0
25	Buildings	3%													
26	Warehouse		-	-	-	-	-	-	-	1.3	1.3	1.3	1.3	1.3	6.3
27	Cars - Trucks	17%													
28	Corporate vehicles		-	0.6	0.6	0.9	0.9	1.2	1.2	1.2	1.5	1.5	1.5	1.5	12.8
29	Truck		-	-	-	-	-	-	-	-	-	0.9	0.9	0.9	2.8
30	Equipment	10%													
31	Welding machine		-	-	-	-	-	-	-	1.0	1.0	1.0	1.0	1.0	5.2
32	Office Fixtures and Fittings	14%													
33	Various		-	-	-	-	0.7	0.7	0.7	0.7	0.7	0.7	0.7	0.7	5.7
34	IT infrastructure	20%													
35	Software		-	-	-	-	0.3	0.6	1.0	1.0	1.0	1.0	1.0	1.0	6.8
36	Hardware		-	-	-	-	0.8	0.8	0.8	0.8	1.0	1.0	1.0	1.0	7.3
37	Total depreciation		-	0.6	0.6	0.9	4.7	5.4	5.8	8.1	8.5	9.5	9.5	9.5	63.0

EXHIBIT 4.25   CAPEX plan and depreciation schedule for the first fiscal year of NewCo

gross fixed assets to give the net fixed assets. At the same time, depreciation will be charged to the income statement to offset against the cost of the asset on the balance sheet (Exhibit 4.26).

Gross fixed assets:	€1,862k
(–) Accumulated Depreciation:	€63k
Net fixed assets:	€1,799k

EXHIBIT 4.26   NewCo's balance sheet as of end of year 1

You will recall from Chapter 2 that the overall formula for CAPEX and depreciation in relation to fixed assets is:

$$\text{Beginning Value} + \text{CAPEX} - \text{Depreciation} = \text{Ending Value}$$

| CAPEX (€ 000) | YEAR 2 | | | | | | | | | | | | | YEAR 3 | YEAR 4 | YEAR 5 |
	JAN	FEB	MAR	APR	MAY	JUNE	JULY	AUG	SEP	OCT	NOV	DEC	TOTAL	TOTAL	TOTAL	TOTAL
Cash Outflow																
Land																
Land plot													-	-	-	-
Buildings																
Main office building													-		-	-
Warehouse													-	-	-	-
Cars - Trucks																
Corporate vehicles													-	-	-	-
Truck													-		-	-
Equipment																
Welding machine						124							124	-	-	-
Office Fixtures and Fittings																
Various					5				5				10	10	10	10
IT infrastructure																
Software													-	-	-	-
Hardware													-	-	-	-
Total CAPEX	0	0	0	0	5	124	0	0	5	0	0	0	134	10	10	10

Depreciation	JAN	FEB	MAR	APR	MAY	JUNE	JULY	AUG	SEP	OCT	NOV	DEC	TOTAL	TOTAL	TOTAL	TOTAL
Buildings																
Main office building	2.0	2.0	2.0	2.0	2.0	2.0	2.0	2.0	2.0	2.0	2.0	2.0	24.0	24.0	24.0	24.0
Buildings																
Warehouse	1.3	1.3	1.3	1.3	1.3	1.3	1.3	1.3	1.3	1.3	1.3	1.3	15.0	15.0	15.0	15.0
Cars - Trucks																
Corporate vehicles	1.5	1.5	1.5	1.5	1.5	1.5	1.5	1.5	1.5	1.5	1.5	1.5	18.3	18.3	18.3	18.3
Truck	0.9	0.9	0.9	0.9	0.9	0.9	0.9	0.9	0.9	0.9	0.9	0.9	11.3	11.3	11.3	11.3
Equipment																
Welding machine	1.0	1.0	1.0	1.0	1.0	2.1	2.1	2.1	2.1	2.1	2.1	2.1	19.6	24.8	24.8	24.8
Office Fixtures and Fittings																
Various	0.7	0.7	0.7	0.7	0.8	0.8	0.8	0.8	0.8	0.8	0.8	0.8	9.3	11.4	12.9	14.3
IT infrastructure																
Software	1.0	1.0	1.0	1.0	1.0	1.0	1.0	1.0	1.0	1.0	1.0	1.0	12.0	12.0	12.0	12.0
Hardware	1.0	1.0	1.0	1.0	1.0	1.0	1.0	1.0	1.0	1.0	1.0	1.0	12.0	12.0	12.0	12.0
Total depreciation	9.5	9.5	9.5	9.5	9.5	10.6	10.6	10.6	10.6	10.6	10.6	10.6	121.6	128.9	130.3	131.8

EXHIBIT 4.27 CAPEX plan and depreciation schedule of NewCo for years 2 to 5

When we plan for a new company, we are asked to prepare at least a 5-year plan. For the first couple of years we usually present a CAPEX plan and a depreciation schedule on a monthly basis whereas for the rest of the forecast period an annual presentation is fine. We can extend the Excel worksheet shown in Exhibit 4.25 to include another year presented on a monthly basis plus 3 more years on an annual basis. Exhibit 4.27 presents the additional expenditure of €124k on another welding machine during the second year of operation plus €10k in various office expenses each year starting from year 2.

We can see that the CAPEX for year 2 is €134k and €10k for each consecutive year whereas the depreciation for year 2 is €121,6k and for the rest of the years €128,9k, €130,3k, and €131,8k respectively. Let us see how these numbers are derived. As we mentioned previously, the depreciation in any given month or year is made up of 2 components, the depreciation of the existing assets and the depreciation of any new asset. So the depreciation of the various assets during the first 4 months of the second year is the same and equals that of the last month of the previous year (year 1) since there are no new assets in place.

The depreciation of the office fixtures and fittings will increase in May of the second year since €5k worth of new assets are put in place. The new depreciated amount for May will be:

$$\underbrace{60*14\%/12}_{\substack{\text{Comes from}\\\text{Year 1}}} + \underbrace{5*14\%/12}_{\substack{\text{Comes from}\\\text{Year 2}}} = €0.8k$$

Similarly, the depreciation of the welding machine is doubled in June of the second year since another machine of equal cost is put in place. Finally when we move to years 3 to 5 the depreciation equals that of the previous year plus the one arising from the new assets put in place for the current year. The balance sheet account of the net fixed assets for the 5-year forecast period would then be as shown in Exhibit 4.28:

Balance Sheet	Year 1	Year 2	Year 3	Year 4	Year 5
Gross fixed assets	€1,862k	€1,996k	€2,006k	€2,016k	€2,026k
(−) Accumulated Depreciation	€63k	€184.6k	€313.4k	€443.8k	€575.5k
Net fixed assets	€1,799k	€1,811.5k	€1,692.6k	€1,572.2k	€1,450.5k

EXHIBIT 4.28   Net fixed assets of NewCo for the 5-year forecast period

The gross fixed assets for year 2 are the gross fixed assets for year 1 (€1,862k) plus the CAPEX for year 2 (€134k). The gross fixed assets for the following years are derived similarly.

Please note that if the forecast period was 10 years instead of 5 and you use the concept that the depreciation in any given period is made up of the depreciation of the existing assets and the depreciation of any new asset, some of the assets with a shorter useful life than 10 years would be fully depreciated and thus the existing depreciation that comes from the previous periods should be adjusted properly.

4.5.1 Forecasting CAPEX and Depreciation for Existing Companies

So far we have covered the construction of a CAPEX plan and a depreciation schedule for a business where we had inside information about the asset class, cost, and timing of purchases of its various assets. If we are modelling for our own company or the company we work for, such information is normally available. When we want to forecast the financials of a third company, such information is very difficult to find and we have to use other approaches to forecast both CAPEX and depreciation. In the absence of such information, as you have probably guessed, we may forecast CAPEX for further years either by adopting the percent-of-sales approach or by using regression analysis between CAPEX and sales. We could use the historic financials the FP&A manager gathered for SteelCo, described in Chapter 3, to see the effect of these approaches on future CAPEX values although it would not be a good idea since the sales decreased between 2011 and 2012 but CAPEX increased anticipated a market upturn. For example, the percent-of-sales method would result in decreasing CAPEX year after year since sales are decreasing. Nevertheless, for a going concern company there is a minimum CAPEX necessary to keep operations running smoothly. We could have reached similar results by applying regression between CAPEX and sales. In any case the interested reader can easily apply these approaches the way we did for OPEX costs in the previous section.

What we could do to forecast the CAPEX for 2018 is to use a linear trend function on the gross fixed assets of SteelCo for the years 2011 to 2017 and forecast the gross fixed assets for 2018. Then the CAPEX of 2018 can be derived indirectly from the forecast gross fixed assets for 2018:

$$CAPEX_{2018} = \text{Gross Fixed Assets}_{2018} - \text{Gross Fixed Assets}_{2017} = €64,037k - €63,040k = €997k$$

To forecast the gross fixed assets of 2018 recall that we simply select all the cells (after being converted to numbers) of CAPEX between 2011 and 2017 and then drag them to the right. Alternatively we could use Excel's *forecast* function. The figure of €997k can be easily justified since 2018 was forecast to be the first year with increased sales after 6 years of a downturn (see Section 4.3).

Exhibit 4.29 shows the forecast gross fixed assets of SteelCo for 2018. To forecast the accumulated depreciation we will use the percentage on gross fixed assets first, to estimate the yearly depreciation and then we will add it to the accumulated one of the previous year. You may recall from Chapter 3 that the percentage on gross fixed assets we used to derive depreciation was 3.6%. Then the accumulated depreciation for 2018 is:

$$\text{Accumulated Depreciation}_{2018} = \text{Accumulated Depreciation}_{2017} + \text{Depreciation}_{2018} = €28,315k + 3.6\% * €64,037k = €30,620k$$

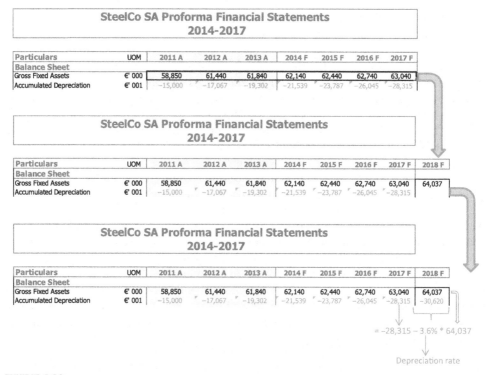

EXHIBIT 4.29 Forecasting CAPEX and depreciation for SteelCo

Thus, in case we want to prepare a full balance sheet statement the net fixed assets would be:

$$\text{Net Fixed Assets}_{2018} = \text{Gross Fixed Assets}_{2018} - \text{Accumulated Depreciation}_{2018} =$$
$$\text{€64,037k} - \text{€30,630k} = \text{€33,417k}$$

As a final note to this section we should stress the fact that capital expenditures should always be treated as a function of how fast a company is growing or is expected to grow. High growth companies will have much higher capital expenditures than low growth ones. Therefore assumptions about capital expenditure can never be made independently of assumptions about growth in the future.

4.6 FORECASTING WORKING CAPITAL AND FUNDING NEEDS

In this final section of the chapter we will see why working capital is one of the most important metrics for gauging a company's efficiency and financial health especially in the post-crisis era where companies start to deleverage their balance sheets. Working capital, in its accounting sense, is defined as: current assets − current liabilities. Nevertheless for the purposes of this book when we refer to working capital we mean commercial working capital defined as:

Commercial Working Capital = Accounts Receivable + Inventory − Accounts Payable

Moreover we will see why a company can be always short of cash, even though it is selling more than ever before. While it may sound impossible, a company can be short of cash because things are going rather well with its operations and it faces high growth. Rapid growth can often cause cash strain on the company. A growing business normally *burns cash*, as we say in financial jargon. The demands of increasing sales in working capital funds can rapidly soak up all extra revenues flowing in when the sales numbers are rising. Not only does the company need to invest more resources in inventory and fixed costs, but receivables typically grow along with sales. So the more its sales volume increases the more cash is tied up in working capital and the higher its funding needs are.

For example, consider Exhibit 4.30 which presents a simple tool, provided in the website accompanying the book, showing the funding needs in accounts receivable for a certain credit policy and turnover. The user can choose the pace at which both the turnover and the DSO grow. The vertical axis shows the annual turnover and the pace at which it grows whereas the horizontal axis presents the DSO and the pace at which they grow. This table is a useful decision-making tool because it provides relevant and reliable information for predicting the working capital needs arising from the accounts receivable. For example, we see that for an annual turnover of €500k we need €95,890 at 70 credit days, €123,288 at 90 and so on. For every 20 days we need incremental funds of €27,397 (figure at cell J13) at the level of €500k annual turnover. If we move vertically instead of horizontally, we see that for every €100k increase in turnover we have extra funding needs which depend on the DSO the company operates. For example at 70 credit days the extra funds amount to €19,178 (figure at cell G14), at 90 credit days €24,658k (figure at cell J14) and so on. Thus the commercial manager of the company who insists that he or she could increase sales from €500k to €1,000k if he or she could increase credit to the customers from 70 days to 110 days, can see immediately that this decision requires an increase in funding from €95,890 (cell E13) to €301,370 (cell K23), that is, more than 200%.

	A	B	C	D	E	F	G	H	I	J	K	L	M	N	O	P
2								Assumptions								
3																
4	Annual Turnover (€)										500,000					
5	Increase sales by (€)										100,000					
6	Days Sales Outstanding (Days)										70					
7	Increase days by (Days)										20					
8																
9																
10	Days Sales Outstanding															
11							70			90			110		130	

12	Annual Turnover	Δ	Funding Needs	Δ	Funding Needs	Δ	Funding Needs	Δ	Funding Needs	Δ
13	500,000		95,890		123,288	27,397	150,685	27,397	178,082	27,397
14		100,000		19,178		24,658		30,137		35,616
15	600,000		115,068		147,945	32,877	180,822	32,877	213,699	32,877
16		100,000		19,178		24,658		30,137		35,616
17	700,000		134,247		172,603	38,356	210,959	38,356	249,315	38,356
18		100,000		19,178		24,658		30,137		35,616
19	800,000		153,425		197,260	43,836	241,096	43,836	284,932	43,836
20		100,000		19,178		24,658		30,137		35,616
21	900,000		172,603		221,918	49,315	271,233	49,315	320,548	49,315
22		100,000		19,178		24,658		30,137		35,616
23	1,000,000		191,781		246,575	54,795	301,370	54,795	356,164	54,795
24		100,000		19,178		24,658		30,137		35,616
25	1,100,000		210,959		271,233	60,274	331,507	60,274	391,781	60,274

EXHIBIT 4.30 Tool calculating funding needs for certain annual turnover and credit days

The figures in the table in Exhibit 4.30 have been derived by using the following formula already described in Chapter 2:

$$\text{Funding Needs} = \text{Accounts Receivable} = \text{Annual Turnover} \times \text{DSO} / 365$$

Using similar formulae we may forecast the inventory and accounts payable given a certain Cost of Goods Sold (COGS) figure. Following this approach we have forecast the balance sheet accounts of accounts receivable, inventory, and accounts payable for SteelCo, as shown in Chapter 3, for years 2014 to 2017. When we have to forecast working capital this is how we will always do it:

1. We will forecast revenues and annual turnover as we discussed in Section 4.3.
2. We will forecast COGS directly or indirectly as we discussed in Section 4.4.
3. We will make assumptions about the future Days Sales Outstanding (DSO), Days Payable Outstanding (DPO), and Days Inventory Outstanding (DIO), and
4. Based on the figures of the above steps we will forecast accounts receivable, accounts payable, and inventory.

A more "quick and dirty" approach would be to estimate the working capital as a percentage of sales, for the historic period, and either use this percentage or follow the trend, if there is one, for the forecast period. For a starting business for which there are no historic data, we could use industry averages. For example, working capital consultancy REL conducts annual surveys analyzing the largest publicly traded European and US companies by revenue. REL, in its "2013 Working Capital Survey: Lessons from Top Performers" provides benchmarks for Days Working Capital (DWC), DSO, DIO, and DPO and shows the best and worst corporate performers in more than 40 industries.[9] Nevertheless for an existing company, like SteelCo, we need to observe whether there is a trend or not. For example, for SteelCo the working capital as a percentage of sales is shown in Exhibit 4.31:

Year	2011	2012	2013	2014f	2015f	2016f	2017f
WC as a % of sales	49%	50%	52%	36%	33%	30%	30%

EXHIBIT 4.31 SteelCo's working capital as a percentage of sales for both the historic and the forecast period

During 2011 to 2013, for which historic data are available, this percentage is fairly constant at around 50%. If we were about to use this percentage as a proxy for future years we would deviate from the company's decision to reduce working capital needs as a remedy for its reducing business activity and the difficulty in accessing liquidity from traditional external sources. This decision is depicted in the forecast (by the FP&A in Chapter 3) of working capital rates as a percentage of sales for years 2014 to 2017 which follow a reducing trend. Based on this trend we may forecast (by selecting the cells and dragging them to the right) that this ratio in 2018 will be 27%. Then, based on the sales of 2018, forecast in Section 4.3, the working capital of 2018 would be:

$$WC_{2018} = WC2018 \text{ as a } \% \text{ of Sales} \times Sales_{2018} = 27\% \times €95,811k = €25,869k$$

We should point out here that the way in which we have handled working capital forecasts is not as meticulous as an analytical budgeting process would require since this would be beyond the scope of this book. For example, companies have dedicated teams dealing with inventory level forecasts in order to ensure that they produce or stock the right level of goods to satisfy their customers' needs without creating an overcapacity situation where too much inventory remains on the shelf. Equally, inventory forecast must not fall short leaving the company without stock to fulfil customers' orders. Failure to maintain accurate inventory levels can be financially catastrophic. And this applies to the other working capital parameters: accounts receivable and accounts payable. Working capital management, in general, has gained wide publicity since the onset of the crisis where working capital efficiency became a vital tool for sustained performance. With less business activity, companies have less access to liquidity from traditional external sources. Kevin Kaiser and S. David Young surveyed many companies for their *Harvard Business Review* article entitled: "Need Cash? Look inside your company" and found that the traditional business focus on the bottom line actually ties up working capital, setting managers on a death march towards bankruptcy. They found that many companies have a lot of capital tied up in receivables and inventory and that this could be turned into cash by challenging the working capital policies.[10] This is confirmed by a different survey conducted by REL for 2013 (as mentioned above) which found a substantial discrepancy between top-performing companies in the top quartile of the survey and median performers. On average, top performers have 55% less working capital tied up in operations, collect from customers more than 2 weeks faster, pay suppliers about 15 days slower, and hold 68% less inventory than median companies. This translated into €762 billion and $1.1 trillion currently tied up in excess working capital in Europe and the US respectively. These extraordinary amounts of capital are roughly equivalent to 6% of the European Union's entire Gross Domestic Product (GDP) and 7% of US GDP, respectively![9] And since working capital levels are inseparable from the funds a company needs to operate, the capital tied up in the companies surveyed is unreasonably high.

As a final note to this section, we should mention the importance of working capital in stock market valuations as a key performance indicator. Companies that are unable to rely solely on top-line revenue growth, are focusing on increasing their efficiency by decreasing their working capital levels and thus the required internal or external funding needs. In the next chapter we will see the monumental role that the working capital level of 2018, determined as a percentage of sales, played in SteelCo's forecast value per share.

4.6.1 Forecasting Funding Needs

To forecast the funding needs of a company, one should forecast first the following:

(a) the amount of new assets that are required to be in place during the forecasting period;
(b) the working capital levels; and
(c) the profitability of the company.

Profits are the only internal long-term source of funds. Generally speaking there are only 2 basic sources of funding – *externally* generated funds and *internally* generated funds. External sources of funds can either be in the form of a Share Capital Increase (SCI) from the present and/or new owners/investors or borrowings in the form of long- or short-term loans. Internal funds, as we said above, are considered to be the profits the company generates. A healthy business must be able to make as high a percentage profit as would be needed to provide all the funds necessary for its operations and future growth. Another source of internal funds is the freeing of cash tied up in working capital or the disposal of company assets. As a financial modeller you should bear in mind that, as the company you model grows and investments in machinery, equipment, and working capital rise, so does the amount of capital invested in it. Share capital increases, unless absolutely necessary, are not the commonest form of capital you will be asked to model. Rather you will be asked either to free some cash tied up internally or use debt as a last resort. Remember that the FP&A of Chapter 3 financed SteelCo's losses by reducing working capital. You can always improve short-term liquidity whether by increasing the company's obligations to vendors (accounts payable), or by reducing inventory, or by reducing the collection period from the company's customers (accounts receivable). Nevertheless, short-term liquidity achieved by deferring payments of current obligations is not a panacea and sooner or later the company's ability to generate cash flow in this way will be exhausted. Not to mention that companies that pay on time develop better relationships with suppliers, are in a position to negotiate better deals and, most importantly, they are receiving goods when they need them. Bad debts are also a particular drag on working capital in tough times and can often be reduced by making more rigorous credit checks on new customers and managing credit limits more carefully.

Returning to the topic of debt, for the purposes of this book you will need to consider only 2 categories: *short-term* and *long-term*. Typical forms of short-term debt include short-term loans, credit lines, and factoring or forfeiting trade finance instruments. The important decision you will have to make is which asset of the balance sheet to finance with short-term debt and which with long-term. There is an old rule of business finance that advocates matching the length of financing of an asset to its useful life. It is very dangerous to attempt to finance long-term capital needs with short-term capital sources. Only the seasonal or cyclical fluctuations of a growing business should be financed by short-term debt. Short-term sources of financing should be used only for the purchase of short-term assets, such as that portion of inventory that is truly seasonal and will, therefore, be sold during the term of the financing.

BIBLIOGRAPHY AND REFERENCES

1. Few, S., *Information Dashboard Design* (O'Reilly, 2006).
2. Tennent, J. and Friend, G., *Guide to Business Modelling* (3rd edition). The Economist Series (John Wiley & Sons, 2011).
3. "Time Series: The Art of Forecasting", Sacramento University, Prof. Hopfe, http://www.csus.edu/indiv/h/hopfem/timeseries.ppt.
4. Rogers, E. M., *Diffusion of Innovations* (5th edition) (New York, NY: Free Press, 2003).
5. Mansfield, E., "Technical Change and the Rate of Imitation" (October 1961) 29 *Econometrica* 741–766.
6. Mahajan, V., Muller, E., and Bass, F., "New Product Diffusion Models in Marketing: A Review and Directions for Research" (1990) 54 *Journal of Marketing* 1–26.
7. Bass F., "The Adoption of a Marketing Model: Comments and Observations", in V. Mahajan and Y. Wind (eds), *Innovation Diffusion of New Product Acceptance* (Cambridge, MA: Ballinger Publishing Company, 1986).
8. Aswath Damodaran's website, http://people.stern.nyu.edu/adamodar/pc/datasets/uValuedata.xls.
9. REL Consultancy, "2013 Working Capital Survey: Lessons from Top Performers", http://www.relconsultancy.com/research/2013/relwcsurvey-eu/.
10. Kaiser, K. and Young, S. D., "Need Cash? Look inside your company" (May 2009) *Harvard Business Review* 64–71.

5

Business Valuation

Chapter 5 describes the valuation of a company based on the Discounted Cash Flow (DCF) technique. DCF modelling is pretty much the gold standard for valuation and the free cash flow (operating cash flow minus capital expenditures, at its simplest level) is the best proxy for corporate financial performance. The step-by-step building of a free cash flow model is presented in a comprehensive way. The discount rate is calculated using the Capital Asset Pricing Model (CAPM) and the cash flow estimates are discounted into an estimated New Present Value (NPV). One row serves to hold the year-by-year cash flow estimates, while the rows which follow hold the discount factors and the cash balances.

Estimating the terminal value is the next step. The terminal value is then discounted and its present value is added to the NPV. As part of this process, the terminal value is applied after the calculation of explicit cash flows for 5 years. Finally the net cash/debt is added/subtracted from the total NPV and the result is divided by the number of the company's shares outstanding to calculate its intrinsic value.

5.1 VALUATION APPROACHES

There are many valuation approaches and methods that one could use to value a company. Amongst the most common approaches are the following:

1. the net asset approach,
2. the market approach, and
3. the income approach.

The net asset approach treats the business as a set of assets and liabilities where their net difference represents its net equity. Before applying the net asset approach both assets and liabilities should have been adjusted to their fair market values. The fair market value as described by the International Financial Reporting Standards (IFRS) is the price, in terms of cash or its equivalent, that a buyer could reasonably be expected to pay, and a seller could reasonably be expected to accept, if the business were offered for sale on the open market for a reasonable period of time, with both buyer and seller being in possession of the pertinent facts and neither being under any compulsion to act.

The drawback of this approach to valuation as outlined above is that it fails to capture the value of a company's intangible assets. Most companies have some intangible value that stems from brand-name recognition, relationships with clients and customers, reputation, experience, and knowledge, along with a variety of other values that are not captured in accounting numbers. For example, the value of Apple or Microsoft has little to do with its land, buildings, and equipment; rather their value is derived from their worldwide brand recognition. The net asset approach is most often used in cases where a business is not viable as a *going concern* and is about to be liquidated (*liquidation value*) or where there are no intangible assets and its value as a going concern is closely related to the liquidation value of its underlying assets (e.g. a real estate holding company). In the latter case the net asset approach is used as an aid to assess the risk associated with the other valuation approaches, i.e. what could be the worst case scenario.

The market approach determines the value of a business based on comparisons with similar companies for which values are known. It compares the subject company to the prices of similar companies operating in the same industry that are either publicly traded or, if privately owned, have been sold recently. Under this approach 2 broad categories of multiples are calculated:

Listed comparable multiples
> The Enterprise Value (EV)/sales, EV/EBITDA and P/E multiples are derived from *comparable listed companies* and are then applied to sales, EBITDA, and net income of the subject company in order to obtain its enterprise value (EV) or its market value (P/E method);

Comparable transactions multiples
> The EV/sales, EV/EBITDA, and P/E multiples in recent *comparable transactions* are observed and then are applied to the sales, EBITDA, and net income of the company to be valued in order to obtain its enterprise value or its market value (P/E method);

This measure of value, the so-called "Enterprise Value" or EV of a business, is the value of its debt plus its Market Capitalization (Mkt Cap) minus the cash deposits that it holds.

$$\text{Enterprise Value} = \text{Mkt Cap} + \text{Debt} - \text{Cash},$$

where Mkt Cap = No of shares outstanding × Price per share

Exhibit 5.1 presents typical values of the 3 most common multiples derived from listed companies. For example, a company with an EBITDA of €3.2 million would have an EV according to the mean value of the EV/EBITDA multiple of 2014:

$$\text{Enterprise Value} = 15.6 \times \text{€3.2 million} = \text{€49.9 million}$$

Similarly Exhibit 5.2 presents typical values of 2 common transaction multiples derived from recent transactions between companies operating in the same or similar industries as the company to be valued. For example, the above company with an EBITDA of €3.2 million would have an EV according to the mean value of the EV/EBITDA multiple of 2013:

$$\text{Enterprise Value} = 8.9 \times \text{€3.2 million} = \text{€28.4 million}$$

The drawback for this approach is that for privately owned businesses there is a lack of publicly available comparable data. Moreover it is difficult to construct a representative and

				Listed Multiples				
				EV/Sales		P/E	EV/EBITDA	
Company	Price	Market Cap	EV	2013	2014	2014	2013	2014
Company 1	€ 15.3	€ 7,256	€ 7,579	10.2x	11.2x	18.1x	11,05x	10,65x
Company 2	€ 17.0	€ 3,202	€ 3,802	11.3x	10.7x	11.2x	21.6x	20,85x
Company 3	€ 8.0	€ 8,537	€ 9,737	12.7x	12.8x	7.1x	32,55x	32,65x
Company 4	€ 13.2	€ 3,296	€ 3,096	17.1x	16.1x	8.5x	6,35x	5,95x
Company 5	€ 6.7	€ 892	€ 1,015	3.1x	3.5x	13.3x	7,05x	7,65x
Mean		€ 4,637	€ 5,046	10.9x	10.9x	11.6x	15.7x	15.6x
Median		€ 3,296	€ 3,802	11.3x	11.2x	11.2x	11,05x	10,65x
Low		€ 892	€ 1,015	3.1x	3.5x	7.1x	6,35x	5,95x
High		€ 8,537	€ 9,737	17.1x	16.1x	18.1x	32,55x	32,65x

EXHIBIT 5.1 Typical presentation of comparable multiples derived from listed companies

adequate benchmark set of comparable peers in terms of size, markets, product range, and country of operations. This approach can be used in conjunction with the other approaches in order to effect the so-called "triangulation" of results. This involves determining the fair value of a company by using all relevant methods in order to cross check one with another. Sometimes the value of the company is derived as a weighted average of all the relevant results by various methods.

Finally, the income approach estimates the value of a company by considering the income (benefits) it generates over a period of time. This approach is based on the fundamental valuation principle that the value of a business is equal to the present worth of the future benefits of ownership. The term income does not necessarily refer to income in the accounting sense but to future benefits accruing to the owner. The most common methods under this approach are capitalization of earnings and discounted cash flow. Under the *capitalization of earnings* method, normalized historic earnings are capitalized at a rate that reflects the risk inherent in the expected future growth in those earnings. The *discounted*

		Transaction Multiples			
		EV/Sales		EV/EBITDA	
Target	Acquirer	2012	2013	2012	2013
Company 1 (UK)	Company 2 (FR)	3,2x		17,8x	
Company 3 (UK)	Company 4 (UK)	6,0x		15,2x	
Company 5 (US)	Company 6 (US)	1,2x		4,6x	
Company 7 (CAN)	Company 8 (US)		2,5x		8,2x
Company 9 (LUX)	Company 10 (NL)		4,4x		9,6x
Mean		3,5x	3,5x	12,5x	8,9x
Highest		6,0x	4,4x	17,8x	9,6x
Lowest		1,2x	2,5x	4,6x	8,2x

EXHIBIT 5.2 Typical presentation of comparable multiples derived from recent company transactions

cash flow method discounts projected cash flows back to present value at a rate that reflects the risk inherent in the projected flows. This rate, sometimes called the hurdle rate, discount rate, or simply the opportunity cost of capital, is frequently the company's WACC (Weighted Average Cost of Capital), which reflects the company's financial structure and the risk related to the sector.

Before continuing further I would like to explain briefly the concepts of present value and opportunity cost of capital. The concept of present value is based on the so-called "time value of money" which states the obvious fact that getting €1,000 today makes more sense than getting it a year from now because you could invest the money and have more than €1,000 in a year's time. The sooner you get the money, the more it is worth to you. Present value is closely related to future value in the sense that if you invest today €100 at 10% in a year's time you will get €110. The €100 is referred to as the present value of the investment whereas the €110 is termed the future value of the investment after 1 year. Their relationship between the 2 values can be expressed in mathematical terms as:

$$€110 = €100 \times (1 + 10\%), \text{ or}$$
$$FV = PV \times (1+r)$$

where r is the interest rate you will get in a year.

If instead of 1 year you invest the €100 for n years, the above equation can be rewritten as:

$$FV = PV \times (1+r)^n,$$

or

$$PV = \frac{FV}{(1+r)^n}$$

Note in the above equation that the factor:

$$\frac{1}{(1+r)^n}$$

is less than 1 since r is greater than zero and n is greater than or equal to 1. This factor is called the *discount factor* and is the value of €1 received in the future. It is usually expressed as a reciprocal of 1 plus a rate of return which in turn represents the reward to investors for accepting delayed payments. The above equation calculates the Present Value (PV) of an investment of Future Value (FV) at the year n from now discounted at a rate of return r. It is the backbone of the DCF technique and we will go back to it later in this chapter. Let us now come to the opportunity cost of capital. The time value of money is represented by the opportunity cost of capital which is fundamental to investment decisions, and is a significant input to a DCF analysis. The opportunity cost of capital or hurdle rate or discount rate is so-called because it represents the return forgone by investing in a specific asset rather than investing in securities. You can think of it as the rate offered by equivalent investment alternatives in the capital market.

Let us now return to the DCF technique – we said that it expresses the present value of a business as a function of its future cash earnings capacity. This methodology works on the premise that the value of a business is measured in terms of future cash flow streams, discounted to the present time at an appropriate discount rate. If we denote by CF_i the future cash flow of a business at year i, where $i = 1 \dots n$, and r is the appropriate discount rate then the value of the business is given by the following equation:

$$\text{Value of a Business} = \frac{CF_1}{(1+r)^1} + \frac{CF_2}{(1+r)^2} + \frac{CF_3}{(1+r)^3} + \frac{CF_4}{(1+r)^4} \dots + \frac{CF_n}{(1+r)^n}$$

Although there are different notions of value, for the purposes of this book, when we discuss the value of a business from now on we refer to the *fair market value* as described above. The objective of any valuation is to estimate the fair market value of a company at a specific point in time (i.e. at a given date). There are a large number of factors to consider when estimating the common stock value of any business entity. These factors vary for each valuation depending on the unique circumstances of the business enterprise and general economic conditions that exist at the effective date of the valuation. However, fundamental guidelines of the factors to consider in any valuation have been established.

The most commonly used valuation guidelines require careful consideration of each of the following:

(a) The nature of the business and its history since inception.
(b) If it has a sustainable competitive advantage that is a competitive advantage not easily copied by rival companies and thus maintained over a long period of time.
(c) The economic outlook in general and the condition and outlook of that specific industry in particular. Michael Porter's 5 forces model provides a framework that models an industry as being influenced by (1) the threat of new entrants; (2) the bargaining power of suppliers; (3) the threat of substitute product or services; (4) the bargaining power of customers; and (5) the rivalry amongst existing competitors. This framework is a useful tool for industry analysis.
(d) The financial condition of the business in terms of liquidity and solvency.
(e) The earning capacity of the company.
(f) The market price of stocks of corporations engaged in the same or a similar line of business having their stocks actively traded in a free and open market, either on an exchange or over the counter.

Moreover, the Discounted Cash Flow (DCF) method is used to determine the present value of a business on the assumption that it is a going concern. In the normal case, a company is established to operate for an indefinite period in the future. So, on the basis of the going concern, we should always assume that the business under valuation will continue its operations in the future.

A final note, before we proceed onto the next section, is that the DCF method ignores *control* issues; this is unlikely with the comparable transaction method which includes what is known as a control premium and hence results in a higher valuation. Valuing a controlling block of shares of a company gives a different result compared to valuing just a few shares of that company. This difference is the so-called *control premium* and is the premium a buyer is willing to pay in order to acquire control of the company and be able to run it in their own way (the assumption being that it will be run more effectively and efficiently). Control premiums make sense for the following reason. If the buyer attempts to buy a large number of shares of a company on the market, he will probably have to offer more than the current market price per share. As he buys more and more shares, the price will go up. In addition, the gossip that someone is trying to take over the company will keep forcing up the share price. In general the value of a controlling block of shares is greater than the market value, since the controlling shareholder can actually decide on the fate of the company and derive considerable benefits by improving its performance. Nevertheless the value of control will vary across firms and it is greater for poorly managed firms that present more room for improvement. As a rule of thumb, control premiums can vary between 5% and 30% or even higher depending on the particular firm, the industry in which it operates, the timing of the acquisition, the room for improvement in the way it is managed, etc.

In the rest of this chapter, we will describe the DCF method in more detail and apply it to the case of SteelCo described in Chapter 3 in order to find its enterprise value and its value per share.

5.2 STEPS FOR APPLYING THE DCF METHOD

When valuing a business on a DCF basis, the objective is to determine the net present value of the Cash Flows ("CF") arising from the business over a future period of time (say 5 years); this period is known as the explicit forecast period. So the *first step* of the DCF method is to decide on the explicit forecast period and estimate future cash flows. This is where the question of which cash flows to estimate comes in. According to Professor Damodaran,[1] the most important types of cash flow are free cash flows (cash flows available to satisfy both the shareholders' and creditors' return requirements) and equity cash flows (cash flows available to shareholders). The choice of cash flow determines whether you are valuing the whole firm or just the equity of that firm. That is, if you are doing a firm valuation you need to consider the free cash flows which are available to both claimholders of the firm, that is, cash flows that include all inflows and outflows prior to the debt serving such as taxes, the amount invested in working capital (WC), and capital expenditure. In case of an equity valuation the cash flows after subtracting interest payments are considered. The most frequently used approach is that of *free cash flows* and this is the approach we will follow for the rest of this chapter.

The *second step* of the DCF method is to estimate the rate at which future cash flows and terminal value will be discounted back to their present values. One of the advantages of DCF is that it permits the various elements that make up the discount rate to be considered separately, and thus the effect of the variations in the assumptions can be modelled easily. As we mentioned earlier, in most valuation cases the WACC is used as the discount rate. The principal elements of WACC are cost of equity (which is the desired rate of return for an equity investor given the risk profile of the company and associated cash flows), the post-tax cost of debt, and the target capital structure of the company (a function of the debt to equity ratio). In turn, cost of equity is derived, on the basis of the CAPM, as a function of the risk-free rate, *beta* (an estimate of the risk profile of the company relative to the equity market) and equity risk premium assigned to the subject equity market. We will deal with the analytical derivation of WACC in Section 5.5.

Under the DCF methodology, value must be placed on both the explicit cash flows as stated above, and the ongoing cash flows a company will generate after the explicit forecast period. The latter value is known as the terminal value and comprises the *third step* of the DCF method as we will see later on.

Value of a Company = {Sum of PV of Free Cash Flows} + {PV of Terminal Value}

The terminal value is derived from the last projected free cash flow of the explicit forecast period and normally represents between 60% and 80% of the company's total value. It is obvious that the longer the period covered by the projection, the less reliable the projections are likely to be. Therefore, the accuracy of this projection will determine the accuracy of the terminal value. For this reason, this approach must be used to value businesses where the future cash flows can be projected with a reasonable degree of reliability. For example, in a fast-changing market the explicit period typically cannot be more than 5 years. Any projection beyond that would be mostly speculation and the same will apply to the terminal value. On the other hand if we want to reduce the impact of the terminal value on the total value of a company we should extend the explicit forecast period as far as possible. This can apply to mature markets where forecasting for more than 5 years is possible. In general, the further the cash flows are projected, the less sensitive the valuation is to inaccuracies in the estimated terminal value.

Finally the *fourth step* of DCF is to discount, using the WACC of step 2, to the present value the free cash flows of the explicit forecast period as well as the terminal value.

If we want to apply these steps to SteelCo's case, as described in Chapter 3, in order to estimate its fair market value, we should tackle the problem following the 4 steps below:

Step 1: Forecast SteelCo's future cash flows for an explicit period of 5 years.

Step 2: Calculate SteelCo's Weighted Average Cost of Capital (WACC).

Step 3: Estimate its terminal value based on the free cash flow of year 5.

Step 4: Use the WACC found in step 2 to discount to the present value the future free cash flows estimated in step 1 and the terminal value estimated in step 3.

The following sections are devoted to the abovementioned DCF steps. Before proceeding to step 1, I would like to quote Professor Damodaran on the myth that the more quantitative a DCF model is, the more precise the valuation results are. He states that the truth is rather that:

1. One's understanding of a valuation model is inversely proportional to the number of inputs required for the model, and
2. Simpler valuation models work much better than complex ones.

Based on the above statements we will try to keep our DCF model as simple as possible.

5.3 REWRITING FINANCIAL STATEMENTS – CALCULATION OF FREE CASH FLOWS

In this section we will derive the free cash flows of a company by rewriting its income statement and balance sheet. There are 2 approaches that we can use to derive the free cash flow of a company. The bottom-up approach and the top-down approach. Let us examine them in turn.

The bottom-up approach starts from the net income of the company. Net income comes right off the income statement and includes any tax or interest expense that must be paid for the period. Since we are talking about cash flows we should add back any non-cash items such as amortization and depreciation that have been taken into consideration in the income statement. Moreover since we want to derive the free cash flows, that is, free to be distributed to all security holders including debt holders, we should add back interest expense which is directed to them. The company will be valued as a going concern, as we mention above, that is, on the basis that it will operate in the foreseeable future. Due to this fact it needs to make the necessary investments in CAPital EXpenditure (CAPEX) and working capital in order to attain revenue growth forecasts. Thus any necessary capital expenditure as well as investments in working capital will be subtracted. The resulting figure is the so-called Free Cash Flow to the Firm (FCFF).

The other approach, the top-down, starts with the estimation of future revenues and operating expenses (including depreciation) to find Earnings Before Interest and Taxes (EBIT) for each year. Then we subtract taxes to find the so-called Net Operating Profit After Tax (NOPAT) for each year. NOPAT is a crucial measure in a variety of financial analyses because it gives a clearer view of the operating efficiency of a company, a view that is not clouded by how leveraged the company is or how big a bank loan it was able to obtain. After the derivation of NOPAT we have to add back any non-cash costs (e.g. depreciation) that have already been subtracted in estimating EBIT. Remember in Chapter 3 we mentioned that, for practical reasons, it is better to gather all depreciation expense categories (cost of goods sold; selling, general, and administrative) in one place (after EBITDA) in the income statement. Had we done so we would not have needed to make any adjustments for depreciation. Finally we subtract capital expenditures and increases in working capital or add back any decreases in working capital.

You will recall that in Chapter 2 we showed that an increase in an asset is a cash outflow whereas a decrease in an asset is a cash inflow. Similarly, we showed that an increase in a liability is a cash inflow whereas a decrease in a liability is a cash outflow. Therefore, since capital expenditure increases the assets of the company, they cause cash outflows and thus have to be subtracted from the operating cash of the company. Moreover, as we mentioned in Chapter 2, the working capital of a company is derived by subtracting its current liabilities from its current assets. So any increase in working capital comes either from an increase in current assets or a decrease in current liabilities or a combination of both. In any case all of the above constitute cash outflows and thus have to be subtracted from the operating cash of the company. Similarly, decreases in working capital come either from decreases in current assets or increases in current liabilities or a combination of both and as such represent cash inflows and have to be added to the company's operating cash. Exhibit 5.3 shows graphically the top-down approach of the derivation of free cash flows to the firm.

Now we have finished with the theoretical part of the derivation of free cash flows let us apply the top-down approach to SteelCo's figures as described in Chapter 3. Since the explicit forecast period is 5 years and the FP&A manager has prepared the proforma financial statements up to 2017 we need to forecast an extra year. To do so we could follow the same methodology as that described in Chapter 3 and forecast a complete income statement and balance sheet for 2018 or follow a more *quick and dirty* approach. We could forecast directly both the EBITDA and the working capital figures as a percentage of sales. We could keep CAPEX constant as that of 2017. Taxes will be assumed to be zero for 2018. The company has so many accumulated losses from 2013 to 2017 that even if 2018 is an extraordinarily good year and presents profits, their taxable amount will be eliminated by the losses carried forward.

So let us start building a new worksheet with all the relevant information that we will need in order to structure a simple DCF model. The first piece of information will be the figures from the financial statements of SteelCo that make up the free cash flow. So the first part of the worksheet will look like the one shown in Exhibit 5.4.

EBIT is derived by subtracting depreciation from EBITDA. Depreciation and EBITDA figures read directly from the forecast income statement of SteelCo as described in Chapter 3.

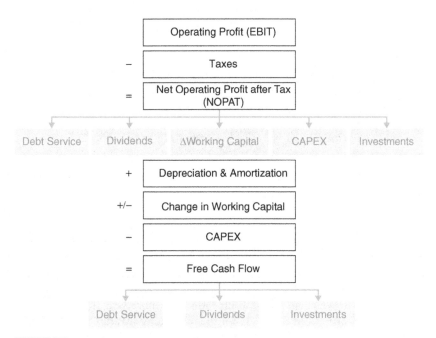

EXHIBIT 5.3 Top-down approach to derive free cash flows

Depreciation for 2018 was set equal to that of 2017 (instead of the figure of € 2,305k estimated in section 4.5.1). The EBITDA for 2018 was calculated using the formula below:

$$EBITA_{2018} = \frac{EBITDA_{2017}}{Sales_{2017}} \times Sales_{2018}$$

That is, we used the EBITDA margin of 2017 as a proxy for the EBITDA margin of 2018. The sales for 2018 were estimated using the polynomial regression methodology we described in Chapter 4:

$$Sales_{2018} = 2,406.8 * x^2 - 34,206*x + 215,424$$

	B	C	D	E	F	G	H	I	J
6	YEAR			2013	2014	2015	2016	2017	2018
7	Period			0	1	2	3	4	5
8									
9	EBIT			4,047	2,557	1,445	611	−7	78
10	Depreciation			2,235	2,237	2,248	2,259	2,269	2,269
11	EBITDA			6,282	4,794	3,693	2,869	2,262	2,348
12	Net Change in Working Capital Needs			8,668	26,216	7,159	5,605	1,805	2,659
13	Operating Cash Flow			14,949	31,011	10,852	8,475	4,067	5,007
14	Taxes			− 0	0	0	0	0	0
15	CAPEX			−400	−300	−300	−300	−300	−300
16	Free Cash Flow			14,549	30,711	10,552	8,175	3,767	4,707

EXHIBIT 5.4 Forecasting the free cash flow for SteelCo for years 2014 to 2018

where x equals the period under forecast and the range is from 1 to 8 (3 years' actual sales figures plus another 4 years of estimates plus an extra year we want to forecast). So the sales for 2018 equal:

$$\text{Sales}_{2018} = 2{,}406.8 * 8^2 - 34{,}206*8 + 215{,}424 = \text{€}95{,}811k$$

and the EBITDA$_{2018}$

$$EBITDA_{2018} = \frac{\text{€}2{,}262k}{\text{€}93{,}915k} \times \text{€}95{,}811k = \text{€}2{,}348k.$$

Moreover the working capital (WC) for 2018 is derived by the following equation:

$$WC_{2018} = WC_{2018} \text{ as a \% of Sales} \times Sales_{2018}$$

The WC as a percentage of sales, as we calculated it in Chapter 4, for the fiscal years 2011 to 2013 was 49%, 50%, and 52% respectively. We can see that it followed an increasing trend. Nevertheless this trend seems to have been reversed in the forecasting period 2014 to 2017. The WC as a percentage of sales for this period is 36%, 33%, 30%, and 30% respectively. We discussed in Chapter 4 whether this is a plausible assumption or not. Moreover we discussed how we could forecast this ratio for 1 more year. The ratio was found to be 27% (see Section 4.6). Suffice it to say for the time being that this ratio for 2018 will be 26%. We will discuss the consequences of the ratio being 27% further towards the end of this chapter. So:

$$WC_{2018} = 26\% \times \text{€}95{,}811k = \text{€}24{,}911k$$

Since we are interested not in the working capital per se but in working capital increases or decreases across the years the ΔWC_{2018} is:

$$\Delta WC_{2018\text{-}2017} = WC_{2018} - WC_{2017} = \text{€}24{,}911k - \text{€}25{,}570k = -\text{€}2{,}659k$$

The negative number declares a decrease in working capital and thus cash inflow. That is why we add it to the operating cash of the company.

Finally, the CAPEX for 2018 has been chosen as equal to that of 2017, which is €300k (instead of the figure of €997k estimated in section 4.5.1).

The free cash flow for 2018, then, is:

$$FCF_{2018} = EBITDA_{2018} - \Delta WC_{2018\text{-}2017} - CAPEX_{2018} =$$
$$\text{€}2{,}348k - (-\text{€}2{,}659k) - \text{€}300k = \text{€}2{,}348k + \text{€}2{,}659k - \text{€}300k = \text{€}4{,}707k.$$

Having finished with the derivation of the free cash flows for the explicit forecast period, next we proceed to the estimation of the weighted average cost of capital.

5.4 CALCULATING THE WEIGHTED AVERAGE COST OF CAPITAL

As we mentioned in Section 5.1 the Weighted Average Cost of Capital (WACC) is the rate used to discount the company cash flows to their present value. The idea behind the discount rate is that it is the rate of return at which the *informed investor* would be just as happy to invest in the company as he would be to invest in some alternative investment with a known rate of return. The WACC equation is the cost of each capital component multiplied by its proportional weight and then summing:

$$WACC = \frac{D}{D+E}K_d(1-T) + \frac{D}{D+E}K_e$$

where

K_e: Cost of equity

K_d: Cost of debt

E: Market value of equity

D: Market value of debt

T: Tax rate.

Gearing (G = D/(D + E))
This is the company's capital structure, that is, the ratio of its debt to the market value of its equity.

Cost of debt (K_d)
The cost of debt reflects the cost that a company has to bear in order to get access to short- and long-term loans. For each company the cost of debt is estimated as the projected interest (cost) on its loans.

Tax rate (T)
The tax rate reflects the effective tax rate for a company operating in a certain country.

Cost of equity (K_e)
The cost of equity can be defined as the minimum return that an investor will require in order to purchase shares of the company. This return has been calculated according to the CAPM based on the following formula:

$$K_e = R_f + [R_m - R_f] \times \beta$$

where

K_e: Cost of equity

R_f: Risk-free rate. This is the amount an investor could expect from investing in securities considered free from credit risk, such as government bonds.

$R_m - R_f$: Market risk premium or the expected return on the market portfolio minus the risk-free rate. The market portfolio is a portfolio consisting of all the securities available in the market where the proportion invested in each security corresponds to its relative market value. The expected return of a market portfolio, since it is completely diversified, is identical to the expected return of the market as a whole.

β: This is the so-called *beta* (also known as levered *beta*) of a stock that measures the risk associated with that particular stock, i.e. how sensitive is the particular stock to movements of the whole market portfolio.

The CAPM was developed back in the fifties by Sharpe and Lintner and assumes 2 types of return for the investor of a particular stock: the risk-free return (e.g. of government bonds) and *beta* times the return on the market portfolio. The first type of return (risk-free) relates to the time value of money concept (see Section 5.1) and the second type of return relates to the risk associated to the particular stock.

Depending on the continent in which the valuation is taking place, a good proxy for the risk-free rate is the 10-year US Treasury Bill or the Euro Area's 10-year Government Bond[2] or the UK 10 Year Gilt, details of which are available on Bloomberg[3] or similar financial sites.

The market risk premium denoted by $[R_m - R_f]$ is the premium required above the risk-free rate that an investor would require in order to bear the additional risk inherent in equity returns on a risky asset. Values for this parameter are published by the Stern School of Business (see Professor Damodaran's[1] website). Moreover, if you are interested in the approach to computing the market risk premium, you can download his latest paper ("Equity Risk Premiums: Determinants, Estimation and Implications") from the following web address: http://papers.ssrn.com/sol3/papers.cfm?abstract_id=2238064.

Beta is a measure of the risk of a specific asset relative to the market risk and reflects the extent to which possible future returns are expected to co-vary with the expected returns of the market as a whole. A *beta* value greater than 1 declares that the investment entails more risk than the market as a whole. On the other hand a *beta* value less than 1 corresponds to a lower risk investment. For a listed company it is easy to estimate its *beta* and it is a function of its average monthly returns, over let us say a couple of years, against the general index returns (market return) of the country in which the company is listed.

$$\beta = \frac{\text{Covariance of General Index (Market Return) with Stock (Listed Company) Return}}{\text{Variance of General Index (Market Return)}}$$

Although we will not elaborate on the formulae of covariance and variance, since on the one hand Excel provides both the COVAR () and the VAR () functions and on the other this would be beyond the scope of this chapter, it will suffice to mention Investopedia's[4] definition of covariance. Covariance is a measure of the degree to which returns on 2 risky assets move in tandem. A positive covariance means that asset returns move together. A negative covariance means returns move inversely. Moreover the *variance* of the general index let us say the S&P 500, is a measure of its volatility. The higher the volatility, the more risky is the index. Recall from your mathematics class that the *variance* of a variable is a measure of how dispersed its values are from its expected values as expressed by its mean.

So the calculation of *beta* is simply the covariance of the 2 arrays of returns (that of a particular stock and that of the index) divided by the variance of the array of returns of the index. If we apply the above relationship to the sample general index and stock data of November 2013 of a stock exchange as shown in Exhibit 5.5 then the *beta* of the stock would be 1.7. The returns are calculated as the closing stock or index price minus the opening stock or index price divided by the opening stock or index price.

$$Beta = \text{COVAR (C2:C26, E2:E26) / VAR (E2:E26)} = 0.256 \times 10^{-3}/ 0.149 \times 10^{-3} = 1.7$$

Calculating *beta* is a bit more complicated in the case of a non-listed company, that is, a private company. Price information is not available for a private company and its *beta* is usually found by identifying either a listed company with a similar business risk profile and using its *beta* or a group of companies that are part of the sector the private company participates in and estimating the average *betas* for the listed companies of this sector. However, when selecting an appropriate *beta* from a similar company, we have to take into consideration the

	A	B	C	D	E
1	Date	General Index	General Index returns	Particular Stock	Particular Stock returns
2	29/10/2013	5.289.22		7.38	
3	30/10/2013	5.310.88	0.410%	7.26	−1.626%
4	31/10/2013	5.334.50	0.445%	7.22	−0.551%
5	1/11/2013	5.264.71	−1.308%	7.02	−2.770%
6	2/11/2013	5.284.20	0.370%	7.10	1.140%
7	5/11/2013	5.246.56	−0.712%	6.96	−1.972%
8	6/11/2013	5.309.92	1.208%	7.10	2.011%
9	7/11/2013	5.305.79	−0.078%	7.02	−1.127%
10	8/11/2013	5.228.19	−1.463%	7.00	−0.285%
11	9/11/2013	5.148.13	−1.531%	6.94	−0.857%
12	12/11/2013	5.124.97	−0.450%	6.80	−2.017%
13	13/11/2013	5.129.24	0.083%	6.72	−1.176%
14	14/11/2013	5.177.09	0.933%	7.12	5.952%
15	15/11/2013	5.117.42	−1.153%	6.90	−3.090%
16	16/11/2013	5.096.04	−0.418%	6.98	1.159%
17	19/11/2013	4.995.31	−1.977%	6.72	−3.725%
18	20/11/2013	4.960.31	−0.701%	6.46	−3.869%
19	21/11/2013	4.818.26	−2.864%	6.00	−7.121%
20	22/11/2013	4.824.93	0.138%	5.64	−6.000%
21	23/11/2013	4.925.78	2.090%	5.90	4.610%
22	26/11/2013	4.906.46	−0.392%	5.56	−5.763%
23	27/11/2013	4.864.62	−0.853%	5.24	−5.755%
24	28/11/2013	4.951.70	1.790%	5.38	2.672%
25	29/11/2013	4.973.59	0.442%	5.24	−2.602%
26	30/11/2013	5.053.87	1.614%	5.22	−0.382%

EXHIBIT 5.5 Sample month's data of a particular stock and the general stock market index

gearing ratio (financial risk) involved. And we have to do so because the *beta* factor of a company reflects both its business risk (resulting from its business model) and its finance risk (resulting from its level of gearing). So in order to be able to use a *beta* of company A (which is listed) to value company B (which is private) we have to unlever or degear the *beta* of company A and relever or regear it using the so-called Modigliani-Miller formulae, presented below:

$$\beta_{\text{private company}} = \beta_{\text{ungeared}} * (1 + (1 - \text{tax rate}) (\text{private company's Debt/Equity})), \text{ where}$$
$$\beta_{\text{ungeared}} = \beta_{\text{listed company}} * 1 / (1 + (1 - \text{tax rate}) (\text{listed company's Debt/Equity})).$$

Sometimes the β_{ungeared} is called Asset *beta*, βa, and reflects the business risk of the sector. Moreover the $\beta_{\text{private company}}$ or the *beta* of a listed company calculated in Exhibit 5.5 is called equity or geared *beta* or levered *beta*, βe, and reflects both the industry risk of the company and the company-specific risk because of its financial gearing.

If we want to summarize how to estimate *beta* from the raw data of a publicly traded company provided from the stock market on which it is listed, we would follow the steps below (steps 6 and 7 apply to *beta* estimation of private companies):

1. Obtain historical stock price data for the company's stock price for the past 2 years.
2. Obtain historical values of an appropriate general index (say S&P 500) for the same period.

3. Convert the share price values into daily return values by using the following formula: return = (closing stock price − opening stock price)/opening stock price.

4. Convert historical stock market index values into daily return using the above formula.

5. Using the formula: βe = COVAR (Index, Stock) / VAR (Index) to estimate the βe of the company.

6. In case we want the *beta* of a private company unlever or degear the *beta* of the listed company, βe in order to find βa.

7. Relever or regear βa with the private company's debt to equity ratio in order to find its βe.

There are other ways to calculate the *beta* (β) of a stock but what we have said so far will suffice. Anything more would be beyond the scope of this book. For the DCF valuation practitioner, MSCI's Barra[5] and Morningstar's apostrophe Ibbotson Associates[6] are subscription services that offer up-to-date equity market risk premium rates and *betas* for public companies.

5.4.1 Calculating the Weighted Average Cost of Capital of SteelCo

Having finished with the brief description of the theory behind WACC let us apply it to calculate SteelCo's WACC. To do so we will need to figure out values for the key components of WACC as shown in Exhibit 5.6.

Let's start with the cost of debt. This figure is relative easy to figure out. If we recall how the FP&A manager modelled interest expense in Chapter 3, he kept constant the cost of both short-term debt and long-term debt up to 2017 at 6.7% and 5.7% respectively. So one way to find the cost of debt (*Kd*) could be to take the average of these 2 costs. Nevertheless since Short-Term Debt (STD) and Long-Term Debt (LTD) are not equal in value, it would be more appropriate to take the weighted average cost of these debts for each year from 2014 to 2017 and then take a plain average of these four numbers. The *Kd* for 2014 would then be equal to 6.0%.

$$Kd\ 2014 = \frac{STD2014 \times 6.7\% + LTD2014 \times 5.7\%}{STD2014 + LTD2014}$$

$$= \frac{24.6m \times 6.7\% + 50.2m \times 5.7\%}{24.6m + 50.2m} = 6.0\%$$

Following the same methodology, *Kd* 2015, *Kd* 2016, and *Kd* 2017 are all found to be equal to 6.0%. That is because the ratio between the short-term debt and the long-term debt

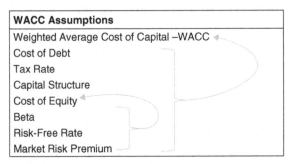

WACC Assumptions
Weighted Average Cost of Capital –WACC
Cost of Debt
Tax Rate
Capital Structure
Cost of Equity
Beta
Risk-Free Rate
Market Risk Premium

EXHIBIT 5.6   Weighted average cost of capital assumptions

of the company across the years remains fairly constant. Thus the *Kd* we will use in order to calculate SteelCo's WACC is set to 6.0%.

The next parameter is the tax rate. The tax rate is the effective tax rate calculated as the actual taxes paid divided by earnings before taxes. Again, this parameter has been estimated by the FP&A manager in Chapter 3 at 33%. Nevertheless, years 2014 to 2017 are loss-making years, and there are no profits against which to offset the losses. The effective tax rate is therefore uncertain because of volatility in operating profits. We will assume that the company will return sooner than later to profitability and any potential loss will be carried forward and set off against future profits. Without this assumption we should ignore the tax deductibility of the cost of debt. Reinhart and Rogoff, in their paper entitled "The Aftermath of Financial Crises"[7] examine the depth and duration of past financial crises and conclude that the mean historic duration of the downturn after the crisis is 6 years. We may then make the bold assumption that SteelCo, after suffering 6 years of losses, will return to profitability again in the 7th year.

The parameter following tax rate is the gearing or capital Structure. The gearing ratio of SteelCo was estimated taking into consideration the projected debt and equity estimated by the company's forecast financial statements. We made the assumption that the market value of SteelCo's equity equals its book value. The capital structure, then, is given by the ratio *Debt/ (Debt + Equity),* where the debt is the sum of both the short-term debt and the long-term debt. The average debt derived for 2014 to 2017 will be used for the WACC calculation. The gearing ratio for 2014 is 77%.

$$G_{2014} = \frac{Debt_{2014}}{Debt_{2014} + Equity_{2014}} = \frac{€74.8m}{€74.8m + €30.2m} = 77\%$$

Using the above equation for 2015, 2016, and 2017 the gearing ratio is found to be 71%, 71%, and 72% respectively. The average gearing ratio for SteelCo, then, is 73% and this is the figure that will be used for the WACC calculation.

Next is the *beta* estimation. SteelCo is a listed company. We have shown above how to estimate the beta (*β*) factor provided that there are available stock market returns for the particular share and the general stock market index. Moreover we have already calculated the *beta* of a particular stock from a month's stock market data and it was found to be 1.7. For the time being we will use 1.7 as the value of *beta*; this comes from the data published by Professor Damodaran and the Stern School of Business[1] for 2014 (http://www.stern.nyu. edu/~adamodar/pc/datasets/betaEurope.xls) and is the *beta* value of the steel industry in Europe. By coincidence both values are the same.

Following is the risk-free rate. We have considered as the risk-free rate the yield to maturity of the Euro Area 10-year Government Benchmark bond due to the particular capital markets in which the company operates. The "Yield To Maturity" (YTM) is the rate of return anticipated on a government bond if held until the end of its lifetime. To exclude any short-term fluctuations in the risk-free rates we base our calculations on the 1-year average yields of the annual period up to 31 December 2013, providing us with a risk-free rate of 3.0%. This information was drawn from the statistical data warehouse of the European Central Bank (ECB).[2]

Finally the market risk premium needs to be derived. For this purpose the data published by Professor Damodaran and the Stern School of Business[1] are used (http://www.stern.nyu. edu/~adamodar/pc/archives/ctryprem12.xls). The market risk premium is chosen to be equal to the Western Europe regional average, which is a simple average of European countries' risk premiums and equals 7.59%.

Now we have examined all the parameters we are ready to calculate SteelCo's WACC. Exhibit 5.6 can be rewritten as shown in Exhibit 5.7:

WACC Assumptions	
Weighted Average Cost of Capital – WACC	7.2%
Cost of Debt	6.0%
Tax Rate	33%
Capital Structure	73%
Cost of Equity	15.9%
Beta	1.70%
Risk-Free Rate	3.0%
Market Risk Premium	7.6%

EXHIBIT 5.7   Weighted average cost of capital parameters for SteelCo

The cost of equity K_e equals 15.9% and has been derived from the following equation described above:

$$K_e = R_f + [R_m - R_f] \times \beta = 3.0\% + 7.6\% \times 1.7 = 15.9\%$$

The WACC equals 7.2% and has been derived from the following equation described above:

$$WACC = \frac{D}{D+E} K_D (1-T) + \frac{E}{D+E} K_e = 73\% \times 6.0\% \times (1 - 33\%) + 27\% \times 15.9\% = 7.2\%,$$

where the gearing ratio $\left(\dfrac{D}{D+E}\right)$ is equal to 73% so the complementary ratio $\dfrac{E}{D+E}$ is $1 - 73\%$ or 27%.

Before we proceed to the next step of the DCF method and estimate the terminal value of a business, this section would not be complete if we did not mention anything about some additional premiums, like the *country risk-premium* and the *size premium*, frequently met in valuation engagements. The idea behind the first premium is the following. A business that operates in an emerging country, such as some countries in Latin America, Southeast Europe, and Asia, is considered riskier than a business in a large, developed market such as the USA, Japan, and some Western European countries. To reflect the increased risk associated with a business operating in an emerging country, a Country Risk Premium (CRP) is added to the market risk premium when using the CAPM. For example while the CRP for the USA is zero the CRP for Greece as of the updated data published by Professor Damodaran[1] on January 2014 is 15%! (http://pages.stern.nyu.edu/~%20adamodar/New_Home_Page/datafile/ctryprem.html).

The methodology for calculating risk premiums is far beyond the scope of this book but Professor Damodaran's site is a good place to start for the interested reader.

The idea behind the size premium is as follows. Empirically small companies have earned a higher return than predicted by CAPM. That is, the average rate of return of publicly traded companies, defined as small-cap, has outperformed large-cap stocks. And that sounds rational from the point of view that the size of small companies is compensated by their returns. So if we try to value a company smaller than its peer group we should add a size premium to its cost of equity.

Finally an additional premium may be added to the CAPM, based on a particular company-specific risk profile. This adjustment reflects the extent to which a company might be expected to have a higher perceived risk than its peer group companies.

So, by taking the above premiums into consideration, the revised CAPM equation takes the following form:

$$K_e = R_f + \beta * [R_m - R_f] + \text{CRP} + \text{Size Premium} + \text{Company Specific Premium}$$

where CRP is the country risk premium.

The Ibbotson *SBBI Valuation Yearbook*[6] or Duff & Phelps' *Risk Premium Report*[8] are good sources for further information about country risk premiums and size premiums.

5.5 ESTIMATING THE TERMINAL VALUE

This particular step of the DCF approach to valuation has to do with a company's terminal value estimation as we saw in Section 5.2. The terminal value represents the projected worth of the company at the end of the explicit forecast period. There are various approaches to calculating the terminal value. Amongst the most common approaches are:

- Exit multiples, where the terminal value is calculated using some comparable company multiple like EBITDA or EBIT (e.g. the terminal value of the company should be worth 5 times its EBITDA), and
- The perpetuity growth method, where terminal value is calculated using the following formula:

$$\text{Terminal value} = \frac{FCF_{N+1}}{r - g}$$

where FCF_{N+1} is the free cash flow of the year following the end of the explicit forecast period (which, let us say, lasts for N years),

r is the discount factor as we described it in Section 5.1 and is represented by the company's WACC, and

g is a constant growth rate that cannot exceed the growth rate of the economy which may be assumed to lie in a range between 1.5% and 5%.

According to Professor Damodaran[1] one simple proxy for the growth rate of an economy is its risk-free rate described above. Another could be the forecast average Gross Domestic Product (GDP) growth of the economy over the forthcoming years.

The whole idea with the terminal value is that since we cannot estimate cash flows forever, we estimate them over a period during which the company holds a competitive advantage relative to its competition (this is the explicit forecast period) and then make the assumption that the growth of the company will converge to the industry norm (i.e. it will be constant and not differ substantially from the growth of the economy).

We will use the perpetuity growth method for the case of SteelCo because it is the one most often used and the more technically sound. We will rewrite the above equation as:

$$\text{Terminal value} = \frac{FCF_N * (1 + g)}{r - g}$$

where FCF_N is the free cash flow for the last year (the 5th) of the explicit forecast period. That is, the free cash flow for the year following the end of the explicit forecast period, FCF_{N+1}, equals the free cash flow of the last year (N=5) increased by $g\%$:

$$FCF_{N+1} = FCF_N * (1+g)$$

So in order to estimate the terminal value of SteelCo at the end of year 5 we need the free cash flow for year 5, the discount rate, and to decide on the constant growth rate g. If we choose a constant growth rate g *equal* to 2.0% then its terminal value equals:

$$\text{Terminal value} = \frac{FCF_N * (1+g)}{r-g} = \frac{€4.7m * (1+2\%)}{7.2\% - 2\%} = €91.9m$$

Please note that we could use as the constant growth rate g a value equal to 3.0%, which is the risk-free rate. This would give a higher terminal value (€114.8m), and thus a higher valuation. Nevertheless, for reasons of prudence we choose a lower growth rate which is by the way very close to the 1.8% growth in the global steel sector that can be found at Professor Damodaran's site under the "Fundamental growth rate in EBIT by sector Dataset" data file[1]. Moreover in case the industry SteelCo operates in is a cyclical one, the free cash flow for the last year could correspond to a downturn and thus it is not a representative one. In that particular case we could use instead an average FCF of the explicit forecast period or an average of the explicit forecast period and the previous 3–5 years in order to accommodate cyclicality.

5.6 DCF SUMMARY – ENTERPRISE VALUE ADJUSTMENTS

This is the final step of a DCF valuation where we will gather the workings of the previous steps together. We see in Exhibit 5.8 the free cash flows of the 5-year explicit forecast period as well as the terminal value of SteelCo. The discount rate has been set to 7.2%. Then the discount factor of each period is calculated based on the following equation:

$$\text{Discount factor of period } n = \frac{1}{(1+r)^n}, \text{ or}$$

$$\text{Discount factor of period } 1 = \frac{1}{1+7.2\%} = 0.93, \text{ Discount factor of period } 2 = \frac{1}{(1+7.2\%)^2} = 0.87$$

and so on. Finally, the present value of each of the free cash flow streams is given by multiplying the FCF with the relevant discount factor.

The sum of the present values of the free cash flows of period 1 to period 5 plus the present value of the terminal value gives the enterprise value of SteelCo.

$$\text{EV of SteelCo} = \frac{€30.7m}{(1+7.2\%)^1} + \frac{€10.6m}{(1+7.2\%)^2} + \frac{€8.2m}{(1+7.2\%)^3} + \frac{€3.8m}{(1+7.2\%)^4} + \frac{€4.7m}{(1+7.2\%)^5}$$

$$+ \frac{€91.9m}{(1+7.2\%)^5}$$

or

$$\text{EV of SteelCo} = €115.5m$$

	B	C	D	E	F	G	H	I	J	K
5	Values in Euro '000					DCF Valuation				
6	YEAR			2013	2014	2015	2016	2017	2018	Terminal Value
7	Period			0	1	2	3	4	5	5
8										
9	EBIT			4,047	2,557	1,445	611	−7	78	
10	Depreciation			2,235	2,237	2,248	2,259	2,269	2,269	
11	EBITDA			6,282	4,794	3,693	2,869	2,262	2,348	
12	Net Change in Working Capital Needs			8,668	26,216	7,159	5,605	1,805	2,659	
13	Operating Cash Flow			14,949	31,011	10,852	8,475	4,067	5,007	
14	Taxes			-	0	0	0	0	0	
15	CAPEX			−400	−300	−300	−300	−300	−300	2.0%
16	Free Cash Flow			14,549	30,711	10,552	8,175	3,767	4,707	4,801
17	Cash Deposits			7,000	37,711	48,262	56,437	60,204	64,911	
18	Terminal Value									91,945
19										
20	Discount Rate @		7.2%		0.93	0.87	0.81	0.76	0.71	0.71
21	Present Value				28,642	9,178	6,632	2,850	3,321	64,881

Σ

Enterprise Value of SteelCo   115,505

EXHIBIT 5.8 DCF valuation model for SteelCo

Please note that apart from SteelCo's free cash flows, we present just below them its cumulative cash deposits [Cells (E17:J17) of Exhibit 5.8]. It is typical to present in similar valuation engagements a combined graph of the evolution of free cash flows and the cumulative cash deposits over time. The graph of the cumulative cash flows in cases of new companies and start-ups sometimes takes the form of the letter J and thus is known as the J-curve graph (see Exhibit 5.9).

Exhibit 5.9 shows a typical J-curve divided into 3 phases (initial period, growth period, and maturity period). These phases appear discrete, but this is purely to make the diagram easier to read. The timing of each stage depends largely on the characteristics of each company and the environment in which it operates. In the early stage of the J-curve the free cash flows of the firm are negative. Gradually they become positive at an increasing rate and finally they stabilize. Any valuation arising from the above cash flows will be determined on one

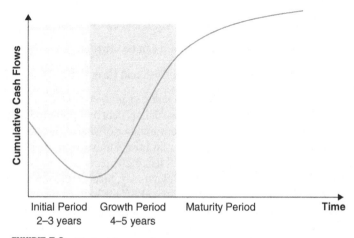

EXHIBIT 5.9 Typical J-curve for start-ups

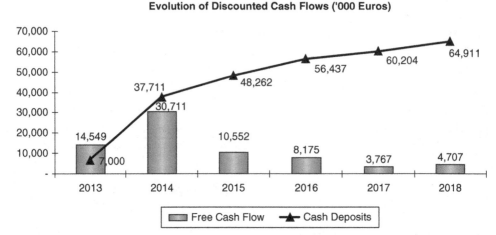

EXHIBIT 5.10   Evolution of discounted cash flows for SteelCo

hand by the depth and duration of the trough and on the other by the trajectory and extent of the upswing. SteelCo is not a start-up and its cumulative cash deposits graph looks like the one in Exhibit 5.10.

Another point of concern is that the terminal value was discounted by the discount factor of the last period of the explicit forecast period, that is, the fifth period and *not* the next one. We have also kept the discount rate constant for both the explicit forecast period and the terminal value. In this way we have assumed that SteelCo's leverage and the other WACC parameters (risk-free rate, market premium, etc.) stay fairly constant during that period. We could have used different discount rates for each year if we had to value a company with significant changes in its leverage ratio or if it operated in an environment where changes in risk-free rates and country risk premiums were expected.

Returning to SteelCo, if we want to find its equity value (shareholder value) or the so-called "intrinsic" value per share we need to make some adjustments to the enterprise value according to the following equation:

Enterprise Value = Value of equity − Value of Cash and Cash Equivalents + Value of Debt

or if we solve for the value of equity, the equation can be rewritten as:

Value of Equity = Enterprise Value + Value of Cash and Cash Equivalents − Value of Debt

SteelCo is a public company and its equity value or market capitalization is derived after subtracting from its total value all senior claims such as debt and preferred stock. It is calculated as the current share price multiplied by the number of shares outstanding. To find the number of shares outstanding, you need first to find the number of basic shares on the front of the latest company SEC filing in case of a US listed company (e.g. 10-K, 10-Q, 20-F) or a similar one in case of another stock exchange. If, let us say, SteelCo has 4.6 million shares outstanding then its intrinsic value per share is estimated to be €3.88, as shown in Exhibit 5.11.

We start with SteelCo's enterprise value of €115,505k as calculated above and we then subtract its total debt which equals €104,663k. When calculating total debt, be sure to include both the long-term debt and the short-term debt. The market value of debt should be used in the

Company Worth in Euro '000	115,505
– Debt	–104,663
+ Cash Deposits	7,000
+/– Other adjustments	-
= Shareholders Value	17,841
Shares Outstanding	4,600,000
Price per Share	3.88

EXHIBIT 5.11 The intrinsic value per share of SteelCo

calculation of enterprise value. However, in practice we can usually use the book value of the debt by assuming that the debt trades at par. The figure of debt we subtracted corresponds to the total debt of the company at the time the valuation takes place. We consider that the valuation takes place at the end of 2013 so the debt that we subtract is the one as at 31 December 2013.

Then we add up cash and equivalents. SteelCo holds €7,000k in cash as at 31 December 2013. If there were any balance sheet items such as property, plant, and equipment *available for sale* then we should add them up as well. Since there is no such information about SteelCo we leave the other adjustments line empty. The shareholders value then equals €17,841k.

Value of Equity (Shareholders Value) = €115.5m + €7.0m – €104.7m = €17.8m

And if we divide shareholders value by the number of shares outstanding (4.6m):

$$\text{Price per Share} = \frac{\text{Shareholders Value}}{\text{Number of Shares Outstanding}} = \frac{€17,841k}{4,600k} = €3.88$$

This price is at a discount of almost 50% compared to SteelCo's book value per share which is €6.97 as of 31 December 2013:

$$\text{Book Value per Share} = \frac{\text{Book Value of Equity}}{\text{Number of Shares Outstanding}} = \frac{€32,030k}{4,600k} = €6.97$$

We can invoke many reasons for a discrepancy between the book value (accounting value) per share and its intrinsic value. As far as SteelCo's case is concerned, the most obvious one is that the book value reflects the past performance of the company whereas the intrinsic value reflects the future performance. In particular, in contrast to book value, the intrinsic value as estimated by the DCF method reflects the absence of future growth potential of the company at least in the short term. The intrinsic value derived by the DCF can come closer to the book value by adjusting the growth potential of SteelCo during the explicit forecast period in terms of both sales and profits.

As a final note to this chapter I would like to warn the user of the DCF method about its drawbacks. Although the concept of DCF valuation is simple, is less exposed to market perceptions and forces you to think about the underlying business model of the company, it is very sensitive to its inputs (which are sometimes difficult to estimate). For example, small changes in the discount rate may have a big impact on the value of a company. Apart from the discount rate, DCF is very sensitive in estimating the value of a company to changes in the growth rate of the terminal value. Moreover it can easily be manipulated by a savvy modeller in order to provide the conclusion he or she wants. In order to make the above crystal clear let us examine the following situation.

Part of the calculation of the free cash flow for 2018 was the working capital difference between years 2018 and 2017. To estimate the working capital for 2018 we made the authoritative assumption that it would be 26% of 2018 sales. Before we proceed further with our thinking keep in mind that 2018 is the last year of the explicit forecast period. Moreover the free cash flow for 2018, after being increased by the perpetual growth rate, is the main constituent of the terminal value which in our case represents 80% of SteelCo's total value. Let us see what would be the value of SteelCo had we assumed that the working capital of 2018, given the sales we have already forecast, was 27% instead of 26%. The working capital of 2018 would be €25,869k instead of €24,911k and the difference between the working capital of 2018 and the working capital of 2017 would be €1,701k instead of €2,659k. Then the free cash flow of 2018 would be €3,749 instead of €4,707k and the terminal value, keeping all other parameters the same, would be €73,229k instead of €91,945k. Finally, the total value of SteelCo would be €101,622k instead of €115,505k and its intrinsic value per share would be just €0.86 instead of €3.88. That is, for a slight increase in working capital requirements of 3.85% {(27% − 26%)/26%} the intrinsic value per share of SteelCo plummeted by 77.8%. The interested reader can play with the assumptions of the DCF valuation model on the website accompanying the book and see their impact on the company's value.

BIBLIOGRAPHY AND REFERENCES

1. Professor Aswath Damodaran's web site. Probably the best valuation source you can find online, http://www.damodaran.com.
2. Statistical data warehouse of the European Central Bank (ECB), http://sdw.ecb.europa.eu/quickview.do?SERIES_KEY=143.FM.M.U2.EUR.4F.BB.U2_10Y.YLD.
3. Bloomberg site, http://www.bloomberg.com/markets/rates-bonds/.
4. Investopedia web site, http://www.investopedia.com/terms/c/covariance.asp.
5. Barra Integrated Model, http://www.msci.com/products/risk_management_analytics/barra_integrated_model/.
6. Ibbotson Associates, http://www.ibbotson.com.
7. Reinhart, C. M. and Rogoff, K. S., "The Aftermath of Financial Crises" (May 2009) 99(2) *American Economic Review*, American Economic Association, 466–472, http://www.nber.org/papers/w14656.
8. Duff & Phelps, http://www.duffandphelps.com/Pages/default.aspx.

Two

Planning for Uncertainty

6

Using Sensitivity Analysis

Chapter 6 examines the use of sensitivity analysis in apportioning the uncertainty of a model's output to the different sources of uncertainty concerning its inputs. Sensitivity analysis is one of the most important tools in financial analysis. It allows a modeller to quickly modify inputs to see how specific key performance indicators of interest will react. This chapter focuses on a quick and painless way to run multiple scenarios without having to change inputs manually each time by making use of Excel data tables. Step-by-step examples walk the reader through the preparation of sensitivity analysis tables. In addition the chapter explains the use of Excel's Goal Seek function and presents through examples the preparation of Tornado charts, as a means of assessing the importance of various model input variables.

6.1 INTRODUCTION

The second part of the book deals with how to introduce uncertainty into our financial forecasting models. As we have seen in the first part, a financial model is used to assess a company's performance on both a historical and a projected basis. It provides a way for the analyst to organize the company's operations and analyze its results. Nevertheless the parameter values and assumptions of any financial model are subject to change and error. In this particular chapter we will focus on sensitivity analysis as a means of investigating these potential changes and errors and their impacts on the conclusions to be drawn from the model.[1] Sensitivity analysis is an important tool in the financial model building process and generally refers to the variation in output of a model with respect to changes in the values of its input(s). It attempts to provide a ranking of the model inputs based on their relative contributions to model output variability and uncertainty. We could say that sensitivity analysis is possibly the most useful and widely used technique available to modellers to support the decision-making process. Decision-making is by its nature connected to strategic planning. The latter sets the direction and the road-map of the company while the former deals with the kind of resources (capital, people, time, effort & systems, etc.) needed to achieve the company's strategic goals. Strategic planning is the layout of a vision of future events precise enough to be captured in a long-term financial plan. In today's global economic crisis the macroeconomic environment is highly uncertain and there are many drivers affecting long-term strategic plans. Executives will eventually be called to face uncertainty by evaluating alternative scenarios and test how sensitive their plans are to changes in these key drivers. The McKinsey & Company site is an invaluable source on how to incorporate uncertainty into strategic planning. Their featured article "Strategy under Uncertainty"[2] or the eighth working paper from a series of working papers on risk called "Shaping Strategy in an Uncertain Macroeconomic Environment"[3] are useful examples.

Nevertheless we must highlight here the fact that neither sensitivity analysis nor any other technique for dealing with uncertainty can bulletproof the financial modeller or a company from black swan-type events. A "black swan" is an unpredictable, rare, and high impact event, such as the 9/11 attacks or the 2008 global financial crisis, first introduced by Nassim Nicholas Taleb, the author of the best-selling book *The Black Swan: The Impact of the Highly Improbable*.[4] For most companies, a black swan event would be a risk that has not been explicitly considered and that would lead to a major setback for the company or even a complete failure. Sensitivity analysis by its nature cannot be used to identify black swan-type events.

For the rest of this chapter and the second part of the book, while we will keep in mind that forward-looking assumptions rarely hold true and thus the future cannot be predicted with any certainty, we will use various techniques for dealing with uncertainty to facilitate decision-making based on incomplete, unknown, or uncertain data.

6.2   ONE-DIMENSIONAL AND 2-DIMENSIONAL SENSITIVITY ANALYSIS

In this section we will deal with the creation of 1-dimensional and 2-dimensional tables in Excel as a means of sensitivity analysis. We have already considered the concept of sensitivity analysis in Chapter 4. You may recall that, based on SteelCo's financial model, we built a control panel where we were able to change dynamically certain input parameters and see the changing outcomes of the model. You may also recall that in Section 4.1 we concluded that if the covenants were not to be breached in 2014, a much higher gross margin should be achieved than the one originally planned. This particular kind of uncertainty handling is called *What if* analysis and is often used to compare different scenarios and their potential outcomes based on changing conditions.

Now consider the following example. A company plans to take on a project that is forecast to give the cash flows in Exhibit 6.1 (cells C5:G5). The initial cost of the project is estimated at €10,000. It is important to calculate an estimate of how profitable the project will be since the company has an internal policy of accepting projects with an Internal Rate of Return (IRR) higher than 10%. Internal rate of return is used for investment appraisal and is the discount rate at which the Net Present Value (NPV) of an investment becomes zero. In other words, IRR is the discount rate which equates the present value of the future cash flows of a project with the initial outflow. You will recall from Chapter 5 that the NPV formula is used to determine the present value of the project by adding the discounted cash flows received from the project. The formula for the discounted sum of all cash flows is written as:

$$NPV = -Cf_0 + \sum_{i=1}^{T} \frac{cf_i}{(1+r)^i}$$

where Cf_0 is the initial cash outflow of the project and r the discount rate.

	A	B	C	D	E	F	G	H	I
1									
2	Growth rate (g)=	5%							
3	Discount rate (r)=	10%							
4	Year	0	1	2	3	4	5		
5	Cash outflow / inflow	−10,000 €	2,400 €	2,520 €	2,646 €	2,778 €	2,917 €	=F5*(1+$B$2)	
6	NPV =	−39 €	=NPV(B3;C5:G5)+B5						
7	IRR =	9.9%	=IRR(B5:G5)						

EXHIBIT 6.1   Simple investment appraisal model presenting selective cell functions

Considering that since the money going out is subtracted from the discounted sum of the incoming cash flows, the net present value of a project always needs to be positive in order to be considered a viable project.

The above model has 2 inputs: the growth rate of cash flows from the second year onwards and the discount rate. The project will bring in €2,400 in the first year of implementation and then it is assumed that each following year the cash inflow will be that of the previous year increased at a constant growth rate (in our case Cell B2 = 5%). Thus year 2 cash inflow will be:

$$\text{Year}_2 \text{ Cash Inflow} = \text{Year}_1 \text{ Cash Inflow} \times (1+5\%) = €2,400 \times 1.05 = €2,520$$

and so on. Moreover the company's cost of capital, which is roughly 10% (see Cell B3), is used as the discount rate. Instead of calculating discount factors manually as we did in Chapter 5 and then multiplying them with the future cash flows, we will use Excel's **NPV** function to calculate the net present value of the project immediately (cell B6). Finally we will use another Excel function (**IRR**) to calculate the Internal Rate of Return of the project (cell B7). Please note that while we included cells B5 to G5 in the **IRR** function (that is we included the initial cash outflow), we excluded cell B5 from the **NPV** function for the calculation of net present value. We just added cell B5 to the result of the **NPV** function instead (see cell B6 of Exhibit 6.1). The reason is that the cash outflow is considered to take place at the beginning of year 1 whereas the first cash inflow is considered to take place at the end of year 1. The first input value in the **NPV** function is discounted by the discount rate and that is why we exclude cash outflow at year 0. This should not be discounted at all. The function of cell B6 {NPV(B3;C5:G5)+B5} results in the discounted sum of all cash flows from years 1 to 5 described above.

We see from Exhibit 6.1 that the NPV of the project, under the specific assumptions of growth and discount rate, is negative. That is, the project is "No Go" as we say in finance jargon. Moreover the IRR is below 10%. Again the project is No Go. The project manager wants to know under what circumstances he can improve the project outcome. In order to help him, we could start changing the input assumption manually. Or instead we can use Excel's **Data Table** command to perform sensitivity analysis for a range of values for the growth rate at first and then for both the growth rate and the discount rate. To start building a data table for the IRR, as a function of the growth rate, we need a set of possible values for the growth rate. Let us say that the possible growth rate's values range from 3% to 8%. That is, we surround the growth base assumption with higher and lower estimates as shown in Exhibit 6.2. Then, to build the 1-dimensional sensitivity analysis table we just need to copy the formula calculating the IRR in the adjacent cell 1 row below to the left of the range values (cell C11) as shown in Exhibit 6.2 and select the cell range of both rows (cells C10:I11).

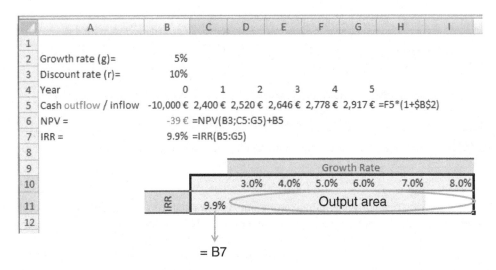

EXHIBIT 6.2   Constructing a 1-dimensional data table

Next, in the Excel ribbon we choose **Data**, then the **What If Analysis** tab, and finally the **Data Table** option. A **Data Table** dialog box like the one in Exhibit 6.3 appears. Since we want to construct a 1-dimensional data table in order to see how the IRR of the project varies with respect to changes in growth rate values, we need to fill in only the row input cell with cell B2. Finally we click the **OK button**. The various IRRs according to the different growth rates appear on the worksheet (cells D11:I11) as shown in Exhibit 6.4. Instead of a row, we could use a range of values in a column. In that case we would use the **Column input cell** of Exhibit 6.3.

As we can see from Exhibit 6.4, the project can succeed with an IRR greater than 10% assuming growth rates starting from 6% onwards.

At this point, one might ask the obvious question: at which exact growth rate is the IRR 10%? To answer this question we will use another feature of Excel, that of **Goal Seek**. **Goal Seek** helps you find what inputs you need to assign to a variable of a function in order to get a certain output. To do that, we choose **Data**, then the **What If Analysis** tab, and finally the **Goal Seek** option (Exhibit 6.5a). The **Goal Seek** window has 3 input options (Exhibit 6.5b): the cell that we want to change (**Set cell**), the value that we want this cell to take (**To Value**), and last the cell that we will change in order to achieve the requested value of the **Set cell** (**By changing cell**). In other words **Goal Seek** helps us *set a cell* at a certain *value by changing*

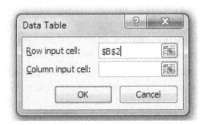

EXHIBIT 6.3   Data Table dialog box. We input the cell we want to vary with a range of values.

▲	A	B	C	D	E	F	G	H	I
1									
2	Growth rate (g)=	5%							
3	Discount rate (r)=	10%							
4	Year	0	1	2	3	4	5		
5	Cash outflow / inflow	-10,000 €	2,400 €	2,520 €	2,646 €	2,778 €	2,917 €	=F5*(1+$B$2)	
6	NPV =	-39 €	=NPV(B3;C5:G5)+B5						
7	IRR =	9.9%	=IRR(B5:G5)						
8									
9						Growth Rate			
10				3.0%	4.0%	5.0%	6.0%	7.0%	8.0%
11		IRR	9.9%	8.5%	9.2%	9.9%	10.5%	11.2%	11.9%

EXHIBIT 6.4 One-dimensional data table presenting various IRR values according to various growth rates

another *cell*. So what we want is to set cell B7 (the IRR) at a value of 10% by changing cell B2 (the growth rate). Once we press **OK** the **Goal Seek** function will find the closest value to achieve the goal and will display it in the cell denoted in the **Set cell** input option. This value is 5.2% and the growth rate is adjusted automatically to 5.2% once we push the **OK** button.

What we have done so far is to change a single variable in our simple model and monitor how the output of the model reacts to this change. Now let us try to change 2 variables at the same time and see how the output of the model responds. The real value of sensitivity

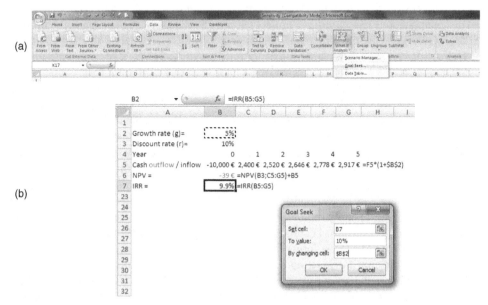

EXHIBIT 6.5 Using the Goal Seek function to find the required input of growth rate that gives an IRR of 10%

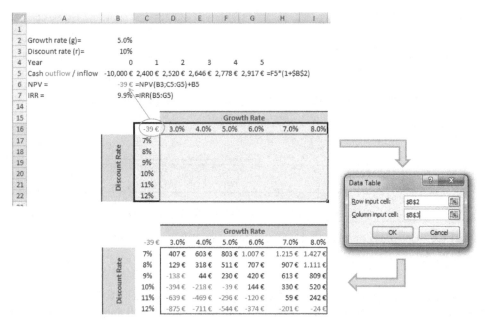

EXHIBIT 6.6 Two-dimensional sensitivity analysis table of a project NPV

analysis resides in the 2-dimensional data tables. The reason for this is simple. If we were to calculate manually the outcome of the 1-dimensional data table of Exhibit 6.4, we would need to change the growth rate cell 6 times. In a 2-dimensional 6 × 6 data table we would need to make 36 changes! Let us illustrate the point with another example of how we can automate this. Let us construct the table in Exhibit 6.6 in order to see which combinations of growth rate and discount rate give rise to positive project net present values. Note that, again, the first row of the table contains the possible input values for the growth rate whereas the first column of the table contains the possible input values for the discount rate. We have copied the formula calculating the NPV at the top left corner of the table (cell C16 of Exhibit 6.6). We set cell B2 as the row input cell in the **Data Table** dialog box (the growth rate input variable) and as the column input cell we set cell B3 (the discount rate input variable). Then by clicking **OK** the values of the table appearing at the bottom of Exhibit 6.6 fill the table range D17:I22.

We see a range of possible NPV values according to the particular growth and discount rates respectively. We can easily identify the pairs of growth and discount rates that result in a positive NPV. Moreover, by using the so-called conditional formatting feature of Excel we can easily visualize the positive and the negative NPV values. **Conditional Formatting** is an Excel tool that enables us to distinguish patterns and trends that exist in raw data. With conditional formatting we can apply formatting to 1 or more cells (in our case the whole sensitivity table ranging from cell D17 to I22) based on the value of the cell. We simply have to select the cells that we want to add the formatting to and then, in the Excel ribbon, in the **Home tab** to click the **Conditional Formatting** command. A drop-down menu will appear. The Conditional Formatting menu gives us various options (see Exhibit 6.7). We select the **Highlight Cells Rules** and then the **Greater Than** option where, for example, we indicate that we want NPVs higher than €1,000 to be presented in a dark colour. In the **Less Than** option we choose negative NPVs to be presented as gray text.

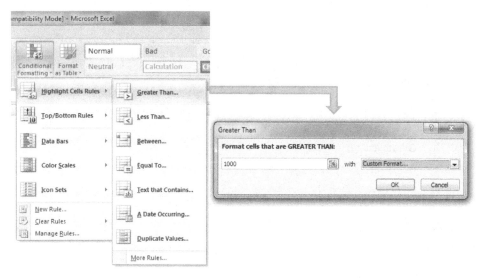

EXHIBIT 6.7 Conditional formatting: entering a value and formatting style

Make sure that you always use conditional formatting, when working with 2-dimensional sensitivity analysis tables, to visualize the desired pairs of variables that give the requested output.

The model described above had only 2 input variables: growth rate and discount rate. Therefore we did not have much choice as to which variable to choose in the sensitivity analysis. Recall that SteelCo's "Assumptions" worksheet in Chapter 3 included more than 20 variables. The question which may be asked is how we know which variables to choose in the sensitivity analysis. The next section deals with this question.

6.3 CHOOSING THE VARIABLES TO CHANGE

In this section we will deal with how to choose the right variables in sensitivity analysis. In most financial models there are many variables. Even in the model of the previous section if I were to ask you which variable (assumption) had the single most important impact on the NPV of the project, it is unlikely that you could answer immediately. Probably you should vary the variables one at a time, and see which one has the greatest impact on the NPV. In case of more variables we should repeat this procedure, identify the most sensitive variables, and use them to drive the sensitivity analysis. A very useful chart in Excel which helps in presenting the variables according to their importance in the model output is the so-called **Tornado chart**. A Tornado chart is a pictorial representation of a sensitivity analysis of the model, and is very useful for communicating the relative significance of different input variables. The chart is obtained by changing each input variable at some consistent range (e.g., ±10% from the base case) one at a time, and comparing their results to the base case. Then we can use Excel to plot them as horizontal bars ranked in descending order, as shown in Exhibit 6.8.

From the graph of Exhibit 6.8 it is obvious that by far the most critical variable, as far as the NPV of the project is concerned, is the discount rate. The graph of Exhibit 6.8 plots the difference from the base case at +10% and −10%, as we will see later on. Thus the point at

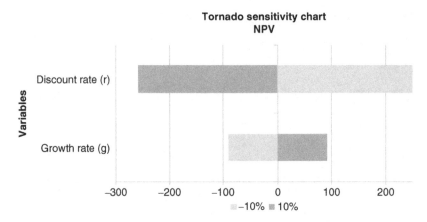

EXHIBIT 6.8 Tornado chart of the relative significance of the input variables of the NPV of the project in Section 6.2

which the vertical axis meets the horizontal one is at zero (0) difference from the base case NPV (which is –€39). We see that by increasing the discount rate by 10% the project loses almost 7 times more value compared to the base case NPV. Similarly by reducing the discount rate by 10% the project's NPV increases by more than 5 times.

When dealing with sensitivity analysis it is good to include Tornado sensitivity charts in your models in order to visualize the most critical variables – or critical success factors as they are called in management jargon – which the decision-maker should take into consideration. For a model with, let us say, 6 variables the Tornado chart will look like the one in Exhibit 6.9. We can see that variable number 4 is the most critical one followed by variable number 2.

Thus, when the time for sensitivity analysis comes we will construct a 2-dimensional data table between variables 4 and 2.

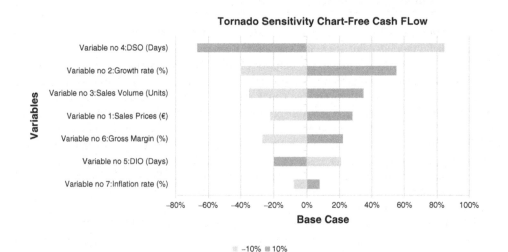

EXHIBIT 6.9 Tornado chart showing the relative importance of 6 variables

Base case input values	
Growth rate	5%
Discount rate	10%
Base case output value	
NPV	−€39

EXHIBIT 6.10   Base case input and output values that the Tornado chart will be built on

For the rest of this section we will consider how to construct the Tornado chart shown in Exhibit 6.8. First we need to derive the data values plotted in the Tornado chart. We agree that the base case values are those shown in Exhibit 6.10:

Now let us flex each variable at 10% from the base case. That is, the growth rate will take values (1 − 10%)* 5% = 4.5% and (1 + 10%)* 5% = 5.5%. Similarly the discount rate will take values (1 − 10%)* 10% = 9% and (1 + 10%)* 10% = 11% respectively. Exhibit 6.11 shows the NPV values for each flexed variable keeping all other inputs the same. For example, at growth rate 4.5% (10% of the base case) the NPV of the project is −€129 (keeping the discount rate the same). Similarly, at a discount rate 9.0 % (−10% of the base case) the NPV of the project is €230 (keeping the growth rate the same). We can see that for each input variable we calculate the range between the 2 extremes (−10% + 10%). That is, for the growth rate the range is 129 + 52 = 181 whereas for the discount rate it is 230 + 296 = 527. The variable with the greatest range is obviously the most critical one. If we had 10 variables we could use the sort feature of Excel (**Data tab**, **Sort & Filter** group) to sort them in ascending or descending order to achieve a presentation like the one in Exhibit 6.11.

Please note that the values of NPV plotted in Exhibit 6.8 are not the ones presented in Exhibit 6.11 but their difference from the base case value. As we mentioned previously, the vertical axis meets the horizontal at zero (0) difference from the base case NPV. To derive the values plotted in Exhibit 6.8 we simply subtract the base case NPV (−€39) from the output NPV values at −10% and 10% as you can see in Exhibit 6.12. So the numbers we finally plot are the following:

We first select the range K3:M4 and then click on the **Insert tab** on the excel ribbon; select **Bar** from the **Charts** group and then the second on the right from the **2-D Bar** section

	Input values			Output value - NPV			
	Base Case	−10%	10%	Base Case	−10%	10%	Range
Growth rate	5%	4.5%	5.5%	−39	−129	52	181
Discount rate	10%	9.0%	11.0%	−39	230	−296	527

EXHIBIT 6.11   NPV values after flexing base case input values by ± 10%

	J	K	L	M	N
1					
2		Variable	-10%	10%	
3		Growth rate (g)	-90	91	
4		Discount rate (r)	269	-258	
5					

EXHIBIT 6.12   Difference in project's NPV for various growth and discount rates

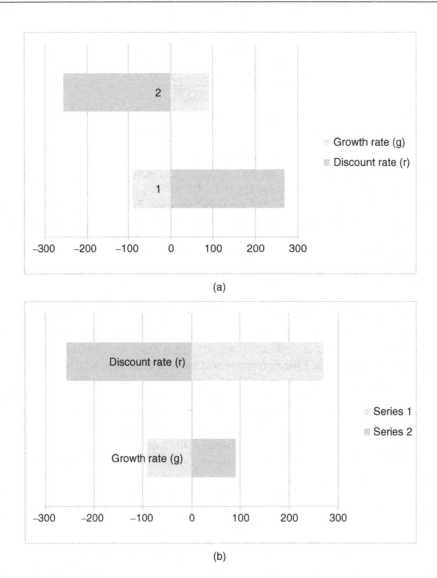

EXHIBIT 6.13 Different phases in the construction of a Tornado chart

(**Stacked Bar**). Then a chart like the one in Exhibit 6.13a appears on the current worksheet. This chart has little to do with the one in Exhibit 6.8. Let us format it, then, like that of Exhibit 6.8.

1. With the chart selected, on **Chart Tools, Design tab** we click the **Switch Row/Column tab** from the **Data** group (second group in the ribbon). The chart now starts to resemble the one in Exhibit 6.8 (Exhibit 6.13b). The reason we did this is because Excel plotted the rows of data on the vertical axis, and the columns of data on the horizontal axis. After we switch rows to columns in the chart, the columns of data are plotted on the vertical axis, and the rows of data are plotted on the horizontal one.

2. Then, we select the legend of the chart, which is on the right, and by right clicking on it a popup window appears. We select the last option – **Format Legend** – and from the new

popup window that appears we choose **Bottom** instead of the **Right** that is preselected. The legend of the chart moves immediately to the bottom. Then instead of Series 1 and Series 2 we give names to the series in the way we described in Chapter 4. From the **Select Data** tab, we select Series 1, Edit the name, and select cell L2 (−10%). In the same way we rename Series 2 to 10%.

3. Then, we right click on the vertical axis and select **Format Axis** from the popup window and change **Axis Labels** to **Low** in the drop-down box instead of **Next to Axis** that is preselected.
4. Finally, we add a chart title (click on the **Chart Tools**, **Layout tab** and then select **Chart Title** from the **Labels** group, then **Above Chart** and then enter the title that appears on Exhibit 6.8) and a vertical axis title (similarly, from the **Labels** group choose **Axis Titles**, then **Primary Vertical Axis Title** and type "Variables").

Now the chart should not be dissimilar to the one in Exhibit 6.8.

The interested reader, who finds Tornado charts useful but not very straightforward to construct, may find a lot of free add-ins that perform this kind of analysis automatically. A useful add-in, called the sensitivity toolkit, can be found on the MBA site of the Tuck School of Business of Dartmouth College.[5] This toolkit supports 4 different forms of sensitivity analysis.

6.4 MODELLING EXAMPLE

In this section we will apply sensitivity analysis to selected input variables of the model the FP&A manager built in Chapter 3 and we will try to establish under what circumstances the company can return to profitability in year 2015. We will follow the steps listed below:

1. Select the most sensitive variables to change.
2. Assign them the proper range of values.
3. Construct the 2-dimensional sensitivity analysis table.
4. Interpret the results.

6.4.1 Selecting the Variables to Change

If you construct a tornado chart with various SteelCo variables you will see that its profitability is most sensitive to sales volume and gross margin as a percentage of sales. So the variables we choose to analyse in a 2-dimensional data table are these two. We will need a new worksheet dedicated only to sensitivity analysis tables. Let us name this worksheet "Sensitivity analysis". Then we must draw on paper the layout as a single A4 sheet. When presenting numerical data, it is important to present them in such a way as to maximize their impact and ensure that they are easy to read and interpret. If we imagine our "Sensitivity Analysis" worksheet as a 1-page A4 report, then we definitely need a title at the top denoting what it is. Then we have to decide the area that we allocate on the 2-dimensional table. To do so, we must first decide the range of values the 2 variables will span.

6.4.2 Assigning a Range of Values

The best practice is to assign a symmetrical range around the base case value of the variable of interest. In doing so the range consists of an even number of entries where the median is the base case. Thus, regarding the gross margin percentage, we decide to vary it symmetrically with 4 values on each side. The base case is 9.5% and we present it in a row range. That is from 7.5% to 9% with a step of 0.5%, on the left, and from 10% to 11.5% with the same step on the right (see Exhibit 6.14):

% Gross Margin								
7.5%	8.0%	8.5%	9.0%	9.5%	10.0%	10.5%	11.0%	11.5%

EXHIBIT 6.14 Range of values for the gross margin percentage variable

The above range will form the horizontal axis of the table. The vertical axis will present the various sales volumes. Let us vary the sales volume symmetrically from 120,000 Metric Tons (MTs) to 200,000 MTs with a step of 5,000 MTs and present them in a column. Recall from the model of Chapter 3 that the base case sales volume, in year 2015, is 160,596 MTs. When we build a sensitivity table it is good to see the base case scenario somewhere in the middle of the table. Since the base case is not a multiple of 5,000 MT we will have to present the base case as well. Nevertheless the figure of 160,596 MTs is very close to 160,000 MTs so we will present the former sales volume instead of the latter one. The vertical axis of the table will look like the column in Exhibit 6.15:

Sales Volume Variation (MT)
120,000
125,000
130,000
135,000
140,000
145,000
150,000
155,000
160,596
165,000
170,000
175,000
180,000
185,000
190,000
195,000
200,000

EXHIBIT 6.15 Range of values for the sales volume variable

You will appreciate that we have given specific attention to the titles of each axis. It is important that the user of the model can see at once which variable is presented on each axis and what its unit of measurement is. When we deal with a horizontal axis we can select the cells spanning the row above the varying range and merge them using the **Merge & Center** command of the **Home tab** in the Excel ribbon. Then we can type the name of the variable there and format the borders of the cell with a solid line in order to emphasize it. To do so we select the cell we want to format and click the **down arrow** beside the **Borders button** in the **Font** group of the **Home** tab. We select the **More Borders** option from the drop-down menu that appears. There we can choose the type of line, the thickness, and the colour of the borders we want to apply to the cell selection. Although each individual has their own aesthetics and there are no universal standards regarding cell formatting, it is important to format your Excel models properly because this makes it easier for others to read and understand. Formatting literacy comes with experience. For the reader that wants to elaborate more on Excel formats and styles I would recommend visiting[6] and downloading the *Best Practice Spreadsheet Modeling Standards, Commentary & Examples,* a 280-page document developed by the Spreadsheet Standards Review Board (SSRB) and the Best Practice Modelling (BPM) organization to promote universal spreadsheet modelling standards.

6.4.3 Constructing the 2-dimensional Sensitivity Analysis Table

Returning to the sensitivity analysis, so far we have designed a 9 × 17 table by deciding on the range of the heading row and heading column, naming and formatting them. You will recall from Section 6.1 that we must copy the formula calculating the measurement we want to analyze (Profit before Tax - PBT) in our case) at the top left hand corner of the table. This cell reads from the bottom line of the income statement, located in the "Workings" worksheet, the PBT row, and especially the cell that corresponds to 2015. That is at the intersection of the row and column of the input variables, there is a reference to the output variable we want to monitor. If we try to create the data table, we will need to select a row input cell and a column input cell in the **Data Table** dialog box. Usually the input cells that drive the table are located in the same worksheet as the Data Table. That means that the row and column input cells must refer to a cell on the active worksheet. But the row and column input cells that we want to vary are located in the "Assumptions" worksheet. This is not a problem since there is a workaround. Instead of placing the raw numbers of the input variables, for year 2015, in the "Assumptions" worksheet, we can define 2 cells in the active worksheet of "Sensitivity Analysis" and use linking formulae ("=Sensitivity analysis!A7") and ("=Sensitivity analysis!B7") to feed the values of these cells into the "Assumptions" worksheet (see Exhibit 6.16). In this

Sales Volume Variation (MT)	−2,595	7.5%	8.0%	8.5%	9.0%	9.5%	10.0%	10.5%	11.0%	11.5%
120,000		−6,212	−5,783	−5,355	−4,927	−4,499	−4,071	−3,643	−3,214	−2,786
125,000		−6,048	−5,602	−5,156	−4,710	−4,264	−3,818	−3,372	−2,926	−2,480
130,000		−5,885	−5,421	−4,957	−4,494	−4,030	−3,566	−3,102	−2,638	−2,175
135,000		−5,722	−5,240	−4,759	−4,277	−3,795	−3,314	−2,832	−2,350	−1,869
140,000		−5,559	−5,059	−4,560	−4,060	−3,561	−3,061	−2,562	−2,062	−1,563
145,000		−5,396	−4,878	−4,361	−3,844	−3,326	−2,809	−2,292	−1,774	−1,257
150,000		−5,232	−4,697	−4,162	−3,627	−3,092	−2,556	−2,021	−1,486	−951
155,000		−5,069	−4,516	−3,963	−3,410	−2,857	−2,304	−1,751	−1,198	−645
160,596		−4,887	−4,314	−3,741	−3,168	−2,595	−2,022	−1,449	−876	−303
165,000		−4,743	−4,154	−3,565	−2,977	−2,388	−1,799	−1,211	−622	−33
170,000		−4,580	−3,973	−3,367	−2,760	−2,153	−1,547	−940	−334	273
175,000		−4,416	−3,792	−3,168	−2,543	−1,919	−1,295	−670	−46	579
180,000		−4,253	−3,611	−2,969	−2,327	−1,684	−1,042	−400	242	884
185,000		−4,090	−3,430	−2,770	−2,110	−1,450	−790	−130	530	1,190
190,000		−3,927	−3,249	−2,571	−1,893	−1,215	−537	140	818	1,496
195,000		−3,764	−3,068	−2,372	−1,676	−981	−285	411	1,106	1,802
200,000		−3,601	−2,887	−2,173	−1,460	−746	−33	681	1,395	2,108

Report Title — Sensitivity Analysis

Table Title — PBT for 2015

% Gross Margin

Volume 2015 = 160,596   %GM 2015 = 9.50%

='Workings'!H35

Column & Row input cells — Both feeds the Assumptions page

Base Case Scenario

EXHIBIT 6.16 Sensitivity analysis report

way the input cells are on the same worksheet as the Data Table which in turn feed the relevant input cells on the "Assumptions" worksheet.

Notice that in this way we have both input and output cells on the same worksheet. Remember that when we were describing the basic modelling principles in Chapters 1 and 3 we stressed the fact that all the assumptions of the model should be located on a separate worksheet: the "Assumptions" one. Each time we change an assumption or an input variable, the workings of the model change respectively and thus the output of the model. Different outputs of the model may exist in different worksheets. We saw in Chapter 4 that in order to facilitate the monitoring of SteelCo's loan covenants we built the control panel. Moreover as we will see in the Appendix of the book there exists a worksheet, called "Ratios", where we have calculated all the different ratios described in Chapter 2. While the "Ratios" worksheet is purely an output worksheet, the way in which we built the "Control panel" permitted us to change some input variables, which in turn fed the "Assumptions" worksheet, which in turn fed the "Workings" worksheet, which in turn fed the control panel's output area. The functionality of the "Sensitivity Analysis" worksheet is similar to that of the control panel. The output variable we want to monitor will be presented in the table area. Each time an input variable varies according to the row or column ranges, it will feed the relevant variable into the "Assumptions" worksheet, which in turn will feed the "Workings" worksheet, which in turn will feed the output of the table. Exhibit 6.16 shows the "Sensitivity Analysis" worksheet presented as an A4 report.

As you notice immediately, the base case scenario of the losses before tax for 2015 is €2,595 as had been forecast in Chapter 3 (see Exhibit 3.19). It is highlighted to track attention and it is located at the centre of the table. It corresponds to a sales volume equal to 160,596 MT and a gross margin percentage equal to 9.5%. As we move towards the left hand corner of the table, losses increase. This is expected since the sales volume decreases and gross margin percentage decreases as we move diagonally to the top left corner. On the other hand, as we move diagonally to the bottom right hand corner of the table, losses vanish gradually and the company starts to make profits. We can see that, out of the 153 different table outcomes, 138 are loss making and 15 profit making. Thanks to conditional formatting these outcomes are easily identified. The same applies to the combinations of the 2 input variables that give rise to these positive outcomes.

We should stress once again here the importance of consistent and meaningful formatting not only as a means of communicating results clearly and powerfully, but also of reducing the risk of error. To this end we placed titles on top of cell A7 (Volume 2015) and B7 (% GM 2015) denoting which one should be used as the *row input cell* and the *column input cell* at the *Data Table* popup window. To gain some space we reduced the width of both A7 and B7 cells and used the **Wrap Text** command (**Home** tab) so that the title folds into 2 lines. Moreover we used a title at the top of the sensitivity table. Since the "Sensitivity Analysis" worksheet may contain more than one table it is wise to denote what is the output of each table. We **Merge and Center** the cells over which the title will be typed. To distinguish the title of the sensitivity table (PBT for 2015) from the title of the row input variable (% gross margin) we format-ted the former with light shading. Although you can use Excel's different pre-set formatting styles to add colour and shading to your worksheet (**Styles** options located on the **Home** tab of the ribbon) you should not overdo it, as this can destroy the spreadsheet's aesthetics and produce the opposite effect. Note that the header at the top of the worksheet (the report title) is quite minimal as it is bold, gray coloured, uses a larger font size, and is bordered with a thin gray line.

Moreover we have removed the grid lines. It is often confusing to distinguish between borders and gridlines in Excel. By removing the grid lines (from the **View** tab of the Excel ribbon we deselect **Gridlines**) we improve the readability of the spreadsheet.

Finally we have chosen a clear and readable font like Calibri throughout the whole worksheet for the titles, the subtitles, and the input and output values. Using too many different fonts can be very distracting. To find out more about how to create stylish spreadsheets you can visit TechRepublic's *Windows and Office* blog.[7]

Now, coming back to our modelling example, let us say that the management of SteelCo instruct us to go a step further and present them with another table showing the combinations of working capital parameters and especially DSO and DIO under which the Operating Cash Flow (OpCF) of the company remains positive in 2015. What we need to do is to add to the "Sensitivity Analysis" worksheet another 2-dimensional table the way we did before. Let us put on the horizontal axis the Days Sales Outstanding (DSO) and on the vertical one the Days Inventory Outstanding (DIO). The set of possible values for the DSO will vary from 60 days to 100 days with a step of 5 days. In the same way we choose the range of possible values for the DIO to vary from 55 days to 115 days with a step of 5 days. Again, we will set the row and column input cells on the active (sensitivity analysis) worksheet which will feed the "Assumptions" worksheet as described previously. The formatting will be similar to the one in the table for 2015 PBT. That is, positive OpCF will be presented in plain text whereas negative OpCF will be presented in shaded text. Exhibit 6.17 shows what the "Sensitivity Analysis" report will look like prior to its submission to SteelCo's management. We have removed the Row and Column headings from the report. The use of headings is only for pedagogical reasons. Instead we added a footer (line of text that prints at the bottom of the spreadsheet page) to present information about the filename of the Excel file in use (bottom left hand corner of the page), the date the report is printed (the bottom centre of the page), and the spreadsheet author (the bottom right hand corner of the page).

6.4.4 Interpreting the Results

The management of SteelCo holding this report can immediately see the combinations of gross margin and sales volume for 2015 that give rise to profits as opposed to the base case scenario which bear losses. Moreover it is obvious that both DIO and DSO could deteriorate and still the OpCF of the company remains positive.

So far we have dealt with the technical part of how to create and format a professional and neat sensitivity analysis report. Nevertheless the interpretation of the report findings is much more important than its construction. It is the raison d'être of its creation in the first instance. It should trigger management action. SteelCo's management should figure out how to achieve both increased sales volume and gross margin in a declining market. Or how to decrease both inventory levels and the credit given to customers in order to minimize SteelCo's working capital requirements and thus improve its liquidity.

Increasing sales volume in a declining market means increasing SteelCo's market share whereas increasing profit margins may mean increasing its sales prices or reducing its costs or changing its product mix or differentiating or all of these. Buzzell, Gale, and Sultan in their 1975 *Harvard Business Review* article "Market Share – a Key to Profitability"[8] argued that as market share increases, a business is likely to have a higher profit margin, a declining purchases-to-sales ratio, a decline in marketing costs as a percentage of sales, higher quality, and higher priced products. Moreover Raynor and Ahmed in their 2013 article "Three Rules for Making a Company Truly Great"[9] in the same journal argued that the many and diverse choices that made certain companies great were consistent with (1) differentiating in areas other than price and (2) prioritizing increasing their revenue over reducing their costs. The third rule was that companies should follow Rules 1 and 2. We could suggest various strategies that SteelCo could follow to increase market share and improve profitability. Nevertheless

Sensitivity Analysis

Volume 2015	%GM 2015
160,596	9.50%

PBT for 2015

Sales Volume Variation (MT) / −2,595	% Gross Margin								
	7.5%	8.0%	8.5%	9.0%	9.5%	10.0%	10.5%	11.0%	11.5%
120,000	−6,212	−5,783	−5,355	−4,927	−4,499	−4,071	−3,643	−3,214	−2,786
125,000	−6,048	−5,602	−5,156	−4,710	−4,264	−3,818	−3,372	−2,926	−2,480
130,000	−5,885	−5,421	−4,957	−4,494	−4,030	−3,566	−3,102	−2,638	−2,175
135,000	−5,722	−5,240	−4,759	−4,277	−3,795	−3,314	−2,832	−2,350	−1,869
140,000	−5,559	−5,059	−4,560	−4,060	−3,561	−3,061	−2,562	−2,062	−1,563
145,000	−5,396	−4,878	−4,361	−3,844	−3,326	−2,809	−2,292	−1,774	−1,257
150,000	−5,232	−4,697	−4,162	−3,627	−3,092	−2,556	−2,021	−1,486	−951
155,000	−5,069	−4,516	−3,963	−3,410	−2,857	−2,304	−1,751	−1,198	−645
160,596	−4,887	−4,314	−3,741	−3,168	−2,595	−2,022	−1,449	−876	−303
165,000	−4,743	−4,154	−3,565	−2,977	−2,388	−1,799	−1,211	−622	−33
170,000	−4,580	−3,973	−3,367	−2,760	−2,153	−1,547	−940	−334	273
175,000	−4,416	−3,792	−3,168	−2,543	−1,919	−1,295	−670	−46	579
180,000	−4,253	−3,611	−2,969	−2,327	−1,684	−1,042	−400	242	884
185,000	−4,090	−3,430	−2,770	−2,110	−1,450	−790	−130	530	1,190
190,000	−3,927	−3,249	−2,571	−1,893	−1,215	−537	140	818	1,496
195,000	−3,764	−3,068	−2,372	−1,676	−981	−285	411	1,106	1,802
200,000	−3,601	−2,887	−2,173	−1,460	−746	−33	681	1,395	2,108

DIO 2015	DSO 2015
80	80

OpCf for 2015

Sales Volume Variation (MT) / 6,812	Days Sales Outstanding								
	60	65	70	75	80	85	90	95	100
55	21,371	19,497	17,624	15,750	13,877	12,003	10,130	8,256	6,382
60	19,958	18,084	16,211	14,337	12,464	10,590	8,717	6,843	4,970
65	18,545	16,671	14,798	12,924	11,051	9,177	7,304	5,430	3,557
70	17,132	15,258	13,385	11,511	9,638	7,764	5,891	4,017	2,144
75	15,719	13,845	11,972	10,098	8,225	6,351	4,478	2,604	731
80	14,306	12,432	10,559	8,685	6,812	4,938	3,065	1,191	−682
85	12,893	11,020	9,146	7,272	5,399	3,525	1,652	−222	−2,095
90	11,480	9,607	7,733	5,859	3,986	2,112	239	−1,635	−3,508
95	10,067	8,194	6,320	4,446	2,573	699	−1,174	−3,048	−4,921
100	8,654	6,781	4,907	3,034	1,160	−714	−2,587	−4,461	−6,334
105	7,241	5,368	3,494	1,621	−253	−2,127	−4,000	−5,874	−7,747
110	5,828	3,955	2,081	208	−1,666	−3,540	−5,413	−7,287	−9,160
115	4,415	2,542	668	−1,205	−3,079	−4,952	−6,826	−8,700	−10,573

EXHIBIT 6.17 Sensitivity analysis report as submitted to SteelCo's management

SteelCo's management actions after the interpretation of the sensitivity analysis report, though by nature very interesting, are beyond the scope of this book. The above *Harvard Business Review* articles provide food for thought for the interested reader.

As a final note to this section I would like to highlight the need to keep track of where the input values of model assumptions are located. By doing so, we not only avoid possible errors in the future but we make it easier for third parties to work with our model. Apart from the "Assumptions" worksheet, values for input variables are located, so far, in the "Control panel" worksheet we built in Chapter 4 and the "Sensitivity Analysis" worksheet. You can keep track using various methods. Since all inputs, wherever they are located, come to the "Workings" worksheet through the "Assumptions" worksheet, I would suggest adding a comment to all those cells of the latter that read from another worksheet indicating the worksheet they read from (see Exhibit 6.18). To add a comment to a cell, click inside the cell on the spreadsheet and from the **Review tab** on the Excel ribbon click on **New Comment**. A textbox will appear to the right of the cell where you can type your comments. On the top left hand corner of the textbox the name of the user account that was set up in Windows appears. Whenever you move your cursor over a cell that contains a comment, you will see the comment appear in a sort of a note. Moreover, cells containing comments have a red triangle in the top right hand corner to remind you that extra care is needed.

Assumptions

Particulars	UOM	2011 A	2012 A	2013 A	2014 F	2015 F	2016 F	2017 F
Price								
Long Products	€/MT	700	670	650	65(	650		650
Flat Products	€/MT	650	680	700	70(	700		700
Volume								
Long Products	MT	200,000	170,000	150,000	133,092	120,447	11,137	104,515
Flat Products	MT	70,000	60,000	50,000	44,364	40,149	37,046	34,838
Total Sales MT	MT	270,000			177,456	160,596	**148,183**	**139,354**
Rate of change	%				−11.3%	−9.5%	−7.7%	−6.0%
Profitability								
% Gross Margin	%	8.2%	9.7%	9.5%	9.5%	9.5%	9.5%	9.5%
Financing								
Deposit rate	%	5.0%			1.0%	1.0%		
Financing Cost - LT	%	−2.5%			−5.7%	−5.7%		
Financing Cost - ST	%	−5.3%			−6.7%	−6.7%		
Working Capital								
Stock Days - DIO	Days	86			85	80		
Customer Days - DSO	Days	115			85	80		
Supplier Days - DPO	Days	41			50	50		
Effective Tax Rate	%	33.0%			33.0%	33.0%		
Depreciation								
Depreciation rate	%	3.7%			3.6%	3.6%	3.6%	3.6%
Cost of sales	€ '000	995	945	1,028	1,029	1,034	1,039	1,044

EXHIBIT 6.18 Keeping track of the input variables' value origin

As we move on to the remaining chapters of the book we will feed selective input variables located in the "Assumptions" worksheet through other worksheets. Each time we do so we will keep track of the origin of the input variable value by inserting a new comment into the relevant cell.

BIBLIOGRAPHY AND REFERENCES

1. Baird, B. F., *Managerial Decisions under Uncertainty. An Introduction to the Analysis of Decision Making* (New York: John Wiley & Sons, 1989).
2. McKinsey Quarterly, "Strategy under Uncertainty", June 2000, http://www.mckinsey.com/insights/managing_in_uncertainty/strategy_under_uncertainty.
3. McKinsey working papers on risk. "Shaping Strategy in an Uncertain Macroeconomic Environment, No 8, December 2008, http://www.mckinsey.com.
4. Taleb, N. N. (2010). *The Black Swan: The impact of the highly improbable*, 2nd edn (London: Penguin, 2010).
5. The Sensitivity Toolkit, Tuck Business School, Dartmouth College, http://mba.tuck.dartmouth.edu/toolkit/.
6. *Best Practice Spreadsheet Modeling Standards; Commentary & Examples*, Version 7, http://www.bestpracticemodelling.com/downloads/knowledge.
7. 20 Excel Tips for Creating Stylish Spreadsheets, http://www.techrepublic.com/blog/windows-and-office/20-excel-tips-for-creating-stylish-spreadsheets/#.
8. Buzzell, R. D., Gale, B. T., and Sultan, R. G. M., "Market Share – a Key to Profitability" (January 1975) *Harvard Business Review* 97–106.
9. Raynor, M. E. and Ahmed, M., "Three Rules for Making a Company Truly Great" (April 2013) *Harvard Business Review* 108–117.

7

Using Scenarios

Chapter 7 deals with scenario analysis. Scenario analysis is a strategic process of analyzing decisions by considering alternative possible outcomes. It may be used as an analytical tool to manage uncertainty. The purpose of scenario analysis is to provide a plausible idea of what might happen into the future. For example, we use scenario analysis to determine the Net Present Value (NPV) of a potential investment under high and low inflation scenarios.

By analyzing various scenarios, we are in a better position to anticipate the outcomes of our model. The examples presented in this chapter use 3 different scenarios: base case, worst case, and best case. The base case is the expected scenario: if all things proceed normally, this is what the expected outcome will be. The worst and best cases are obviously scenarios with less and more favourable conditions, but they are still confined by a sense of feasibility.

7.1 INTRODUCTION

The previous chapter introduced sensitivity analysis as a means of incorporating uncertainty and risk into financial models. Every organization faces a unique set of risks in the current rapidly changing marketplace, full of political and economic uncertainties. As financial analysts and modellers, we have to plan for whatever might go wrong and be ready to support the company's management. Identifying, analyzing, and mitigating what can go wrong can provide peace of mind and a strong competitive advantage to the companies we work for. This chapter goes a step further than the previous one. While sensitivity analysis varies 1 or 2 key input variables in a financial model to see how sensitive the model is to the change in these variables this chapter deals with scenario analysis. A scenario involves a reasonable combination of some or all of the input variables of a financial model and not just 1 or 2. Scenario analysis is the strategic process of analyzing decisions by considering many alternative possible outcomes or scenarios. In practice it does so by changing the input values of each alternative scenario and feeding them into the model of reference. While both scenario and sensitivity analysis can be important components in determining possible future outcomes, only scenario analysis can address many different crucial factors affecting a model all at the same time. For example, a worst case scenario could include:

- cost of funding hikes due to a liquidity crisis in the banking system of the country in which the company operates;
- less than expected sales growth due to an economic downturn;
- net margin decreases due to increasing competition or discount specials or price reductions; and
- unfavourable payment terms to foreign suppliers due to increasing sovereign risk of the country in which the company operates.

Scenario analysis has been receiving increased attention as a tool for considering the future in the midst of a rapidly changing business environment. In the 2014 Risk Survey[1] conducted by the Association for Financial Professionals in collaboration with Oliver Wyman, scenario analysis ranked first (80%) among the various risk-oriented tools used by Financial Planning and Analysis people to analyze business situations, followed by sensitivity analysis, which was ranked at 75%. Nevertheless, we should keep in mind that scenario analysis is not a predictive mechanism, but rather an analytic tool to manage uncertainty today.[2]

7.2 USING SCENARIO ANALYSIS WITH EXCEL'S SCENARIO MANAGER

There are several tools which can be used to create scenarios in Excel. Scenario Manager is one of them and it is located on the Excel ribbon's **Data tab** under **What If** analysis. Through the sample model of the previous chapter we will describe the use of Excel's Scenario Manager. You may recall that Exhibit 6.1 presented the forecast cash flows of a project based on a constant growth rate from year 2 onwards. Moreover, given a base case discount rate it presented the Net Present Value (NPV) of the project. Recall also that by varying the growth rate and the discount rate we constructed 2-dimensional sensitivity analysis tables. What we have ignored in this sample model is inflation. When appraising capital projects using discounted cash flow techniques such as NPV we should take account of inflation. Inflation is a general increase in prices leading to a general decline in the real value of money. In times of inflation, the project appraiser should take into account both the real return for the initial cash outflow (i.e. the required return of the project if there were no inflation in the economy) and an additional return to compensate for inflation. The overall required return is called the money or nominal rate of return and is linked to the real rate of return by the following equation (known as the Fisher equation):

$$(1 + i) = (1 + r) \times (1 + \pi)$$

where

i: money (nominal) rate

r: real rate

π: inflation rate

or as an approximation:

$$i \approx r + \pi$$

So, to take into consideration inflation when calculating NPV we must adjust the discount rate r (assumed here to be equal to the real rate) by adding to it the inflation rate π.

Thus, our simple model now has 3 input variables: growth rate, discount rate, and inflation rate (Exhibit 7.1).

▲	A	B	C	D	E	F	G	H	I
1	Growth rate (g)=	5.0%							
2	Discount rate (r)=	10%							
3	Inflation rate (π)=	2.1%							
4	Year		0	1	2	3	4	5	
5	Cash outflow / inflow	-10,000 €	2,400 €	2,520 €	2,646 €	2,778 €	2,917 €	=F5*(1+$B$2)	
6	NPV =		-568 €	=NPV((B2+B3);C5:G5)+B5					
7									

EXHIBIT 7.1 Simple NPV project appraisal model with 3 input variables

Please note that the base case NPV of the project is now lower than the −€39 value prior to inflation. This was expected since we increased the discount rate by the inflation rate. Generally speaking, the higher the discount rate the higher the risk of a project and the lower its net present value is. Let us now build 3 scenarios concerning the NPV of the project (assuming the cash inflows are presented in nominal terms) based on 3 different values of the input variables for each scenario:

As you have probably noticed, the values for the growth rate and the discount rate for the 3 scenarios are the same as those we used in the sensitivity analysis in Chapter 6. For example, recall that the range for the growth rate varied between 3% and 8% whereas the range for the discount rate varied between 7% and 12%. Whereas the worst case for the growth rate is definitely the lower value, the opposite holds true for the discount rate. Regarding the inflation rate, we used Forbes'[3] 2.1% (see the article by Forbes: "Economic Assumptions for your 2014 Business Plan") as the base case. We then adjusted the base case arbitrarily by 0.5% to come to the best case and worst case scenarios respectively (Exhibit 7.2). It is time now to create the first Excel scenario.

On the Excel ribbon's **Data tab** we click **What If Analysis**, and then choose **Scenario Manager** (Exhibit 7.3a). In the Scenario Manager we click the **Add** button and then we type a name for the scenario, e.g. base case (Exhibit 7.3b). By clicking on the red arrow on the right of the **Changing Cells** box an empty box appears. We then select the cells B1:B3 on the active worksheet. We click the **Comment box** and type *Base Case* just to remember what this scenario is all about. The comment is optional. Finally, by pressing the **OK button** the Scenario Values dialog box opens, with a box for each changing cell (Exhibit 7.4).

The values presented at Exhibit 7.4 are the values currently on the worksheet so we do not need to change them. Finally, by pressing the **OK** button we return to the Scenario Manager.

7.2.1 Adding 2 More Scenarios

Provided that the above scenario is our base case we need to create 2 more scenarios; the worst case and the best case. To do so we open the Scenario Manager again and click the

	Worst Case	Base Case	Best Case
Growth rate (g)	3.0%	5.0%	8.0%
Discount rate (r)	12.0%	10.0%	7.0%
Inflation rate (π)	2.6%	2.1%	1.6%

EXHIBIT 7.2 Worst, base, and best case scenarios input variables

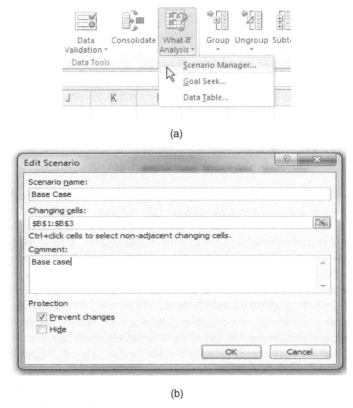

(a)

(b)

EXHIBIT 7.3   Adding a scenario to Excel's Scenario Manager

Add button. The **Scenario name** is now "worst case" but the **Changing cells** remain the same: B1:B3. Then the **Scenario Values** dialog box opens, with a box for each changing cell. Now we need to change the B1 cell box manually to 3% (growth rate under the worst case scenario), the B2 cell box to 12% (discount rate under the worst case scenario), and the B3 cell box to 2.6% (inflation rate under the worst case scenario). Then by pressing the **OK button** we return to the Scenario Manager. Similarly we add another scenario, the best case

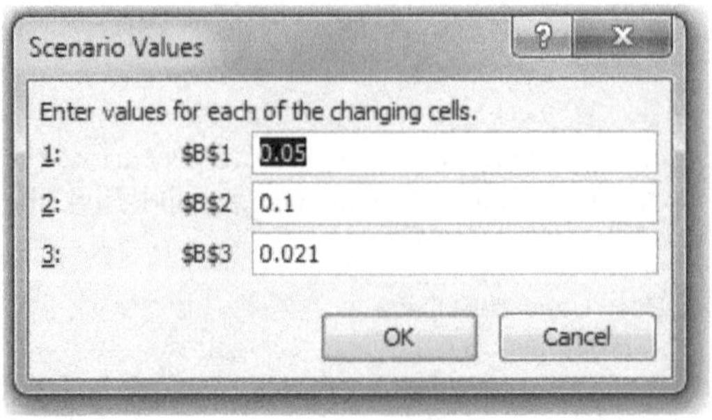

EXHIBIT 7.4   Setting the values to each input variable of the scenario

one, where in the **Scenario Values** dialog box we enter the values of 8% to the B1 cell box (growth rate under the best case scenario), 7% to the B2 cell box (discount rate under the best case scenario), and 1.6% to the B3 cell box (inflation rate under the best case scenario) and then press **OK**. Now the Scenario Manager should look like the one in Exhibit 7.5. We see at the bottom of the Scenario Manager the **Show button**. By selecting a scenario and by clicking the **Show button** we see the output of our model based on the input variables of that scenario. Although by choosing different scenarios and pressing the **Show button** we see the various model outcomes, if we have several scenarios we can quickly forget the results for each one. More importantly, we have no real way of comparing the results of the various scenarios. Each time we change a scenario, the previous one is lost. To address this issue we can use the Scenario Manager's **Summary button** to keep track of all the available scenarios in a consolidated scenario report.

Therefore, in the Scenario Manager, as shown in Exhibit 7.5, if we press the **Summary button**, the **Scenario Summary** dialog box appears (Exhibit 7.6). We then select, for **Report type**, the **Scenario Summary**. Finally, in the **Result cells** box we choose cell B6 which is our simple model's output or the NPV of the project (see Exhibit 7.6). By pressing the **OK button**, a **Scenario Summary** sheet is added automatically to our workbook (Exhibit 7.7).

If we click on the "Scenario Summary" worksheet we see the 3 scenarios we have added to the Scenario Manager plus the current values of the selected changing cells of the model. Note that the current values are the same as the ones of the base case scenario. The same of course applies for the result cell. This happened because when we added the base case scenario and we chose cells B1:B3 as the changing cells we did not change their values but

EXHIBIT 7.5   Three scenarios have been added to the Scenario Manager

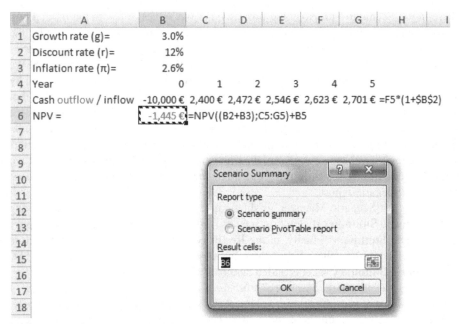

	A	B	C	D	E	F	G	H	I
1	Growth rate (g)=	3.0%							
2	Discount rate (r)=	12%							
3	Inflation rate (π)=	2.6%							
4	Year		0	1	2	3	4	5	
5	Cash outflow / inflow	-10,000 €	2,400 €	2,472 €	2,546 €	2,623 €	2,701 €	=F5*(1+$B$2)	
6	NPV =	-1,445 €	=NPV((B2+B3);C5:G5)+B5						
7									
8									
9									
10									
11									
12									
13									
14									
15									
16									
17									
18									

Scenario Summary

Report type
◉ Scenario summary
○ Scenario PivotTable report

Result cells:
36

OK   Cancel

EXHIBIT 7.6   Choosing the output cell that will be presented in the Scenario Summary report

left them as they were. Thus, column D does not add any value and we may hide it or delete it. Furthermore Row 4 presents the comments typed in each scenario and thus we may either delete it or hide it by clicking the - buttons at the left side of the worksheet.

Finally, we may rename both the changing cells and the result cell. So instead of

$B$1 we may type Growth rate,

$B$2 we may type Discount rate,

$B$3 we may type Inflation rate,

respectively. Similarly, instead of $B$6 we may type the NPV of the project. By doing so it is easier to remember at a future point in time which was the changing variable and it will definitely be easier for a third party to understand the **Scenario Summary** sheet. Now after deleting Rows 11 to 13 and adding the piece of information to the footer as described in Section 6.4 we are ready to print the report for further interpretation.

When the **Scenario Summary** dialog box appeared (Exhibit 7.6), under the **Report type**, there was another option, that of the **Scenario PivotTable** report. A PivotTable report is an interactive table that automatically extracts, organizes, and summarizes a large list of data. Nevertheless, PivotTables are beyond the scope of this book and we will not use them in the context of the scenario analysis described in this chapter.

As a final note to this section, I would like to note that the "Scenario Summary" worksheet is a static report that does not change if the scenario data changes. In this case you can create a new **Scenario Summary** when necessary, copy the renamed changing result cells from the old worksheet to the new one, and then delete the old worksheet. The new "Scenario Summary" worksheet will have the name "Scenario Summary 2".

	Current Values:	Base Case	Worst Case	Best Case
Scenario Summary				
		Base Case	Worst Case	Best Case
		Scenario	Scenario	Scenario
Changing Cells:				
$B$1	5.0%	5.0%	3.0%	8.0%
$B$2	10%	10%	12%	7%
$B$3	2.1%	2.1%	2.6%	1.6%
Result Cells:				
$B$6	-568 €	-568 €	-1.445 €	928 €

Notes: Current Values column represents values of changing cells at time Scenario Summary Report was created. Changing cells for each scenario are highlighted in gray.

EXHIBIT 7.7 "Scenario Summary" worksheet with the 3 scenarios added

7.3 ALTERNATIVE WAYS TO CREATE SCENARIOS IN EXCEL

A commonly used method to adjust your model for changing expectations, apart from Excel's Scenario Manager, is to use Excel's **OFFSET** function and a drop-down box. In this section, we will create a table with 3 possible scenarios like those presented in the previous section and associate the scenario numbers to the linked cell of a drop-down box. In this way the inputs of the model will be linked to the scenario table. Therefore, by choosing a different scenario from the base case, the input values from the table will replace the current ones and the output of the model will change accordingly.

The first step is to describe the **OFFSET** function. The **OFFSET** function returns a cell or range of cells that is a specified number of rows and columns from a cell or range of cells. Its syntax is:

= OFFSET (Reference, Rows, Cols, Height [optional], Width [optional])

where

Reference is the starting point from which the function calculates the desired offset located so many rows and columns away. The *Reference* argument can refer to a single cell or to a range of adjacent cells.

Rows is the number of rows above or below the *Reference* point used in calculating the offset.

Cols is the number of columns to the left or right of the *Reference* point used in calculating the offset.

Height and **Width** are optional and set the height, in number of rows and the width, in number of columns, of the returned offset.

For the purpose of the scenario creation in the present section, the **OFFSET** function will return only a cell, that is the height and width will both be set to 1. For example, the **OFFSET** function of Exhibit 7.8 returns the cell that is 4 rows below and 2 columns to the right of cell C2. The **OFFSET** function returns to cell A2 the value of cell E6 (i.e. 11).

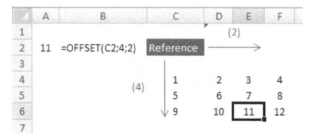

EXHIBIT 7.8 OFFSET function returns to cell A2 the value of 11 (4 rows below and 2 columns to the right of the reference cell C2)

Next we need to set up a combo box (drop-down list) into the active worksheet where the model of Exhibit 7.1 is located. As we have already described in Chapter 4 we first need to activate the **Developer tab** (**Office button/Excel Options/Popular/**check **Show Developer tab** in the ribbon). Then we click on the **Developer tab** and then select the **Insert button** in the **Controls** Section. From a number of **Form Controls** we pick the **Combo Box** (Exhibit 7.9).

By now the cursor should have been changed to a small crosshair. To create the combo box we click and drag the mouse button to an empty space on the worksheet (Exhibit 7.10a). Once we obtain the desired size we release the mouse button and the combo box just appears in our worksheet. The next step is to link it with the list of possible scenarios (the base case, the worst case, and the best case). To do this we first need to create the list. This list can be located on the same or a different worksheet. Let us create it on the same worksheet from cells A18:A20 (Figure 7.10b) to make it easier to follow. Then we right click on the combo box and select the last option, **Format Control medium**. The window of Exhibit 7.10c appears. In the **Input Range** box we simply input the cell range defined earlier (A18:A20) that contains the values that we wish to see in the combo box. Subsequently we select the **Cell link**, i.e. the cell that is linked to the combo box. This cell will display the combo box selection. We type C2. Finally we tick the **3-D shading** box to add some aesthetics to our combo box and click **OK**.

As we see in Exhibit 7.10d when we click on the down arrow of the combo box, we see the list of scenarios shown in range A18:A20. When we select an item in the list, Excel returns

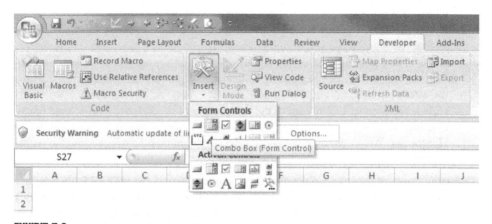

EXHIBIT 7.9 Inserting a combo box in the model worksheet

EXHIBIT 7.10 Setting up a combo box (drop-down list) in our worksheet

the number to the linked cell C2, which corresponds to the selected item. For example when we select the worst case scenario, Excel returns 1 in cell C2, when we select the base case Excel returns 2, and when we select the best case Excel returns 3 in cell C2 respectively.

Having finished with the set-up of the combo box (drop-down list), it is time to link its output to the input variables of the model. Let us first create a table with the 3 different scenario values as shown in Exhibit 7.11a. Then let us use Excel's **OFFSET** function, as described above, to link the table values with the input variables of the model. Exhibit 7.11b shows the syntax of the **OFFSET** function for each one of the input variables of the model. The growth rate input variable will take the value of the cell located 1 row below and C2 columns to the right of the reference cell which is K1 or =OFFSET($K$1;1;$C$2) (Exhibit 7.11b). If the worst case scenario is chosen in the combo box then C2 takes the value of 1 and the growth rate input variable will take the value of the one located 1 row below and 1 column to the right of cell K1 or 3%. If we had chosen the base case scenario then the output cell of the combo box would have taken the value of 2 and the growth rate input variable would be equal to the value of the cell located 1 row below and 2 columns to the right of cell K1 or 5%. Similarly, if we had chosen the best case scenario then the output cell of the combo box would have taken the value of 3 and the growth rate input variable would be equal to the value of the cell located 1 row below and 3 columns to the right of cell K1 or 8%. The same applies for the discount rate and the inflation rate. For example, by choosing the best case scenario the linked cell takes the value 3. Then the discount rate input variable will take the value of the cell located 2 rows below and 3 columns to the right of the reference cell K1 or 7%. Subsequently the inflation rate will take the value of the cell located 3 rows below and 3 columns to the right of the reference cell K1 or 1.6% (Exhibit 7.11c). We see that cell B6, which is the output cell of the model, takes the value of €928. This value is obviously the same as the one presented in the "Scenario Summary" worksheet of Exhibit 7.7 under the best case scenario.

Once you build the scenario analysis capabilities into the model in the way we have presented in this section, you may find it more functional to present various scenarios through a drop-down list. The methodology presented above can be applied to complex models with many alternative scenarios. What you have to do is to build:

(a) a list with the names of all possible scenarios somewhere remotely from your model's area, and

(b) the table with the input variable values of all possible scenarios.

The rest are handled by the **OFFSET** function in the way we have demonstrated above. Nevertheless, the **OFFSET** function has drawbacks and is often used in an unsatisfactory manner. Some modellers avoid it because it makes models less transparent by being harder to review, is difficult to explain, and reduces user confidence in the model since it is not easily understood.

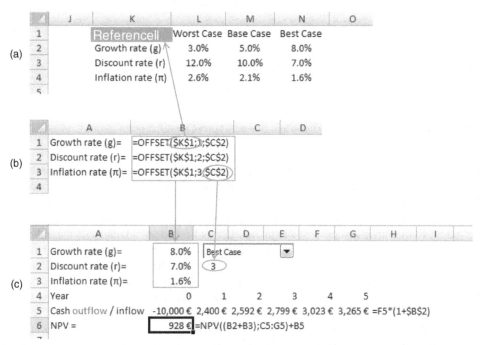

EXHIBIT 7.11 Steps a to c present the use of the OFFSET function to link the inputs of a model to possible scenarios presented in a table

For example OFFSET() can bring up silly answers and present them as valid if you do not notice that it excludes the reference cell when calculating the "rows" and "columns" components, but includes the reference cell when calculating the "height" and "width" components. This can be confusing, and requires extreme care. Of course, there are other techniques, less popular than the one with the use of the **OFFSET** functions described above, which can be used to incorporate scenario analysis into a model. A combination of Excel's **INDEX** and **MATCH** functions is one of them. We do not intend to describe every single technique in this section but if you are still interested you can visit the Wall Street Prep site and read the article "Financial Modelling Techniques: Index & Match"[4] in case you are looking for an alternative to the **OFFSET** function.

7.4 APPLYING SCENARIOS TO STEELCO'S CASE

In the previous 2 sections we have shown how to incorporate scenario analysis into a simple model by using both Excel's Scenario Manager and the **OFFSET** function in conjunction with a drop-down list (combo box). In this final section of the chapter we will apply scenario analysis to the explicit forecasts of future profits and free cash flow of SteelCo as provided in Chapter 3. The problem that arises when making forecasts is that by definition they encompass an unknown and uncertain future. In this section we will deal with this problem by making use of Excel's Scenario Manager. Before we decide which variables are most sensitive to SteelCo's profits and free cash flows we have to decide which year of the forecasting period 2014–2017 we will analyze. You may recall that in Chapter 4 we created a control panel where we could change some input variables of 2014 and monitor dynamically how the 3 covenants responded to these changes. Moreover, in Chapter 6 we created sensitivity analysis tables between the sales volume and the gross margin in order to monitor 2015 profits (losses) before taxes and free cash flows. Recall also that each input variable of SteelCo's model is located in the "Assumptions" worksheet and takes its value from a single source that either is located in another worksheet or is a hardcoded number. Therefore, it would not be wise to choose either 2014 or 2015 variables to vary in our scenario analysis since they have been used in previous chapters and consequently in this chapter we will vary 2016 model inputs as a means of anticipating risk in our model. We will follow the series of steps listed below:

1. Decide on the number of scenarios and input variables under each scenario.
2. Decide on the output variables.
3. Assign values to the input variables under each scenario.
4. Build the scenarios in Excel's Scenario Manager.
5. Interpret the results.

7.4.1 Deciding on the Number of Scenarios and Input Variables under each Scenario

The first steps are to choose (a) which variables to add in each scenario and (b) how many scenarios to analyze. The answer to the second issue is simpler. The best practice, as we mentioned in Section 7.2, is to use 3 different scenarios (worst case, base case, and best case). We will follow this practice in this section as well. The first issue, though, is a more complicated one. The obvious problem in using scenario analysis is to determine which variables have the greatest impact not in the 1 but in the 2, 3, 4, or even more output variables we want to monitor. This is an experience you gain over the years and after building one model after another. After choosing which variables to add in the 3 alternative scenarios, we will have to determine the level (the value) of each variable in each scenario. That is, we will have to come up with a comprehensive outlook with respect to a number of economic variables that represent the most likely outcome of each alternative scenario. Finally, we will have to establish a probability (a percentage) that each scenario is supposed to represent amongst all possible scenarios. For example, we could define the base case scenario as the most probable one (e.g. with a 60% probability of happening), and the other 2, the worst case and the best case, to share 20% equally.

The assumptions (input variables) for 2016 forecasts as presented in Chapter 3 range from sales information (prices and volumes) to company profitability (gross margin percentage) to working capital parameters (DSO, DIO, and DPO) to financing costs, not to mention new capital expenditures and depreciation rates (Exhibit 7.12).

Both sales prices and volumes affect SteelCo's annual turnover. Increasing sales prices will result in increased sales (turnover) and all other things being constant, in increased profitability for SteelCo through higher gross margins in absolute terms. On the other hand, increasing sales prices could lead to higher working capital needs and thus lower free cash flows. The same applies to the sales volumes. So if we were to examine these 2 variables in isolation from the others, we would face the dilemma of where to include the high prices or volumes. We should include them in the best case scenario if we were monitoring profits but in the worst case scenario if we were monitoring free cash flows. In any case increasing sales prices or volumes should be considered in conjunction with decreasing working capital parameters so as to prevent increasing cash needs. So shall we incorporate prices into our various scenarios? Anybody dealing with steel products is aware that the increased volatility in steel prices has diminished any forecasting ability. That means that even if we wanted to add prices to our scenarios it would not be easy to choose which values to consider for the best and the worst case scenarios. So let us forget prices for the time being and examine the other variables of the "Assumptions" worksheet shown in Exhibit 7.12. Sales volumes is definitely a make or break parameter that should participate in the scenario analysis since it directly affects SteelCo's sales, is less volatile than prices, and can be forecast with less uncertainty.

Next comes the gross margin percentage. This is the major variable for SteelCo's profitability and should be included. Then the variables for the cost of funds SteelCo makes use of. Both short-term and long-term borrowing costs should be included. Deposit rates are not that crucial since the amount of cash SteelCo holds is less than 5% of total debt and thus any potential income is insignificant compared to interest expenses. The final parameters under consideration should be those of the working capital (days sales outstanding, days inventory outstanding, and days payable outstanding). These variables are extremely important for calculating the level of working capital and thus SteelCo's free cash flows. The remaining variables presented in the "Assumptions" worksheet are not that crucial either to the profit before tax or to the free cash flow of SteelCo. The doubting reader could construct a Tornado chart to compare the relative importance of the above variables.

7.4.2 Deciding on the Output Variables

Having finished with the input variables, the next step requires us to decide upon which output variables we will present in the summary report. The output of any model depends on the fundamental business decision for which the model is needed. At the beginning of the chapter we said that we wanted to monitor the profits before tax and free cash flows of SteelCo. Let us look at other important indicators we need to consider when analyzing a company from a fundamental

Assumptions

Particulars	UOM	2016 F
Price		
Long Products	€/MT	650
Flat Products	€/MT	700
Volume		
Long Products	MT	111,137
Flat Products	MT	37,046
Total Sales MT	MT	**148,183**
Profitability		
% Gross Margin	%	9.5%
Financing		
Deposit rate		1.0%
Financing Cost - LT	%	-5.7%
Financing Cost - ST	%	-6.7%
Working Capital		
Stock Days - DIO	Days	80
Customer Days - DSO	Days	75
Supplier Days - DPO	Days	55
Effective Tax Rate	%	33.0%
Depreciation		
Depreciation rate		3.6%
Cost of sales	€' 000	1,039
Distribution/Selling	€' 000	1,220
Total	€' 000	**2,259**
% Cost of sales	%	46.0%
% in SG&A	%	54.0%
Investment	€' 000	300
Consume Price Inde	%	2.0%

EXHIBIT 7.12   Potential input variables to scenario analysis

perspective. We should enrich the output variables with SteelCo's annual turnover, EBITDA, working capital, and net debt. Annual turnover is important as it directly affects the bottom line of SteelCo and gives management an estimate of how much of the market the company controls and how much is controlled by rivals. EBITDA on the other hand is the income statement figure commonly used to measure a company's value and how well it performs against its rivals. EBITDA measures the operating excellence of the company before taking into account expenses such as depreciation and interest, which dilute profit figures. Furthermore, working capital is a measurement of a company's operating liquidity and gives some insight regarding its financial soundness. The latter is determined by net debt. Generally speaking, debt gives a glimpse of how healthy a company is in terms of its ability to seize opportunities for growth. Finally, profits are the ultimate measure of success of any business and free cash flow is the best measure of shareholders' value creation. Positive cash flows may finance new projects, new product lines, and thus growth without the need to go to banks to borrow money or sell additional stock to raise capital.

7.4.3 Assigning Values to the Input Variables under Each Scenario

So far we have dealt with with the choice of input and output variables. The next step requires us to decide what values to use, for chosen variables, under the 3 scenarios. We will need to fill in a table like the one in Exhibit 7.13:

Input Variables	Worst case	Base Case	Best case
Volume			
Total Sales MT		148,183	
Profitability			
% Gross Margin		9.5%	
Financing			
Financing Cost - LT		5.7%	
Financing Cost - ST		6.7%	
Working Capital			
Stock Days - DIO		80	
Customer Days - DSO		75	
Supplier Days - DPO		55	

EXHIBIT 7.13 Worst and best case input variables that need to be assigned values

Note that the values of the input variables under the base case scenario have already been filled in. These are the values already presented in Chapter 3. The question posed is what values to choose for the worst and the best case scenarios respectively. Total sales volume is the first variable. The sales volume of the base case scenario already results in losses instead of profits. So the worst case value should present even lower sales volume. If we examine SteelCo's 4-year projection plan we will see that 2017 is even worse, compared to 2016, in terms of sales volume. Actually, it is the worst year in terms of sales volume since, as we forecast in Chapter 5, 2018 will present sales growth. So we may assume that the decline cycle could be accelerated by 1 year. That is, 2017 sales volume, under the worst circumstances, could take place in 2016. The sales volume under the best case scenario must be realistic and may be drawn from the past. Under an optimistic scenario, the economy will not deteriorate any further and SteelCo will sell the amount it did in 2013 (the last historic year with actual data). So under the best case we may assume that sales volume will remain at 2013 levels, that is, 200,000 MTs.

Furthermore, the gross margin has been kept constant across the forecast period at 9.5%. We can see that SteelCo has achieved higher profitability in year 2012 – 9.7% – as well as lower profitability – 8.2% – in year 2011 (see Chapter 3). We could then round the 8.2% gross margin of 2011 to 8% and use it as the worst case scenario and similarly round the 9.7% gross margin of 2012 to 10% and use it as the best case.

Regarding the cost of funding it is assumed that it will remain constant across the forecast period at 5.7% for long-term funds and 6.7% for short-term funds. This cost of funding was the last actual one for 2013. Nevertheless, we can see that back in 2011 the cost of long-term funds was 2.5%. Suddenly, in 2013, this cost rose sharply. Recall that in 2013 SteelCo breached one debt covenant which led to the renegotiation of the terms of debt. The debt, as was likely, was renegotiated on worse terms as a quid pro quo for not demanding immediate repayment. Please note that the cost of short-term debt was much higher than the long-term debt cost before the breach of the covenant. After the onset of the economic crisis the cost of funding increased abruptly as banks experienced unprecedented shocks to their funding models, in terms of both market access and cost. SteelCo's short-term debt cost started to increase from the last quarter of 2008 whereas that of long-term debt remained stable for some time. Remember that SteelCo negotiated the long-term debt in June 2008, 3 months before the onset of the crisis – the day Lehman Brothers collapsed. The spread was 2.5% and the lenders could not change it unless there was an event of default such as the breach of a covenant. We do not think that SteelCo's situation is irreversible but even if it is in a position to meet the covenants in 2016 the cost of funds will not return to 2.5%. So we would suggest that under the best case scenario, where the financials of the company improve and return to profitability, a fairly good cost of funds would be around 4.75%. But how did we come up with that figure? Aswath Damodaran (we are familiar with him as we have used his tools in the valuation in Chapter 5) uses the interest coverage ratio of a firm to estimate a synthetic rating and, through it, its cost of debt.[5] A synthetic rating is a rating assigned to a firm not by a ratings agency like S&P but based upon its financial ratios. For example for a high market capitalization firm with an interest coverage ratio between 1.75 and 2.00 the synthetic rating would be B+ and the cost of debt 4.75%. Back in 2011 SteelCo presented an interest coverage ratio of 2. So, we assume that under the best case scenario the cost, for SteelCo, of both the long- and short-term debt will be 4.75%. Using the same methodology we see[5] that a company with an interest coverage ratio between 0.80 and 1.25 has a synthetic rating of CCC and a cost of debt around 10.00%. This is the one we will use as the cost of debt for the worst case scenario for both long- and short-term debt.

The last variables we have to decide upon under the various scenarios are the working capital variables. Let us start from the Days Sales Outstanding (DSOs) or the number of days a company takes to collect the money from its customers after a sale has been made. If we look at the historic financial statements of SteelCo we see that DSOs have a declining trend ranging from 115 in 2011 to 110 in 2013 and forecast at 75 in 2016. Reducing DSOs to 75 days may already be seen as an optimistic scenario. Nevertheless, since the trend in the industry is declining we may accept 75 day as the base case and 115 as the worst case scenario values. That is, SteelCo instead of improving it could deteriorate its collection period to what it used to be back in 2011, although that would be catastrophic. But this is the essence of scenario analysis: to hope for the best but prepare for the worst. For the best case scenario we could consider a further improvement in DSOs – something like 10 days. It would be too much to assume that in 3 years' time (from 2013 to 2016) DSOs could improve by more than 40% (110 in 2013 vs 65 under the best case scenario in 2016).

Although DSOs followed an improving trend between 2011 and 2013, Days Inventory Outstanding (DIOs) moved in the opposite direction. This is sometimes the result of not anticipating and properly planning for a slowdown in product demand due to an economic downturn. Nevertheless, SteelCo's management forecast in Chapter 3 an improvement of 15 days or 16% in 2016 (from 95 days in 2013 to 80 days in 2016) which forms the base case scenario. As you may have guessed, this is another optimistic target and thus we would suggest that the best case scenario should pose a further slight improvement in DIOs, let us say of 5 days (i.e. to 75 days). On the other hand, we would follow a different approach to establish the worst case value of DIOs. If we plot the historic DIOs we will see that they almost fit a perfect straight line. We can therefore use linear regression and extrapolation, as we did in Chapter 3, to make a prediction outside the range of x values. If we consider as x values the years 2011 to 2013 and we extrapolate DIOs for a year later this would give 100 days. We may consider this value as the worst case one since such a trend will harm SteelCo's liquidity.

Days Payable Outstanding (DPOs) follow the same trend as DIOs. They deteriorated as we moved from 2011 to 2013, declining from 41 to 30. However, the management of the company forecast an improvement of 25 days for 2016 compared to DPOs of 2013 which were 30 or 83.3%. This is already an ambitious target. Since the scenarios we will present must be pragmatic, that is they must have at least some chance of being realized, we may assume that the best case scenario could not present an improvement of more than 100% or DPOs of 60 days, that is 5 days more than the base case which is already ambitious. We could set the worst case scenario values to 25 days. This number is the extrapolated one should we use linear regression to forecast the next number of the following sequence which represents the DPOs for the 3 historic years 2011 to 2013, the same way we did with DIOs:

$$41, 38, 30, ??$$

The table with the various variable values under each scenario should look like the one in Exhibit 7.14:

Input Variables	Worst case	Base Case	Best case
Volume			
Total Sales MT	139,354	148,183	200,000
Profitability			
% Gross Margin	8%	9.5%	10%
Financing			
Financing Cost - LT	10.0%	5.7%	4.75%
Financing Cost - ST	10.0%	6.7%	4.75%
Working Capital			
Stock Days - DIO	100	80	75
Customer Days - DSO	115	75	65
Supplier Days - DPO	25	55	60

EXHIBIT 7.14   The input variables values assigned under each scenario

Before we move on and create the 3 scenarios with Excel's Scenario Manager, let us pay particular attention to 2 issues. The first one is the working capital parameters. Cash flow wise, the lower the working capital needs of a company, the better. This means that the lower the DSOs and DIOs and the higher the DPOs the better. Taking into consideration this perspective, we allocated the highest DSOs and DIOs to the worst case scenario together with the lowest DPOs. There is much debate as to whether a declining working capital is a good sign or not. As Investopedia[6] puts it, declining working capital over a longer time period can be a red flag that warrants further analysis. On the other hand, working capital gives an idea of the company's underlying operational efficiency. If a company is not operating efficiently, it will show up as an increase in working capital. As far as SteelCo's case is concerned, the company is in the midst of an economic downturn, so we consider liquidity to be its first priority and thus reducing working capital needs should rank at the top of management's agenda.

The second issue that should be stressed is that we have used as the base case scenario values the forecast numbers for 2016 as they were presented in Chapter 3. Let us assume that we did not have any forecast for 2016 and that we still wanted to analyze these scenarios. In this case, we could have used industry data to establish the values for the 3 scenarios. Specifically we could use the median value as our base case, the average value of the top performers (defined as the first quartile or 25th percentile of the data set) as the best case, and the average value of the laggards (last 25% of the data set) as the worst case. REL's consultancy survey, mentioned in Chapter 4, "2013 Working Capital Survey: Lessons from Top Performers" provides benchmarks for working capital parameters while it shows the best and worst performers in more than 40 industries. We could use similar surveys to set the base, best, and worst case values of the other input variables under consideration.

7.4.4 Building the Scenarios in Excel's Scenario Manager

Let us proceed now with step 4 and add the 3 scenarios to Excel's Scenario Manager. We have shown how to do this in Section 7.2. In this section we should clarify some further issues. For example, in Section 7.2 in the **Changing cells** box of the Scenario Manager window we chose to change 3 consecutive cells. What about changing cells that are located in remote locations in a worksheet? Exhibit 7.15 presents the cells we decided to change at the beginning of this

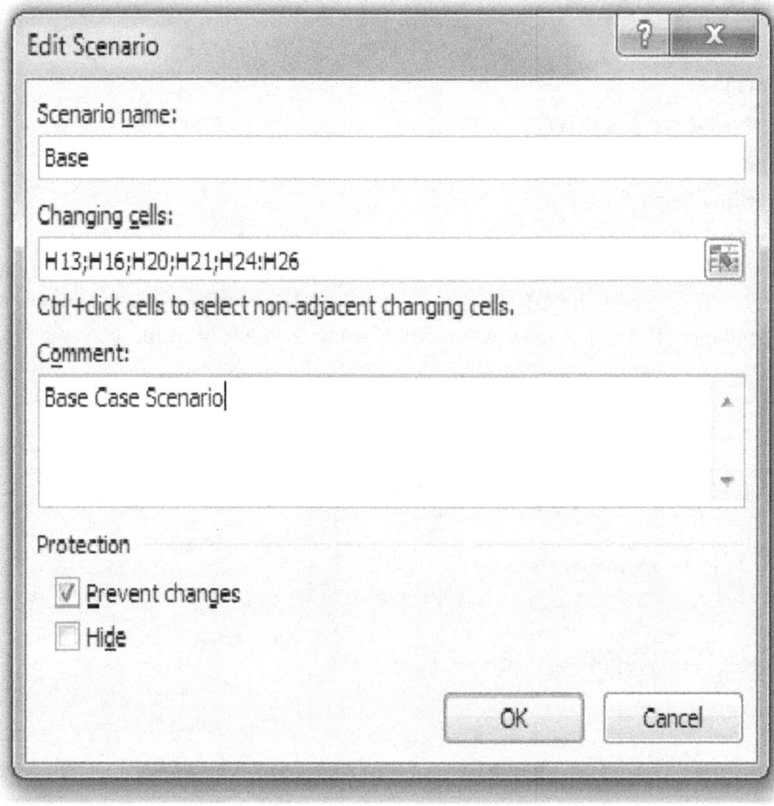

EXHIBIT 7.15 Changing cells that are remotely located in the same worksheet

section. Some of them, e.g. Volume, Profitability, and Financing, are remotely located and are separated by semicolons (H13;H16;H20;H21) whereas the working capital parameters are sequentially located and are listed together (H24:H26). After we add the other 2 scenarios, the worst case and the best case, the way we did with the base case, we need to run the **Scenario Summary** report and present all the resulting scenarios together. Remember that the **Result cells** we will monitor are SteelCo's profits before tax, free cash flows, annual turnover, EBITDA, working capital, and net debt. All of these cells are located in the "Workings" worksheet.

So in the **Result cells** box of the **Scenario Summary** window we enter the cells from the "Workings" worksheet as shown in Exhibit 7.16. When we press the **OK button** we get an error message saying "Reference must be on the active sheet". Remember that we have created the scenarios while being on the "Assumptions" worksheet. One might think it would therefore be better to create the scenarios on the "Workings" worksheet where our output cells are. However, in that case we would still get the above message because the **Changing cells** would be on another worksheet (the "Assumptions" one).

There is a simple workaround to overcome this problem. We will copy some of the most important indicative figures, such as the ones described above at the bottom of the "Assumptions" worksheet (by linking the relevant cells to the "Workings" worksheet). Now the "Assumptions" worksheet will look like the one in Exhibit 7.17.

Thus the **Result cells** of the **Scenario Summary** will be the following cells of Exhibit 7.17 referring to fiscal year 2016:

H45: Turnover,

H47: EBITDA,

H49: Profits before Tax (PBT),

H50: Free Cash Flow,

H52: Working Capital, and

H53: Net Debt.

A "Scenario Summary" worksheet is added automatically to our workbook, as we said in Section 7.2, if we press the **OK button** of the **Scenario Summary** window under Excel's Scenario Manager (Exhibit 7.18a). After doing some formatting in the way we discussed in

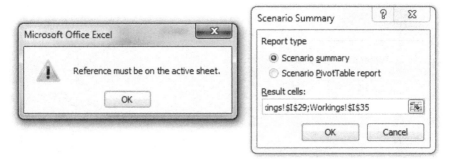

EXHIBIT 7.16   Changing cells and Result cells must be on the same active worksheet. Otherwise an error message appears

Section 7.3, the "Scenario Summary" worksheet begins to take the form of Exhibit 7.18b. First we delete the current values (column D) since these are the same as in the base case scenario and then we follow the cell numbers shown in column C and we link the titles that correspond to these cells to column B. In this way it is easier to follow the variations of the financial figures of interest and you do not have to remember what each cell number corresponds to. After the replacement of the cell references (column C) to titles (column B) we may clear column C (Exhibit 7.18b). The **Scenario Summary** is now ready to be presented to SteelCo's management.

	A	B	C	D	E	F	G	H	I
1				**Assumptions**					
2									
3									
4	Particulars	UOM	2011 A	2012 A	2013 A	2014 F	2015 F	2016 F	2017 F
5									
6	Price								
7	Long Products	€/MT	700	670	650	650	650	650	650
8	Flat Products	€/MT	650	680	700	700	700	700	700
9									
10	Volume								
11	Long Products	MT	200,000	170,000	150,000	133,092	120,447	111,137	104,515
12	Flat Products	MT	70,000	60,000	50,000	44,364	40,149	37,046	34,838
13	**Total Sales MT**	MT	**270,000**	**230,000**	**200,000**	**177,456**	**160,596**	**148,183**	**139,354**
14									
15	Profitability								
16	% Gross Margin	%	8.2%	9.7%	9.5%	9.5%	9.5%	9.5%	9.5%
17									
18	Financing								
19	Deposit rate	%	5.0%	3.0%	1.0%	1.0%	1.0%	1.0%	1.0%
20	Financing Cost - LT	%	-2.5%	-2.5%	-5.7%	-5.7%	-5.7%	-5.7%	-5.7%
21	Financing Cost - ST	%	-5.3%	-5.6%	-6.7%	-6.7%	-6.7%	-6.7%	-6.7%
22									
23	Working Capital								
24	Stock Days - DIO	Days	86	91	95	85	80	80	80
25	Customer Days - DSO	Days	115	113	110	85	80	75	75
26	Supplier Days - DPO	Days	41	38	30	50	50	55	55
27									
28	Effective Tax Rate	%	33.0%	33.0%	33.0%	33.0%	33.0%	33.0%	33.0%
29									
30	Depreciation								
31	Depreciation rate	%	3.7%	3.4%	3.6%	3.6%	3.6%	3.6%	3.6%
32	Cost of sales	€' 000	995	945	1,028	1,029	1,034	1,039	1,044
33	Distribution/Selling	€' 000	1,200	1,122	1,207	1,208	1,214	1,220	1,225
34	**Total**	€' 000	**2,195**	**2,067**	**2,235**	**2,237**	**2,248**	**2,259**	**2,269**
35									
36	% Cost of sales	%	45.3%	45.7%	46.0%	46.0%	46.0%	46.0%	46.0%
37	% in SG&A	%	54.7%	54.3%	54.0%	54.0%	54.0%	54.0%	54.0%
38									
39	Investment	€' 000		2,590	400	300	300	300	300
40									
41	Consumer Price Index	%	2.0%	1.8%	1.7%	2.0%	2.0%	2.0%	2.0%
42									
43									
44	Indicative Figures	UOM	2011 A	2012 A	2013 A	2014 F	2015 F	2016 F	2017 F
45	Turnover	€' 000	185,500	154,684	132,500	117,564	106,395	98,171	92,322
46	Gross Profit Margin	%	8.2%	9.7%	9.5%	9.5%	9.5%	9.5%	9.5%
47	EBITDA	€' 000	9,147	8,997	6,282	4,794	3,693	2,869	2,262
48	Finance cost	€' 000	-4,755	-4,470	-6,357	-4,443	-4,040	-3,778	-3,795
49	PBT	€' 000	2,197	2,459	-2,310	-1,885	-2,595	-3,167	-3,802
50	Free Cash Flow	€' 000	14,000	15,354	8,192	26,268	6,512	4,397	-28
51	Equity	€' 000	32,732	34,380	32,070	30,184	27,590	24,423	20,620
52	Working Capital	€' 000	90,013	77,023	68,355	42,139	34,980	29,375	27,570
53	Net Debt	€' 000	119,971	105,855	97,663	71,395	64,883	60,486	60,514

EXHIBIT 7.17 "Assumptions" worksheet after the copying of some important indicative figures from the "Workings" worksheet so that both Changing and Results cells are on the same worksheet

(a)

	Current Values:	Base	Good	Bad
Scenario Summary				
Changing Cells:				
$H$13	148,183	148,183	200,000	139,354
$H$16	9.5%	9.5%	10.0%	8.0%
$H$20	-5.7%	-5.7%	-4.8%	-10.0%
$H$21	-6.7%	-6.7%	-4.8%	-10.0%
$H$24	80	80	75	100
$H$25	75	75	65	115
$H$26	55	55	60	25
Result Cells:				
$H$45	98,171	98,171	132,500	92,322
$H$47	2,869	2,869	6,509	977
$H$49	-3,167	-3,167	1,320	-10,594
$H$50	4,397	4,397	5,960	-25,096
$H$52	29,375	29,375	32,299	51,441
$H$53	60,486	60,486	58,923	89,980

Notes: Current Values column represents values of changing cells at time Scenario Summary Report was created. Changing cells for each scenario are highlighted in gray.

(b)

Scenario Summary	Base	Good	Bad
Changing Cells:			
Volume	148,183	200,000	139,354
% Gross Margin	9.5%	10.0%	8.0%
Financing Cost - LT	-5.7%	-4.8%	-10.0%
Financing Cost - ST	-6.7%	-4.8%	-10.0%
Stock Days - DIO	80	75	100
Customer Days - DSO	75	65	115
Supplier Days - DPO	55	60	25
Result Cells:			
Turnover	98,171	132,500	92,322
EBITDA	2,869	6,509	977
PBT	-3,167	1,320	-10,594
Free Cash Flow	4,397	5,960	-25,096
Working Capital	29,375	32,299	51,441
Net Debt	60,486	58,923	89,980

EXHIBIT 7.18 Scenario Summary (a) as it appeared automatically in our workbook and (b) after being formatted for presentation purposes

7.4.5 Interpreting the Results

The final step is to analyze and interpret the results of the 3 scenarios. At first glance we may comment that only the "good" one is PBT positive. Moreover, although the good one presents an EBITDA over 100% higher than that of the base case, the net debt decreases by only 2.58% (from €60,486k to €58,923k) since the higher EBITDA covers the higher working capital needs due to the higher turnover. On the other hand, the worst case (bad) scenario is really bad. Free cash flow decreases by more than €30 million and this decrease is presented as an increase in net debt. The real question posed here is whether SteelCo in such a worst case scenario would be capable of drawing this amount of money from banking institutions given both the economic conditions of the market and those of the company. In the best case it will be difficult to do so and in the worst case simply impossible. You can see that under this scenario the determining factor in the net debt increase is the almost €20 million working capital increase due to the deterioration of DSOs, DIOs, and DPOs. Working capital needs and net debt are strongly intertwined.

One could argue that the above analysis is not very informative. After all, it should come as no surprise to know that under the best case scenario the net debt will be lower than that under the worst case scenario. With a range that large (almost €31 million between the 2 scenarios), it will be difficult for SteelCo's management to make any judgement, unless we present to SteelCo's management an expected scenario by assigning probabilities to each of the base, worst, and best scenarios. What probabilities we will assign under each scenario depends on our knowledge of the sector and the expertise of various agencies providing macroeconomic forecasts such as interest rates. For example if we set a probability of 60% for the base case scenario to be realized and another 20% each for the best case and the worst case then the expected scenario would look like the one presented in Exhibit 7.19.

For example the expected net debt will be:

$$\text{Net Debt for } 2016 = 60\%* \ €60,486k + 20\% * €58,923k + 20\%* €89,980k = €66,072k$$

One might question then why we bothered to present 3 different scenarios and did not adjust the current input cells of the 2016 forecast so as to arrive at the expected value scenario output. What you have to understand here is that scenario analysis is a qualitative exercise whose primary benefit is to broaden the thinking of decision-makers. If nothing else, the process of thinking through scenarios is a useful exercise in examining alternative strategies under different macroeconomic environments. For example, what can be done to minimize the effect of downside risk and what to maximize the effect of a potential upside if management's view of the economic downturn turns out to be false? Aswath Damodaran's "Probabilistic Approaches: Scenario Analysis, Decision Trees and Simulations" is a good source for further

	B	C	D	E	F	G
2	Probabilities		60%	20%	20%	100%
3	Scenario Summary		Base	Good	Bad	Expected Value
5	Changing Cells:					
6	Volume		148,183	200,000	139,354	
7	% Gross Margin		9.5%	10.0%	8.0%	
8	Financing Cost - LT		-5.7%	-4.8%	-10.0%	
9	Financing Cost - ST		-6.7%	-4.8%	-10.0%	
10	Stock Days - DIO		80	75	100	
11	Customer Days - DSO		75	65	115	
12	Supplier Days - DPO		55	60	25	
13	Result Cells:					
14	Turnover		98,171	132,500	92,322	103,867
15	EBITDA		2,869	6,509	977	3,219
16	PBT		-3,167	1,320	-10,594	-3,755
17	Free Cash Flow		4,397	5,960	-25,096	-1,189
18	Working Capital		29,375	32,299	51,441	34,373
19	Net Debt		60,486	58,923	89,980	66,072

EXHIBIT 7.19 Presenting an expected scenario by assigning probabilities to each of the base, worst, and best scenarios

reading on the uses and limitations of scenario analysis[7] (you can download it directly from his website).

As a final note to this chapter we should stress some limitations of Excel's Scenario Manager. First, we cannot add more than 32 variables in any scenario. This is the maximum number of variables we can analyze. Secondly, scenarios are static. This means that each time we change something in the model we must re-run the Scenario Manager. Thirdly, both the changing cells and the resulting cells must be on the same worksheet as we saw earlier. Fourthly, the titles of the input variables and output variables are set as the cell names and must be manually adjusted to present something meaningful. Finally, both the input and the output variable values must be entered into a data form rather than picked up directly from a spreadsheet.

BIBLIOGRAPHY AND REFERENCES

1.   2014 AFP Risk Survey, Report of Survey Results, Association for Financial Professionals and Oliver Wyman, January 2014, http://www.oliverwyman.com/content/dam/oliver-wyman/global/en/files/insights/risk-management/2014/Jan/2014AFPRiskSurvey-FINAL.pdf.
2.   https://www.boundless.com/finance/the-role-of-risk-in-capital-budgeting/scenario-and-simulation-assessments/scenario-analysis/.
3.   http://www.forbes.com/sites/billconerly/2013/09/02/economic-assumptions-for-your-2014-business-plan/.
4.   Wall Street Prep website; "Financial Modelling Techniques: Index & Match"; http://www.wall-streetprep.com/blog/financial-modeling-techniques-index-match/.
5.   Aswath Damodaran's website. "Estimating a Synthetic Rating and Cost of Debt", http://pages.stern.nyu.edu/~adamodar/New_Home_Page/valquestions/syntrating.htm.
6.   Investopedia website, http://www.investopedia.com/terms/w/workingcapital.asp.
7.   Aswath Damodaran's website, "Probabilistic Approaches: Scenario Analysis, Decision Trees and Simulations", http://people.stern.nyu.edu/adamodar/pdfiles/papers/probabilistic.pdf.

8

Using Monte Carlo Simulation

Chapter 8 illustrates the use of Monte Carlo simulation in obtaining a range of values for certain financial indicators of a company of interest (e.g. profitability and borrowing).

A company's future profitability, borrowing, and many other quantities are all highly uncertain quantities. This chapter describes the theory and gives practical examples of how to run a simulation. For example, in a simulation analysis, the computer begins by picking at random a value for each of the uncertain variables based on its specified probability distribution. Monte Carlo variables assume that the processes being studied are independent of each other and that each value is a random draw from a distribution. The end result of Monte Carlo simulation is the continuous probability distribution with its own expected value and standard deviation.

Simulation relates to both sensitivity analysis (Chapter 6) and scenario analysis (Chapter 7). It ties together sensitivities and input variable probability distributions in order to give answers to questions such as: What strains on the firm's liquidity may be caused by changes in certain variables such as sales volume and credit granted to customers?

8.1 INTRODUCTION

In the previous 2 chapters we examined sensitivity analysis and scenario planning as techniques to assess the risk associated with financial modelling. Although these techniques are good for assessing the effect of discrete risk they can provide little help when it comes to continuous risk. Simulations, on the other hand, provide a way of examining the consequences of continuous risk. To the extent that most risks we face in the real world can generate hundreds of possible outcomes, a simulation can give us a fuller picture of risk.[1] The kind of simulation that we examine in this chapter is the so-called Monte Carlo simulation. Monte Carlo simulation was first developed back in the 1950s, at Los Alamos, by a group of researchers led by a Greek American physicist called Nicolas Metropolis. Monte Carlo simulation is a problem-solving method that makes use of random numbers and probability distributions. The method is named after the city in Monaco, famous for its casinos, because the uncle of one of Metropolis's colleagues loved to gamble there.[2] After all, casino games are based on chance and involve repetitive events with known probabilities. When rolling a die for example, you know that a number between 1 and 6 will come up with a probability of 1 in 6, but you don't know which one. Similarly, when there is a range of possible financial inputs to a model, its output is uncertain as we don't know exactly which one will materialize. Monte Carlo simulation is a technique that represents uncertainties by specifying model inputs as probability distributions and produces, instead of a single number, a probability distribution of the model's output. Although it will not eliminate uncertainties in business decisions, it can help to understand them in normal business circumstances. In general, *uncertainty* means that a number of different values can exist for a quantity and *risk* means the possibility of loss or gain as a result of these uncertainties.[3] There are various sources of uncertainty that affect the risk associated with a business decision. For example whether or not an event will occur (e.g. will a bank grant a new credit line to a company facing liquidity issues?). Moreover even if the event will occur we must estimate when it will occur (i.e. the date the new line will be granted), its magnitude (i.e. the level of the credit line), and its cost (i.e. the interest rate or spread of the credit line). When building a financial model to facilitate a business decision, uncertainty from the above sources is common and should be considered for a complete assessment.

8.2 BUILDING UNCERTAINTY DIRECTLY INTO THE MODELLING PROCESS

When risk and uncertainty are dominant factors in a business situation it is often better to build them directly into the modelling process. Let us describe the approach we use through an example. Consider the simple model we first built in Chapter 6 to help us decide whether or not to proceed with a new project given the first year's cash flows, the growth rate for every year thereafter, and the discount rate of the project. This model is a so-called deterministic one since its outcome is precisely determined through a known relationship of its inputs without any room for random variation. In deterministic models, a given input always produces the same output. That is, for 5% growth rate, all other things being equal, the NPV of the project will always be negative at –€39 and thus it is "No Go". Consider now that the project manager, after some research on similar projects, has concluded that the growth rate follows a certain probability distribution and he wants to know what the chances are that the project's NPV is over €50. Although we will cover probability distributions later on, it is sufficient to say meanwhile that the project manager has established that the probability distribution of the growth rate looks like the bell-shaped curve of Exhibit 8.1.

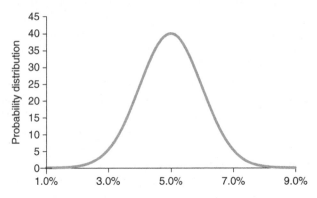

EXHIBIT 8.1   Probability distribution curve of the growth rate of the simple NPV model

This bell-shaped curve is a so-called normal distribution with mean 5% and standard deviation 1%. The horizontal axis (X-axis) represents the dependent variable or the growth rate in our case. The vertical axis (Y-axis) represents the relative likelihood that the values of the growth rate (horizontal axis) will be achieved. As you can see from the shape of the curve, the relative likelihood increases in the centre where the bell is. The likelihood tapers off from the centre in both directions. So, further out in either direction the likelihood gets smaller and smaller until it is nearly zero. You will recall that in Chapter 6, where we performed sensitivity analysis of the growth rate, its values ranged from 3% to 8%. Also in Chapter 7 the worst case scenario value of the growth rate was 3% whereas the best case one was 8%. More or less the same information is presented in the probability distribution of the growth rate, as shown in Exhibit 8.1. That is, the chances of the growth rate being either less than 3% or more than 8% are very slim.

Returning now to the simple model of Exhibit 6.1, we will apply probabilistic modelling (i.e. the Monte Carlo simulation) in order to build uncertainty directly into our model. Probabilistic modelling is any form of modelling that utilizes presumed probability distributions of certain input assumptions to calculate the implied probability distribution for chosen output metrics.[4] Without getting into the technical parts of probabilistic modelling and the Monte Carlo simulation (we will do that later on) the type of output of the model will look like the graph of Exhibit 8.2. It is a so-called frequency distribution chart. We can see that instead of a simple deterministic value –€39 – we now have a range of output values from almost –€500 to €500. But let us examine Exhibit 8.2 closely to understand its context. The overall purpose of this type of output is to present the likelihood (probability in statistical terms) that the NPV of the project will range between certain values. For example, we want to find the probability that the NPV of the project will be positive, or above a certain value, or between a range of values.

The Left Hand Axis (LHA) represents the so-called hits, that is, the number of times during the simulation that a particular NPV fell in a specific range of values or "bin". The simulation was run 500 times, and for each simulation the NPV of the project was noted. If you add up all the hits you see that they sum to 500. As you would expect, the majority of hits come in at around the value of –€39.

The Right Hand Axis (RHA) represents the so-called calculative probability (we will cover cumulative probabilities in the next section) and shows the probability that the NPV of

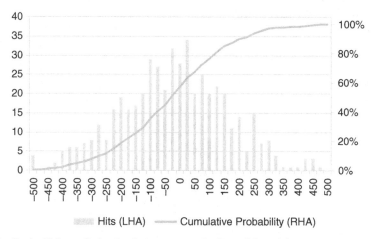

EXHIBIT 8.2 Typical Monte Carlo simulation output of a financial model

the project will be equal to or less than a particular value. For example, it is almost certain (cumulative probability of 100%) that the NPV of the project will be less than €500 but there is a 57% chance that the NPV of the project will be negative. Finally, the horizontal axis shows the distribution of the identified potential model outcomes.

This type of analysis allows a decision-maker to draw the following conclusions:

- There is 68% chance that the NPV of the project will be below €50. That leaves a 32% chance that the NPV of the project will be above €50.
- The average NPV of the project is –€32 with a 43% chance of its being positive.

8.3 PROBABILITIES, CUMULATIVE PROBABILITIES, AND FREQUENCY DISTRIBUTION CHARTS

We saw in the previous section that the application of the Monte Carlo simulation technique to any modelling process involves the use of probability distribution functions, cumulative probabilities, and frequency distribution charts or histograms. In this section we will try to cover the basics of these concepts.

First of all let examine what a probability distribution is and where it is used. A probability distribution is a statistical model that shows the possible outcomes of a particular event or course of action as well as the statistical likelihood of each event. In the context of this book we will use probability distributions as a tool for evaluating risk. The most commonly used probability distribution in the business world is the normal distribution (also known as the bell curve or a Gaussian distribution). The normal distribution is symmetrical around the centre like the one in Exhibit 8.3 (taken from Wikipedia, the free encyclopaedia[5]) and is fully described through the mean (μ) and the standard deviation (σ).

The mean represents the centre of distribution and the standard deviation is a measure of spread or variability from the centre. You can see that about 68% of values drawn from a normal distribution lie within 1 standard deviation σ away from the mean, about 95% of the values lie within 2 standard deviations (2 σ) and about 99.7% are within 3 standard deviations (3 σ). Therefore, when we assumed in the previous section that the growth rate follows a normal distribution with mean 5% and standard deviation 1%, we implicitly assumed that there was a 68% chance that it would lie between 4% and 6%, a 95% chance that it would lie between 3% and 7%, and a 99.7% chance that it would lie between 2% and 8%. In a normal distribution, we can calculate the probability that various values lie within certain ranges or intervals. This probability is the area under the curve within certain ranges or intervals. It is obvious that the

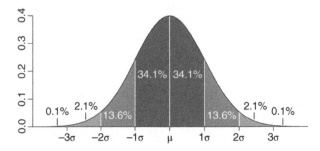

EXHIBIT 8.3   The normal distribution (source: Wikipedia)[5]

total area under the curve is 100% or 1. However, the exact probability of a particular value is zero. That is, the probability that the growth rate is exactly 5% is zero (the area under the curve for a single point is zero). The normal distribution is a so-called continuous distribution and defines the distribution of the values for a continuous random variable through the following equation, known as the Probability Density Function (PDF) $f(x)$:

$$f(x) = \frac{1}{\sqrt{2\pi\sigma^2}} e^{\frac{-(x-\mu)^2}{2\sigma^2}}$$

where both e and π are constants and e = 2.7183 and π = 3.1415 respectively. Continuous random variables span from $-\infty$ to $+\infty$, that is, $-\infty < x < +\infty$ though the shape of the normal distribution makes it very unlikely that extremely large or extremely small values will occur. A random variable is a quantity that varies depending on chance and a continuous random variable can take on an infinite number of possibilities. Assuming that the growth rate follows a normal distribution we assume that it is a continuous random variable although, as we said previously, the chances of values falling outside the range of 2%–8% are very slim.

As far as the probability density function $f(x)$ is concerned, you will be relieved to hear that we will not have to compute it manually since Excel provides the following function:

$$\text{NORMDIST}(x, \mu, \sigma, \text{cumulative})$$

If the *cumulative* argument is FALSE the above function returns the value of the density function as x *but not a probability*. That is, $f(5.5\%)$ equals 35.21:

$$f(5.5\%) = \text{NORMDIST}(5.5\%; 5\%; 1\%; \text{FALSE}) = 35.21$$

Remember that the probability of any specific value, e.g. $P(x = 5.5\%) = 0$ since x is a continuous random variable. Nevertheless if we want to calculate the probability that x (the growth rate) is lower than 5.5% or $P(x < 5.5\%)$, this probability can be represented as the area beneath the bell-shaped curve (Exhibit 8.4a) and can be calculated in Excel by using as a *cumulative* argument the TRUE value in the NORMDIST function:

$$P(x < 5.5\%) = \text{NORMDIST}(5.5\%, 5\%, 1\%, \text{TRUE}) = 0.6914 \text{ or } 69.14\%$$

This is the so-called cumulative probability and usually it is referred to as a probability to the left. Cumulative probabilities refer to the probability that a random variable is less than or equal to a specified value. The Cumulative Distribution Function (CDF) of a continuous random variable x, in general, can be expressed as the integral of its probability density function $f(x)$ as follows:

$$F(x) = \int_{-\infty}^{x} f_x(t)dt$$

Nevertheless we will not have to deal with the above function since Excel provides the **NORMDIST** function. Thus, in case we want to find the probability that the growth rate is higher than 5.5%, then we need to find a probability to the right or $P(x > 5.5\%)$ which is given by the following equation:

$$P(x > 5.5\%) = 1 - \text{NORMDIST}(5.5\%, 5\%, 1\%, \text{TRUE}) = 1 - 0.6914 \text{ or } 30.86\%.$$

As the range of possible probabilities can be no less than 0% and no more than 100% (the cumulative probability for all possible outcomes is 1), when we want to calculate probabilities above a certain value in fact we need to subtract from the total area under the curve (which is 100% or 1) the area under the curve to the left of this value:

$$P(x > a) = \text{(Area under the curve to the right of } a) = 1 - \text{(Area under the curve to the left of } a)$$

Similarly, when we want to find the probability that the growth rate is higher than 5.5% but lower than 6.5% – that is, when we want to find probabilities between certain values – what we need to do is to calculate the areas under the curve between these 2 points (i.e. 5.5% and 6.5%) by subtracting their cumulative probabilities according to the formula (Exhibit 8.4b):

$$P(a < x < b) = \text{NORMDIST}(b,\mu,\sigma,\text{TRUE}) - \text{NORMDIST}(a,\mu,\sigma,\text{TRUE})$$

or

$$P(5.5\% < x < 6.5\%) = \text{NORMDIST}(5.5\%, 5\%, 1\%, \text{TRUE}) -$$
$$\text{NORMDIST}(6.5\%, 5\%, 1\%, \text{TRUE})$$

$$= 69.14\% - 93.32\% = 24.17\%$$

Sometimes, instead of finding a probability given the variable x we may want the reverse. We may want to find the x variable given a certain probability. Excel provides the **NORMINV** function (the inverse of the NORMDIST function) so that it returns the value x such that NORMDIST $(x, \mu, \sigma, \text{TRUE}) = p$:

$$x = \text{NORMINV}(p, \mu, \sigma)$$

The inverse cumulative distribution function, or the quintile as it is called in probability and statistics, specifies for a given probability in the probability distribution of a random variable, the value at which the probability of the random variable will be less than or equal to that probability (Wikipedia[6]). The inverse cumulative distribution function, $F^{-1}(P)$, of a normal distribution is given by a complex equation but the description of that equation need not detain us here. Instead, we will use the NORMINV function to calculate a random variable from a normal distribution. To do so we will make use of another Excel function: **RAND ()**. The **RAND ()** function returns a random number between 0 and 1. That is, we may assume that **RAND ()** generates random probabilities. Therefore, we can use the **NORMINV** function to calculate a random variable from a normal distribution, using this formula:

$$=\text{NORMINV}(\text{RAND }(), \mu, \sigma)$$

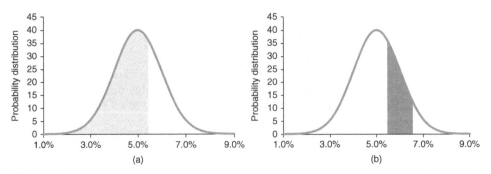

EXHIBIT 8.4   Probability that a random variable is lower than a value (a) or within a range of 2 values (b)

For example, in Section 8.2 we used the function NORMINV (RAND (), 5%, 1%) repeatedly in order to get random values for the growth rate variable. These random numbers followed a normal distribution with mean μ and standard deviation σ. We then fed these numbers into our simple model in order to get multiple instances of the NPV of the project. This is how we obtained the frequency distribution chart (histogram) of Exhibit 8.2.

A frequency distribution chart (or histogram) is a graph that shows a series of values on the horizontal axis and their frequency (how often each value occurs) on the vertical axis. The term distribution refers to the pattern of frequencies of the values on the horizontal axis. The histogram graphically shows the following:

1. centre (i.e. location) of the data
2. spread (i.e. scale) of the data.

The most common form of the histogram is obtained by splitting the range of data into equal-sized bins. Then for each bin, the number of points from the data set that fall into it are counted. The bins can either be defined arbitrarily by the user or via some systematic rule, as we will see in Section 8.4. A frequency distribution chart (histogram) together with a cumulative distribution of the output model variable is the outcome of the Monte Carlo simulation method. A histogram shows the degree of uncertainty in the output model variable, namely the range of the values obtained and how often they occur. The cumulative distribution is a variation of the histogram in which the vertical axis gives not just the counts for a single bin, but rather the counts for that bin plus all bins with smaller values of the variable of interest.

So far we have described only the normal distribution. Some other frequently used probability distributions in Monte Carlo simulation include the triangular distribution and the uniform distribution. Let us describe them in turn.

A triangular distribution is a continuous distribution with a probability density function shaped like a triangle. It is defined by 3 values: the minimum value a, the maximum value b, and the most likely value m. It is bounded by the minimum and maximum values and can be either symmetrical (the most probable value = mean = median) or asymmetrical (Exhibit 8.5a). The probability density function of a triangular distribution is zero for values below a and values above b. It is piecewise linear rising from 0 at a to $\dfrac{2}{b-a}$ at m and then drops down to 0 at b. The formula for the probability density function $f(x)$ is:[6]

$$f(x) = \begin{cases} \dfrac{2(x-a)}{(m-a)(b-a)}, & a \le x \le m \\ \dfrac{2(b-x)}{(b-m)(b-a)}, & m \le x \le b \end{cases}$$

Its probability density function, like that of the normal distribution, has the property that the area under the function is 1. The cumulative distribution function of a triangular distribution is as follows:

$$F(x) = \begin{cases} \dfrac{(x-a)^2}{(m-a)(b-a)}, & a \le x \le m \\ 1 - \dfrac{(b-x)^2}{(b-m)(b-a)}, & m \le x \le b \end{cases}$$

The inverse function of the cumulative distribution function of a triangular distribution is as follows:

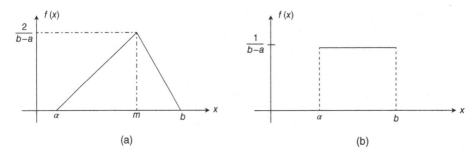

EXHIBIT 8.5 Triangular distribution (a) and uniform distribution (b)

$$F^{-1}(P) = \begin{cases} \sqrt{P(m-a)(b-a)}+a, & \left(P < \frac{m-a}{b-a}\right) \\ -\sqrt{(1-P)(b-m)(b-a)}+b, & \left(P \geq \frac{m-a}{b-a}\right) \end{cases}$$

The derivation of the above formulae does not concern us here. Nevertheless, we do need them since Excel does not provide a built-in function to calculate the inverse cumulative distribution function of the triangular distribution (as it does for the normal distribution) and thus we will have to calculate them manually (see Section 8.4).

Regarding the uniform distribution, it is a continuous distribution bounded by known minimum (α) and maximum (b) values. In contrast to the triangular distribution, the likelihood of occurrence of the values between the minimum and maximum is the same (Exhibit 8.5b). The probability density function of the uniform distribution $f(x)$ is given by the following equation:

$$f(x) = \begin{cases} \dfrac{1}{b-a}, & a \leq x \leq b \\ 0, & \text{otherwise} \end{cases}$$

As with the other probability distribution functions the area under the graph of the random variable is equal to 1. The cumulative distribution function of a uniform distribution is given by the following equation:

$$F(x) = \frac{x}{b-a}$$

The inverse function of the cumulative distribution function of a uniform distribution is given by the following equation:

$$F^{-1}(P) = a + P(b-a)$$

As in the triangular distribution, the derivation of the above formulae is beyond the scope of this book. Nevertheless, as we said previously, we need them in order to calculate the inverse cumulative distribution function since Excel does not provide a built-in function to do so.

Apart from the 3 distributions described above there are some more that could be used in Monte Carlo simulations. For a more detailed description of probability distributions used in Monte Carlo simulations see Professor Damodaran's *Probabilistic Approaches: Scenario Analysis, Decision Trees and Simulations*[1] and PricewaterhouseCoopers' *Uncertainty and Risk Analysis*.[3]

8.4 MODELLING EXAMPLE

So far we have seen that Monte Carlo simulation is a technique that takes the distributions that have been specified on the inputs of a model, and uses them to produce a probability distribution of the output of interest. In this last section of the chapter we will apply Monte Carlo simulation to SteelCo's financial model developed in Chapter 3. The series of steps we will follow is listed below:

1. First we will identify the key risk assumptions (input variables) of the model. A risk assumption is a variable which is critical to the output of the model and a slight variation in its value might have a negative or a positive impact on the output variable of interest. The most critical input variables are typically isolated using Tornado charts in the way we presented in Chapter 6.
2. Then we will identify the probability distribution that each input variable, under analysis, is most likely to follow. For each probability distribution we need to supply the required parameters. For example, in a normal distribution we have to supply its mean and its standard deviation whereas in a triangular distribution we have to supply its minimum, maximum, and the most likely value. A common question to ask is which probability distribution to choose for each variable and how to figure out its characteristic parameters. So, even if we decided that a normal distribution was appropriate for the annual revenue growth rate of the example examined previously, how did we establish that the mean was 5% and the standard deviation 1%? Such answers might be based on historic data, on opinions of management, on our own subjective feelings about the future, or it might be a combination of all of these. This will always be a difficult decision and we should try to choose realistic parameters that are in line with the particular situation.
3. Next we create sampled inputs for the identified variables and perform simulation runs based on these inputs (recalculating the model for each sampled input). On each simulation run, for each input, the Monte Carlo simulation selects a value from the relevant probability distribution at random such that, over a large number of runs, the distribution of the selected values reflects the input probability distribution. For example, in the case of the growth rate in the previous section, it was modelled as a normal distribution of mean 5% and standard deviation 1% and the distribution of its sampled inputs selected during the simulation had approximately mean 5% and standard deviation 1% respectively. Obviously, the more simulation runs, the closer the sampled input distribution comes to the selected probability distribution. Each sample input gives rise to a model output.
4. Next we represent the model outputs graphically by building a histogram (Frequency Distribution Chart).
5. Finally we interpret the results by statistically analyzing the simulation runs. The probability distribution of the output of the model, as presented in the histogram, shows the likelihood of occurrence of all modelled output values. In other words it presents graphically the uncertainty that exists in the output value. Note that it is possible to have as many outputs as necessary instead of a single output.

There are various software packages that could be used to carry out Monte Carlo simulation. The majority of them come as an Excel add-in that allows the user to specify distributions on the inputs of the model and do not require any alterations to the spreadsheet itself, so models can be shared with others who do not have that software package. Oracle's Crystal Ball is the leading spreadsheet-based software suite for predictive modelling, forecasting, simulation, and optimization but there are other add-ins that perform similar work, such as Palisade's @Risk, TreePlan's RiskSim, and Frontline's Solvers Tools for Excel. Instead of using a ready-made add-in, we will construct our own risk model and perform all the above steps by ourselves.

8.4.1 Identifying the Key Risk Variables

You may recall Exhibit 7.12 where all the major assumptions of SteelCo's model were presented. When choosing which parameters to include in the different scenarios of SteelCo (see Section 7.4) we followed a rationale as to which variables are the most critical to the various outputs of the model. In this section we will choose 3 input parameters, 1 for each probability distribution described in the previous section, and after running many simulation steps we will analyze the model's output. Imagine we are requested by the treasurer of SteelCo to advise him what the chances are that the net debt of the company in 2017 will be higher than €60,500. Bear in mind that €60,514 is the net debt for 2017 based on the assumptions presented in Chapter 3. Amongst the most critical inputs that affect net debt are definitely sales volume and Days Sales Outstanding (DSO). The higher the sales volume the higher the working capital needs and the higher the debt level of the company. Moreover, the higher the DSOs the higher the receivables and thus the higher the debt level of the company. The third input variable that is critical to the debt of a company is profitability. Generally speaking, the higher a company's profitability the lower its level of debt.

8.4.2 Choosing a Probability Distribution for Each Input Variable

Let us decide now about the probability distribution for each input variable chosen. Starting with sales volume, we choose the triangular distribution with the most likely value, that of 139,354 which is the 2017 value as forecast in Exhibit 3.7. To define a triangular distribution, apart from the most likely value, we need a minimum and a maximum one. Remember back in Chapter 5 we forecast that 2017 would be the last year of recession and SteelCo's turnover would start rising from 2018 onwards. We may take the view that the recession could end sooner and 2018 sales volume could take place in 2017. We will consider this particular sales volume as the maximum value of the triangular distribution. By using the polynomial regression methodology in Chapter 4 (Exhibit 4.20) we end up with sales revenue of €95,811 in 2018. We need to translate sales revenues to sales volumes considering sales prices for 2018 to be the same as those of 2017, that is €650/MT for the flat products and €700/MT for the long products. The following equation holds between revenues, volume, and prices:

$$\text{Sales Revenues}_{2018} = \text{€650/MT} \times \text{Sales Volume}_{\text{Flat}} + \text{€700/MT} \times \text{Sales Volume}_{\text{Long}},$$

and

$$\text{Total Sales Volume}_{2018} = \text{Sales Volume}_{\text{Flat}} + \text{Sales Volume}_{\text{Long}}$$

Dividing both equations by the total sales volume $_{2018}$ we have:

$$\frac{\text{Sales Revenues}_{2018}}{\text{Total Sales Volume}_{2018}} = \text{€}\frac{650}{\text{MT}} \times \frac{\text{Sales Volume}_{\text{Flat}}}{\text{Total Sales Volume}_{2018}}$$
$$+ \text{€}\frac{700}{\text{MT}} \times \frac{\text{Sales Volume}_{\text{Long}}}{\text{Total Sales Volume}_{2018}}$$

and

$$\frac{\text{Total Sales Volume}_{2018}}{\text{Total Sales Volume}_{2018}} = 1$$

$$= \frac{\text{Sales Volume}_{\text{Flat}}}{\text{Total Sales Volume}_{2018}} + \frac{\text{Sales Volume}_{\text{Long}}}{\text{Total Sales Volume}_{2018}}$$

In Chapter 3 we made the assumption that flat products represent 25% of total volume whereas long products represent 75%. Substituting then:

$$\frac{\text{Sales Volume}_{\text{Flat}}}{\text{Total Sales Volume}_{2018}} = 25\%$$

$$\frac{\text{Sales Volume}_{\text{Long}}}{\text{Total Sales Volume}_{2018}} = 75\%$$

and

$$\text{Sales Revenues}_{2018} = \text{\euro}95,811$$

we find that total sales volume for 2018 = 144,621 MT.

Thus, we could round the value of 144,621 MT to 145,000 MT and use it as the maximum value of the triangular distribution for the 2017 sales volume. If we consider the triangular distribution as symmetrical then the minimum value of the distribution should be around 135,000 MT.

Next we proceed with the profitability input variable of the gross profit margin percentage. We will assume that the gross profit margin percentage follows a uniform distribution. The forecast value for 2017 is 9.5% as shown in Exhibit 3.12. The uniform distribution is defined, as we have seen in the previous section, by 2 parameters a and b (Exhibit 8.5b). Its expected value is defined as:

$$\frac{a+b}{2}$$

If we assume that the expected value of the gross profit margin is 9.5% and we choose one parameter, either a or b, then the other will be derived from the above equation. For example the 2 extreme values we chose for the gross profit margin for the worst and the best case scenarios in Chapter 7 were 8% and 10% respectively. If we choose 8% as the minimum of the uniform probability distribution ($a = 8\%$) then b equals 11% since:

$$\frac{a+b}{2} = 9.5\%$$

Nevertheless, if we look at the historic gross profit margins of SteelCo, they have never exceeded 10% so 11% is far too optimistic. On the other hand, if we choose 10% as the maximum of the uniform probability distribution ($b = 10\%$) then a equals 9%. This is in the range of possible gross profit margins for SteelCo. Therefore we will use $a = 9\%$ and $b = 10\%$ to characterize the uniform probability distribution of the gross profit margins so that the expected value is 9.5%.

Finally we have to choose a probability distribution for the DSOs. As you have already guessed we will use the normal distribution and we will have to choose a mean and a standard deviation. The forecast value of DSOs for 2017 is 75 days as shown in Exhibit 3.10. Therefore we will use this value as the mean of the normal distribution. Now regarding the standard deviation, a common trick to use is to define the possible range within which DSOs could move. Remember that we mention in Section 8.3 that 99.7% of the possible values of a normal random variable X lie between 3 σ on the left and 3 σ on the right of the mean. Then if the range of values lies between DSO_{Min} and DSO_{Max} we may assume that σ equals:

$$\sigma = \frac{DSO_{Max} - DSO_{Min}}{6}$$

Similarly, it must hold that:

$$\mu = \frac{DSO_{Max} + DSO_{Min}}{2}$$

That is, if we assume that =75 and the possible DSO range lies between 60 and 90 then:

$$\mu = \frac{90 + 60}{2} = 75 \text{ and } \sigma = \frac{90 - 60}{6} = 5$$

Exhibit 8.6 presents the probability distributions selected for each input variable of sales volume, gross profit margin, and credit days (DSOs) respectively.

8.4.3 Performing the Simulation Runs

Now we have finished with step 2 it is time to proceed with step 3, which is the core of the Monte Carlo method. In this step we will make use of a random number generator. A random number is a uniformly distributed random variable that is greater than or equal to 0 and less than 1, i.e. the generated random number X that satisfies the rule $0 <= X < 1$. Random numbers can be generated by using the Excel function **RAND** (). This function produces a new random number every time the spreadsheet is recalculated (i.e. by hitting the F9 button). For each random number generated we will assume that it represents a cumulative probability that corresponds to a distribution $F(x) = P (X <= x)$. Then in order to find x we would need the inverse of the cumulative probability function, F^{-1}, so that $x = F^{-1}(P) = F^{-1}(\text{random number})$. We described in Section 8.3 the inverse cumulative distribution functions of the 3 probability distributions we analyzed. Regarding the *inverse* of the cumulative normal probability function, it can be easily calculated in Excel through the function:

NORMSINV (RAND (), mean, standard deviation).

Risk Input Variable	Sales Volume	Gross Profit Margin	Credit Days (DSOs)
Probability distribution	Triangular distribution	Uniform distribution	Normal distribution
	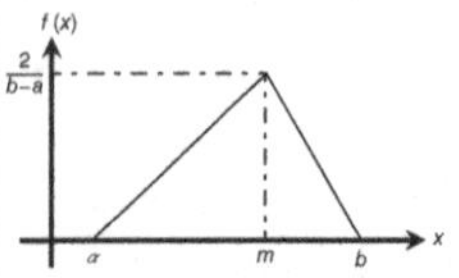	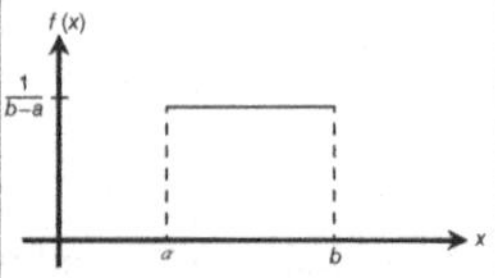	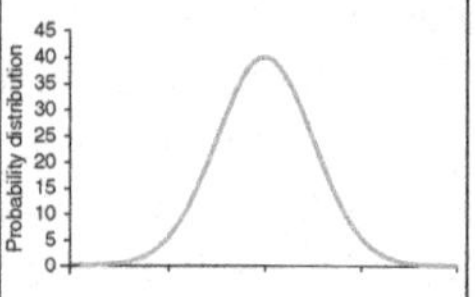

EXHIBIT 8.6   Risk input variables and the relevant probability distributions

That is, the function NORMSINV (0.43879, 75, 5) returns 74.22981, which are the DSOs that have cumulative probability equal to 0.43879 based on a normal distribution with mean 75 and standard deviation 5.

However, Excel does not provide an inverse cumulative probability function for the triangular distribution. We will have to calculate it manually. The inverse of the cumulative triangular distribution, as we mentioned in section 8.3 and described on Wikipedia,[7] is given by the following formula in Excel:

$$= \text{IF}\left(p <= \frac{(m-\alpha)}{(b-\alpha)}, \alpha + \sqrt{(p \times (b-\alpha) \times (m-\alpha))}, b - \sqrt{((1-p) \times (b-\alpha) \times (b-m))}\right)$$

where
p: the probability provided as a random number from RAND (),
α: the minimum value of the distribution,
b: the maximum value of the distribution, and
m: the most likely value of the distribution.

In SteelCo's case $\alpha = 135,000$ MT, $b = 145,000$ MT, and $m = 139,354$ MT. Note that we cannot replace p in this formula with **RAND** (), since that would mean the simultaneous use of RAND cells in one single formula. Instead p will refer to another cell that contains the **RAND** () function.

Finally the inverse cumulative probability function for the uniform distribution is easy to compute and is given, as we mentioned in section 8.3, by the following formula in Excel:[8]

$$= \alpha + RAND() \times (b-\alpha)$$

where
α: the minimum value of the distribution,
b: the maximum value of the distribution, and
RAND () $\times b - \alpha = P(b - \alpha)$.

Since the **RAND** () function generates uniform numbers between 0 and 1, we can extend its value to a larger range by simply multiplying the function value by the desired range. So, to generate a random number X that satisfies $\alpha <= X < b$ we simply multiply the **RAND** () value with $(b - \alpha)$ and add the minimum value of the distribution, α. In SteelCo's case $\alpha = 9\%$ and $b = 10\%$.

We have not yet finished with step 3. We have to run the above functions a number of times, i.e. 500 or 5,000, or even 50,000. Then, for each input we should pick a value from the distribution of that input, feed it into the model, and save the output. The number of times (simulations) that we will need to run the above functions depends on a number of issues, such as the characteristics of probability distributions and the range of outcomes.[1] As you will understand, it would be cumbersome to press F9 500 times so that the model runs with 500 different inputs and save 500 outputs. For this reason we will introduce a very simple VBA code so that you may do as many runs as you please, automatically. However, before we do that, let us present the core modelling of the Monte Carlo simulation worksheet (Exhibit 8.7). At the top of Exhibit 8.7 you see a button called **Simulation**. This button is associated with the VBA code we mentioned above. We will refer to it explicitly in a while. Next to this button there is a check box. The check box links to cell F36. When the check box is not ticked the relative input risk

	A	B	C	D	E	F	G
35							
36		Simulation		☐ Check			
37							
38							
39	**FY 2017 Parameters**						
40	Input						
41	Random Number	0.6804	=RAND()				
42							
43	Days Sales Outstanding	75	=IF(F36=TRUE;NORMINV(RAND();(B45+E45)/2;(E45-B45)/6);75)				
44	Normal Distribution						
45	Range Between 60 and 90	60	· ▮ ·	· ▮ ·	90		
46							
47	Total Sales MT	139,354	=IF(F36=TRUE;IF(B41<=(E49-B49)/(D49-B49);B49+SQRT(B41*(D49-B49)*(E49-B49))				
48	Triangular Distribution		;D49-SQRT((1-B41)*(D49-B49)*(-E49+D49)));139354)				
49	Min, Max, Most Likely Value	135,000		145,000	139,354		
50							
51	% Gross Margin	9.5%	=IF(F36=TRUE;B53+RAND()*(E53-B53);9,5%)				
52	Unifom Distribution						
53	a,b Values	9.0%			10.0%		
54	Output						
55	Net Debt at the end of FY 2017	60,514	=Workings!J61+Workings!J62-Workings!J53				
56							

EXHIBIT 8.7   The core model of the Monte Carlo simulation worksheet

variables take a deterministic value and, in particular, the value that is shown in the "Assumptions" worksheet for 2017 (Exhibit 3.10). That is, DSO take the value of 75, total sales takes the value of 139,354 MT, and gross profit margin takes the value of 9.5%. On the other hand when the check box is ticked the 3 input risk variables take a value from the relative distribution that has been chosen previously. For example, the function of cell B43 starts with an IF statement. If cell F36 = TRUE, that is if the check box is ticked, then cell B43 take a value from a normal distribution with the mean being the average values of cells B45 and E45 and the standard deviation the difference of cells E45 and B45 divided by 6. Cells B45 and E45 represent the DSO_{Min} and DSO_{Max} that we mentioned previously. Note that we have linked these cells with 2 scroll bars so that we change the min and max DSOs in a more stylish way. We have shown in Chapter 4 (Section 4.1) how we import scroll bars and link them with a particular cell.

Moreover, we see in Exhibit 8.7 3 **RAND** () functions. The first is called at cell B41 and feeds cell B47. Cell B47 contains the inverse cumulative distribution function of the triangular distribution representing the total sales volume input variable. The second **RAND** () is part of the inverse normal distribution at cell B43 representing the DSO input variable and the third is part of cell B51, that is, the inverse uniform distribution function representing the gross profit margin input variable.

Furthermore cells B49, D49, and E49 represent the minimum, the maximum, and the most likely values of the triangular distribution whereas cells B53 and E53 represent the α and b values of the uniform distribution.

Finally cell B55 presents the model's output and reads directly from the "Workings" worksheet as shown in Exhibit 8.7. Cells WorkingsJ61, WorkingsJ62, and WorkingsJ53 belong to long-term debt, short-term debt, and cash accounts respectively for year 2017.

8.4.3.1 The Simple VBA CODE

VBA is the acronym of Visual Basic for Applications, Excel's powerful built-in programming language that permits us to incorporate user-written functions easily into a spreadsheet. Although programming is far beyond the scope of this book, we will introduce a simple VBA code to enable the reader to do things that would otherwise be impossible. At the very least, knowing VBA will make it easier to perform time-consuming calculations as in the case of the Monte Carlo simulation. You can use VBA to create either a function or a subroutine. A function performs a task that returns a result (e.g. summing 2 numbers), whereas a subroutine performs a set of actions when invoked. For the purposes of the model we construct here we will make use of a subroutine. A subroutine is a unit of code enclosed between the following start and end statement:

```
Sub


.........


End Sub
```

The easiest way to create a subroutine, for the purposes of this chapter, is to insert a button (ActiveX control) from the **Developer** tab. If it is not activated please activate it from Excel Options in the way we described in previous chapters. ActiveX is a software framework created by Microsoft that allows small applications (like a button) to be shared among different Windows programs. To insert a button, go to the **Developer tab**, in the **Controls** group, click **Insert** and then under **ActiveX Controls** click **Button**. Then click the worksheet location where you want the button to appear and drag accordingly. You should now see a button like the one in Exhibit 8.8 named **CommandButton1**. To change the name of the button from **CommandButton1** to **Simulation** you have to be in "design" mode so that you can edit it (Click the **Developer** tab, go to the **Controls** group and click the **Design Mode** button). Now you can select the button, right click on it, choose the **CommandButton Object** from the popup window, and then click **Edit** (Exhibit 8.8). Replace the **CommandButton1** text with **Simulation.** Then, to add the required VBA code to the button, select it, right click on it, and then click the **View Code** from the popup window.

This starts the Visual Basic Editor. A subroutine called **CommandButton1_Click** appears in the editor as shown in Exhibit 8.9. You see that the subroutine declaration is preceded by the keyword Private. This makes it only available to the current module. It cannot be accessed from any other modules, or from the Excel workbook. Moreover you will see the **End Sub** statement. This tells the computer that it should stop executing the code that is written above.

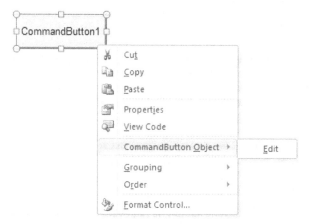

EXHIBIT 8.8   Editing an ActiveX control button

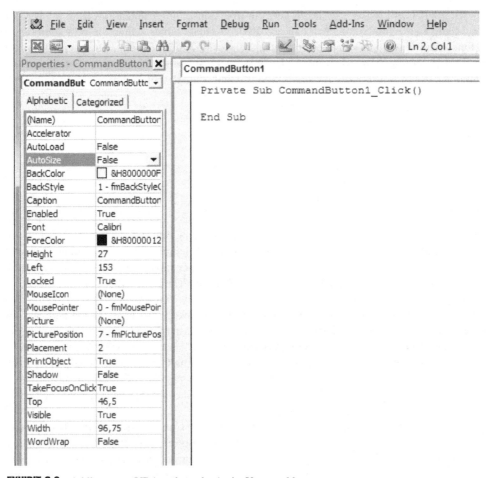

EXHIBIT 8.9 Adding some VBA code to the ActiveX control button

Now let us add the following code to the abovementioned subroutine.

```
Private Sub CommandButton1_Click()
'Loop 500 times to refresh spreadsheet data and save the output of cell b55
     For Row = 62 To 562
            Calculate
            a = Range ("b55")
            Cells (Row, 2) = a
     Next Row
End Sub
```

In VBA, an apostrophe signals the beginning of a comment. Whatever follows it is ignored. A comment usually provides a description of what the VBA code does. Then we make use of a *For Next* statement. The *For Next* statement is a loop that runs the same code over and over a certain number of times. The loop consists of a header which contains a counter variable (in our case the name of the variable is *Row*), a code block and a *Next* statement. That is whatever is between the *For Next* statements will run for 500 times ($562 - 62 = 500$). Under the *For* statement comes the *Calculate* command. This command is used in order to force Excel to recalculate the data in the spreadsheet. In practice when the *Calculate* command is executed, the RAND () functions produce new random variables which in turn produce new values of the input variables. These new input variables give rise to a new model output. Recall from Exhibit 8.7 that the model output (Net debt at the end of FY 2017) is presented in cell B55. Next we feed the value of cell B55 into a variable called *a*. We do so by using the *Range ()* command. This command, as you might have guessed, refers to a cell or a range of cells (in our case it refers to cell B55). Finally we save the value of variable *a* to a new cell. To do so we use the *Cells ()* command. The *Cells ()* command is similar to the *Range ()* command in that it refers to a cell. For example Cells (1,1) refers to the cell of row 1 and column 1 (that is cell A1) whereas *Cells(Row, 2) = a* refers to the cell of row = Row and column = 2 and sets it equal to *a*. That is at the first run cell B62 is equal to *a* which is equal to cell B55 which in turn is the output of the model. At the second run cell B63 takes the value of the new output of the model and so on. At the last run the output of the model is saved at cell B562.

Having finished with the VBA editor we return to Excel by clicking **Close and Return to Microsoft Excel**, on the File menu of the Visual Basic Editor.

Every time we press the *Simulate* button shown in Exhibit 8.7 the range of cells B62:B562 fills with new model output values. To visualize the probability distribution of the model output we need to tabulate the outcomes from the 500 runs. In other words we need to create a histogram (Frequency Distribution Chart) which lead us to step no 4.

8.4.4 Creating a Histogram (Frequency Distribution Chart) in Excel

There are 2 methods to create a histogram (Frequency Distribution Chart) in Excel. The easy but static one and the more difficult but dynamic one. The easy one makes use of the **Histogram Tool** in the **Analysis ToolPak** add-in. If you do not have the Analysis ToolPak add-in already loaded you will have to load it. To do so click on the **Office** Button, select **Excel Options**, click **Add-ins**, select **Analysis ToolPak**, and click on the **Go** button. A screen with activated and non-activated add-ins appears. The Analysis ToolPak add-in should be in the non-activated add-ins. Check the Analysis ToolPak and on the popup window that appears click the **OK** button. Now on the **Data** tab, under the **Analysis** group you will be able to see the **Data Analysis** (Exhibit 8.10). Click on it.

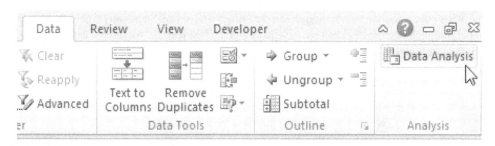

EXHIBIT 8.10 Data Analysis ToolPak add-in

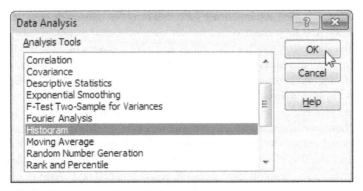

EXHIBIT 8.11   Various tools (including Histogram) under the Data Analysis ToolPak add-in

The histogram pop-up window of Exhibit 8.12 appears:

On the dialog box with the various analysis tools that appear select the Histogram and click **OK** (Exhibit 8.11).

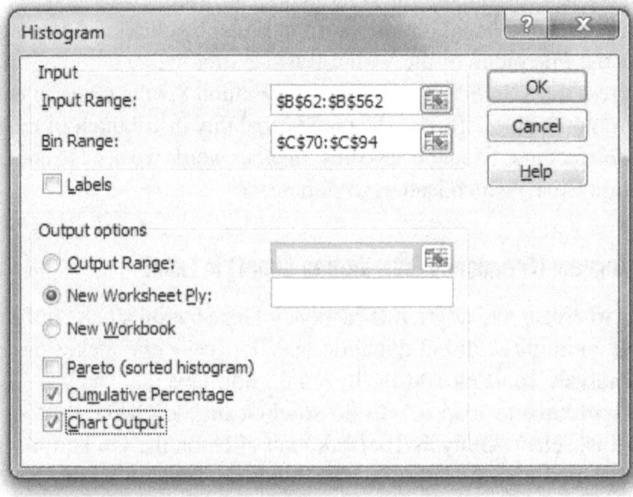

EXHIBIT 8.12   The Histogram popup window

We have to define the **Input Range** first. As you will already have noticed we have selected the range B62:B562 (by clicking in the **Input Range** box). Does this ring a bell? The VBA subroutine we wrote above ran 500 times and saved the results (the output of the model) in range B62:B562. Then we have to define the **Bin Range**. We have selected the range C70:C94 by clicking in the Bin Range box. The **Bin Range** defines the frequency with which the data points of the **Input Range** fall within various ranges. Let us see how we construct the Bin Range. Exhibit 8.13 shows the following information:

- a small part of the output of the subroutine written above (cells B62:B95). There would be no reason to present the total 500 outputs of the simulation.
- the Bin Range (cells C70:C94). You can see that this range spans from 54,500 to 66,500, it is symmetrical around the value of 60,500 (which is gray shaded), and the step between

	A	B	C	D	E	F	G	H	I
62		63,129							
63		64,129							
64		62,753							
65		58,622							
66		63,116							
67		57,253							
68		60,665							
69		60,157							
70		62,015	54,500	0	Average =	60,690	0.0%	0.0%	
71		59,196	55,000	1	Standard Deviation =	1,698	0.2%	0.2%	
72		59,806	55,500	0	Max =	66,064	0.0%	0.2%	
73		61,495	56,000	2	Min =	54,942	0.4%	0.6%	
74		61,005	56,500	3	Max - Min =	11,122	0.6%	1.2%	
75		61,657	57,000	4	No of bins =	25	0.8%	2.0%	
76		60,048	57,500	8	Bin step =	445	1.6%	3.6%	
77		63,574	58,000	4	Rounded Bin step =	500	0.8%	4.4%	
78		58,197	58,500	22			4.4%	8.8%	
79		60,921	59,000	24			4.8%	13.6%	
80		59,285	59,500	57			11.4%	25.0%	
81		63,360	60,000	61			12.2%	37.1%	
82		60,695	60,500	51			10.2%	47.3%	
83		61,238	61,000	56			11.2%	58.5%	
84		61,822	61,500	44			8.8%	67.3%	
85		59,337	62,000	44			8.8%	76.0%	
86		60,307	62,500	46			9.2%	85.2%	
87		62,424	63,000	28			5.6%	90.8%	
88		60,838	63,500	20			4.0%	94.8%	
89		63,682	64,000	17			3.4%	98.2%	
90		60,858	64,500	5			1.0%	99.2%	
91		60,867	65,000	3			0.6%	99.8%	
92		59,528	65,500	0			0.0%	99.8%	
93		63,440	66,000	0			0.0%	99.8%	
94		59,250	66,500	1			0.2%	100.0%	
95		58,412							

EXHIBIT 8.13 Output of the VBA code and bin range construction

2 bins is 500. But how did we come up with this range? Notice that cells F70:F73 show the average value (mean), standard deviation, maximum, and minimum of the range B62:B562. To calculate these values we make use of Excel's functions *average* (B62:B562), *stdev* (B62:B562), *max* (B62:B562), and *min* (B62:B562). The average value is 60,690, the maximum 66,064, and the minimum 54,942 respectively. Therefore we defined the Bin Range so that it contains the whole range of outputs from 54,942 to 66,064 and is centred on the value of 60,500 which is close to the average value of the outputs.

◦ various other calculations in relation to the number of bins, the bin step, and 3 other ranges of data (D70:D94, G70:G94, and H70:H94) the use of which we will refer to later on.

Coming back to Exhibit 8.12 (histogram window), having finished with the inputs of the histogram let us define the outputs. You can see that we checked the **New Worksheet Ply** box so that Excel inserts a new worksheet in the current workbook and pastes the results starting at cell A1. We left the box next to this option empty (we could have entered a name for the new worksheet). We could have checked the **Output Range** option button and selected an output range in the current worksheet. Instead we will construct our own histogram in the current worksheet later on. Moreover we could have chosen the results to be presented in a new **Workbook**. Next we checked the **Cumulative Percentage** button. This button tells Excel to generate an output table column for cumulative percentages and to include a cumulative percentage line in the histogram chart. Finally we checked the **Chart Output** to generate an embedded histogram chart with the output table. By pressing the **OK** button a new sheet is inserted into our worksheet with a data table and a histogram chart similar to that of Exhibit 8.14.

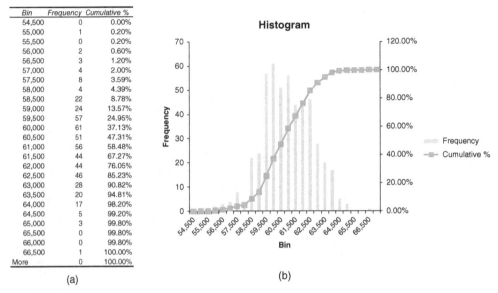

Bin	Frequency	Cumulative %
54,500	0	0.00%
55,000	1	0.20%
55,500	0	0.20%
56,000	2	0.60%
56,500	3	1.20%
57,000	4	2.00%
57,500	8	3.59%
58,000	4	4.39%
58,500	22	8.78%
59,000	24	13.57%
59,500	57	24.95%
60,000	61	37.13%
60,500	51	47.31%
61,000	56	58.48%
61,500	44	67.27%
62,000	44	76.05%
62,500	46	85.23%
63,000	28	90.82%
63,500	20	94.81%
64,000	17	98.20%
64,500	5	99.20%
65,000	3	99.80%
65,500	0	99.80%
66,000	0	99.80%
66,500	1	100.00%
More	0	100.00%

(a)   (b)

EXHIBIT 8.14   Output of the histogram analysis tool

Apart from the tabulation of the outcomes of the 500 runs (Exhibit 8.14a), we see a bell-like frequency chart (bars) and the cumulative distribution line which represents the area under the frequency chart (Exhibit 8.14b). We will interpret the results of this chart later on.

We mentioned earlier that this was the easy method to create a histogram or a frequency chart. The disadvantage of this method is that the chart is static. This means that we have to re-run the tool each time we want to do a new simulation. To create a dynamic histogram we will use the second method we mentioned above by making use of Excel's **FREQUENCY** function. In this way every time we re-run the Monte Carlo simulation, the chart will be automatically updated. First, we have to define the bin numbers, that is, to figure out how many classes (categories) we need to analyze our model outputs. There are no hard and fast rules about how many bins to choose. Normally we pick between 5 and 25 classes making sure that at least a few items fall within each category (bin). A rule of thumb would be to subtract the minimum from the maximum data value and divide by the number of bins we choose. In our case, if we choose 25 bins, the bin step would be:

$$(\text{Maximum} - \text{Minimum}) / \text{No of Bins} = \frac{11,122}{25} = 445$$

We could use the value of 445 to obtain the bin width. Nevertheless it is better to round this number up to 500. So if the centre of the bin range is 60,500, given that we have chosen 25 bins, we need to define 12 bins lower than 60,500 and 12 bins higher than 60,500, separated by the value of 500 (bin step). This is how we created the bin range spanning cells C70:C94 shown in Exhibit 8.13. We will use the same range with Excel's **FREQUENCY** function.

The FREQUENCY function has 2 arguments:

```
FREQUENCY (data_array, bins_array)
```

where **data_array** is the range of cells containing the values that are to be analyzed and **bins_array** is the range of cells containing bins into which the numeric values should be grouped.

Excel's FREQUENCY is an array function and has a special characteristic: we don't simply type it into a cell and press Enter. Instead, we first select the cells where we want to put the **FREQUENCY** function, type the formula, and then press Ctrl-Shift-Enter. **FREQUENCY** will not function correctly if you simply press Enter and try to copy the formula to the adjacent cells. In particular, we selected cells D70:D94 and then typed the following function:

```
= FREQUENCY (B62:B562, C70:C94)
```

and pressed Ctrl-Shift-Enter. Excel filled cells D70:D94 with the **FREQUENCY** function (see Exhibit 8.13) by adding 2 curly brackets around the formula. As we said, these indicate an array function and can only be added by pressing Ctrl-Shift-Enter after you type or edit the formula. Cells D70:D94 count how many data values from the range of B62 to B562 are in each bin. Guess what? The frequencies presented in cells D70:D94 add up to 500. As a last step we use cells C70:C94 as the *x* values and cells D70:D94 as the *y* values to create the frequency bar chart or histogram in Exhibit 8.15a.

Finally, we have to create the cumulative probability distribution based on the frequency distribution table of the bin range (cells C70:C94) and frequencies (cells D70:D94). For this

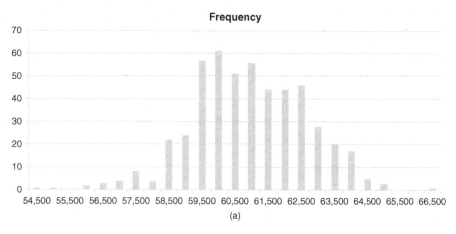

(a)

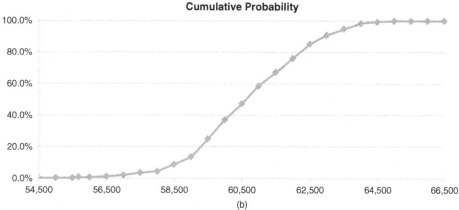

(b)

EXHIBIT 8.15 Similar graph to the Histogram analysis tool output created with Excel's frequency function

reason we will use 2 more columns. In column G we will translate the frequencies (cells D70:D94) into percentages by using the following formula:

$$\text{Cell G70} = \text{D70/SUM(\$D\$70:\$D\$94)},$$

$$\text{Cell G71} = \text{D71/SUM(\$D\$70:\$D\$94)},$$

and so on. Cells G70 to G94 take the values as they are shown in Exhibit 8.13. As you would have expected, cells G70:G94 sum to 1 or 100%. Then to calculate the cumulative probability we use the following sequence:

$$\text{Cell H70} = \text{G70}$$

$$\text{Cell H71} = \text{H70} + \text{G71}$$

$$\text{Cell H72} = \text{H71} + \text{G72}$$

and so on. That is, the first entry is the same as the first entry in column G. The second entry is the sum of the first 2 entries in column G and so on. We fill in the rest of the cumulative probability column H as shown in Exhibit 8.13. You can see that the cumulative probability starts from zero and gradually builds to 1 or 100%. Finally, we use cells C70:C94 as the x values and cells H70:H94 as the y values to create the Y X scatter chart of Exhibit 8.15b. We have shown in earlier chapters how to create bar and line charts. We could have created a chart like the one in Exhibit 8.14 that combined both a frequency bar chart and a cumulative probability distribution. That would require a double axis graph like the one we built back in Chapter 4. We would like to show the reader both options for presenting a histogram chart and leave him or her to decide which one they prefer.

Now that we have finished with step no 4 - have created a histogram (frequency distribution chart) with the output results - let us proceed with step no 5, the raison d'être of the whole Monte Carlo exercise, and interpret the results.

8.4.5 Interpreting the Results

Both Exhibits 8.14 and 8.15 present the same kind of information: a histogram that depicts frequencies of occurrences for specific data values and graphically summarizes the distribution of a data set and a cumulative probability. A cumulative probability corresponding to a particular value is the sum of all the frequencies up to and including that value. Remember that we used Monte Carlo simulation in order to quantify the chances that SteelCo's net debt in 2017 will be over €60,500k. At last we are able to answer this question by properly interpreting the cumulative probability graph. The probability that SteelCo's net debt in 2017 will be below €60,500k is 47.31% which means that the chances that it is over €60,500k are:

$$1 - 47.31\% = 52.69\% \approx 53\%$$

Moreover, based on the above information we could draw the following conclusions:

- SteelCo's net debt has been assumed to be on average €60,690k with a 76% chance of being between €58,500k and €62,500k.
- The shape of the output distribution is approximately normal with a maximum of €66,064k and a minimum of €54,942k.
- The range of SteelCo's net debt at a 95% confidence level will be between €57,362k and €64,018k assuming a normal distribution.

It is easy to find the chances that SteelCo's net debt falls between €58,500k and €62,500k. All you have to do is to subtract $P(x < 58,500)$ from $P(x < 62,500)$. Refer to the table with cumulative probabilities (Exhibit 8.14a) to find that $P(x < 62,500) = 85.23\%$ and $P(x < 58,500) = 8.78\%$. Then

$$P(58,500 < x < 62,500) = P(x < 62,500) - P(x < 58,500) = 85.23\% - 8.78\% = 76.45\% \approx 76\%$$

Moreover the 95% confidence level is defined as 2 standard deviations away from the mean assuming a normal distribution. The mean from Exhibit 8.13 is €60,690k whereas the standard deviation equals €1,698k (see cell F71 in Exhibit 8.13). So the range of SteelCo's net debt at a 95% confidence level is €60,690k ± 2 * 1,698k.

Finally, depending on the debt capacity of SteelCo, the information that there is a greater than 50% chance that the net debt of the company will be over €60,500k might be crucial to SteelCo's management. If SteelCo uses 100% of its credit lines perhaps it needs to address other sources of financing. In any case the above information should, of itself, be enough to trigger management action.

8.4.6 Some Issues of Concern

As a final note to this chapter there are some key issues we have to deal with in the context of using simulations in risk assessment. Although Monte Carlo simulation is a powerful risk analysis tool it can fail when used in the wrong way. Some issues of concern are the following:

- Monte Carlo simulation deals with probability distributions. Every input variable is different. To choose the proper distribution is a complicated procedure. As Professor Damodaran[1] points out, real data may not fit distributions. Even if they fit you may have difficulties in assessing when to use which distribution. PricewaterhouseCoopers' *Uncertainty and Risk Analysis*[3] provides a short guide as to when to use which distribution.
- The "garbage in – garbage out" principle: whether we enter quality inputs or complete garbage, Monte Carlo simulation will still produce some impressive graphs, and you have to be properly trained to assess whether they are meaningless or not.
- Correlated input risk variables: recall that we chose 3 different probability distributions for sales volume, gross profit margin, and DSO for the Monte Carlo model presented in this section. In this way we assumed that the input variables were uncorrelated, that is, there were no interdependent relationships between them (although somebody could argue that DSO and sales volume are correlated since the higher the credit SteelCo provides to its customers the higher the sales volume it can achieve). When there is a strong correlation across input variables, according to Professor Damodaran[1] we can either focus on the variable with the biggest impact on the output of the model or build the correlation explicitly into the model. Although building the correlation into the model is beyond the scope of this book it suffices to say that we should examine input variables for positive or negative correlation. A positive correlation indicates that 2 variables move jointly in the same direction, whereas a negative one indicates that 2 variables move precisely in the opposite way.

REFERENCES AND BIBLIOGRAPHY

1. A. Damodaran, *Probabilistic Approaches: Scenario Analysis, Decision Trees and Simulations,* http://people.stern.nyu.edu/adamodar/pdfiles/papers/probabilistic.pdf.
2. Metropolis, N., "The Beginning of the Monte Carlo Method" (1987) *Los Alamos Science*, Special Issue, http://www.sciencemadness.org/lanl1_a/lib-www/pubs/00326866.pdf.
3. PricewaterhouseCoopers, *Uncertainty and Risk Analysis. A Practical Guide from Business Dynamics* (MCS, 1999).
4. Pergler, M. and Feeman, A., "Probabilistic Modeling as an Exploratory Decision-making Tool", McKinsey Working Papers on Risk, No. 6, September 2008.
5. Wikipedia, http://en.wikipedia.org/wiki/Normal_distribution.
6. Wikipedia, http://en.wikipedia.org/wiki/Quantile_function.
7. Wikipedia, http://en.wikipedia.org/wiki/Triangular_distribution.
8. Wittwer, J.W., *A Practical Guide to Monte Carlo Simulation*, Part 3, from Vertex42.com, 1 June 2004, http://www.vertex42.com/ExcelArticles/mc/GeneratingRandomInputs.html.

Appendix

1. WALKING THROUGH THE EXCEL MODEL PROVIDED WITH THE BOOK (STEELCO SA 4YR BUSINESS PLAN)

Introduction

Through the various chapters of this book we have developed a financial model that comprises the 9 worksheets of Exhibit A1. The model is called "SteelCo SA 4yr Business Plan" and can be downloaded from the website accompanying the book. The model contains each of the worksheets presented as exhibits in the course of the book. It is a macro-enabled Microsoft Office Excel worksheet with the extension (.xlsm) that provides added security. A macro-enabled Microsoft Excel worksheet is used in Excel 2007 and later versions when we work with macros. When we create a macro, such as the one we created in Chapter 8 that runs a Monte Carlo simulation, we must use this format to save our workbook or the macro will not be saved. Make sure that the macro security level in Excel is set either to **Disable all macros with notification** or **Enable all macros**. By default, Excel protects us from running macros, but in this case, where we created our own macro, we will have to change the protective security settings (on the **Developer tab**, click the **Macro Security** button in the **Code group**; the Trust Center dialog box will appear with the **Macro Settings tab** selected. Set the security level either to **Disable all macros with notification** where you will see displayed a security alert when a workbook opens or to **Enable all macros** where the macro will run without a notification. The latter option is more risky especially when using macros from unknown sources.) Apart from the macro security level, to be able to work with the model properly you will have to set the number of iterations to 100, Excel's default, and allow the computer to recalculate automatically. The way we built the plug figure (short-term debt) of the balance sheet and the interest expense of the income statement requires Excel's **Enable iterative calculation** option to be activated (from the top left hand corner choose the **Office button** and then the **Excel Options** menu item; then choose the **Formulas tab** and from the **Calculation Options**, check the **Enable iterative calculation** box, and enter 100 in the **Maximum Iterations** box). The model does not need any kind of installation and there are no minimum systems requirements. Nevertheless, in order to use it we would suggest that your computer should be able to run Microsoft Excel 2007 or later.

Structure of the Model

The structure of the model is shown in Exhibit A1.

The **"Control panel"** worksheet, built in Chapter 4, consists of both input and output variables. The user can perform "what-if" analysis on 2014 key input variables by changing the working capital (i.e. DIO, DSO, and DPO) as well as the sales volume and profitability. The output variables consist of 2014 turnover, profit before tax, EBITDA, free cash flow, and net debt as well as the current ratio, financial leverage, and interest coverage.

The **"Assumptions"** worksheet consists of all the input variables of the model. These variables range from sales prices to sales volumes, gross profit margin percentages, financing costs, working capital parameters, tax rates, depreciation rates, investments, and inflation rates. Some of the above input variables are fed from other worksheets:

- Specific 2014 input variables are fed from the "Control Panel" worksheet.
- Specific 2015 input variables are fed from the "Sensitivity Analysis" worksheet.
- Specific 2016 input variables feed Excel's Scenario Manager to give rise to the good/bad and base case scenarios we examined in Chapter 7.
- Finally, Specific 2017 input variables are fed from the "Monte Carlo Simulation" worksheet.

The "Assumptions" worksheet estimates the above input variables (key forecast drivers) after analyzing the historical financial statements of SteelCo for years 2011 to 2013 and then gives the user the flexibility to forecast his own values for years 2014 to 2017. These values will become the key forecast drivers based on which proforma financial statements will be constructed. Excel's Scenario Manager dictates that selected output variables be placed at the bottom of this worksheet, e.g. turnover, gross profit margin, EBITDA, Finance cost, profit before tax, free cash flow, equity, working capital, and net debt in order to monitor how they change according to the various scenarios built (for a more detailed explanation see Chapter 7).

The **"Workings"** worksheet is the heart of the model. It forecasts the proforma financial statements of SteelCo for years 2014 to 2017, that is, the income statement, the balance sheet, and the cash flow statement based on the forecast drivers described in the "Assumptions" worksheet. The historic financial statements of 2011 to 2013 are also presented in this worksheet for reasons of comparison with the projected ones.

The **"Ratio"** worksheet builds on the theory of ratio analysis provided in Chapter 2. However, it is the only worksheet that has not been covered explicitly in the book. It provides 6 categories of ratios that are most frequently used in analyzing the financial statements of companies. These categories span to the following ratios:

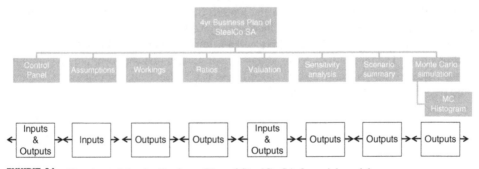

EXHIBIT A1   Structure of the 4yr Business Plan of SteelCo SA financial model

- Profitability ratios
- Return on investment ratios
- Activity ratios
- Liquidity ratios
- Debt ratios
- Coverage ratios

Short explanations are given for the meaning of each ratio. The abovementioned ratios have been calculated for both the historic period and the forecast one.

The **"Valuation"** worksheet provides a 1-page valuation summary of SteelCo. This worksheet contains some assumptions regarding the weighted average cost of capital and terminal value respectively that are necessary for the valuation of SteelCo. Moreover, it calculates the free cash flow of the company for the 5-year forecast period from 2014 to 2018. Finally the value per share of SteelCo is calculated.

The **"Sensitivity Analysis"** worksheet provides a 1-page summary of the various sensitivity analyses we ran in Chapter 6 using Excel's **What-If Analysis Data Table** tool. It is a dynamic worksheet, i.e. every time you change a figure in the model the data tables are updated automatically. This can sometimes be time consuming. When you are working on a different worksheet you may not want Excel to automatically recalculate data tables. Go to the **Calculation Options button**'s drop-down menu on the **Formulas tab** and choose the **Automatic Except for Data Tables** option. By doing so data tables will be recalculated manually whenever you press F9.

The **"Scenario Summary"** worksheet provides a 1-page summary of the good/base/bad scenarios built with Excel's Scenario Manager. In contrast to the "Sensitivity Analysis" worksheet, this is a static one. To change the numbers presented in this worksheet you will have to run the Scenario Manager again.

The **"Monte Carlo Simulation"** worksheet provides a 1-page report of the Monte Carlo simulation built in the model. The various input variable distributions are presented together with a frequency distribution chart (histogram). This worksheet is dynamic. You may run the Monte Carlo simulation and see in real time how the frequency distribution chart builds. In contrast the **"MC Histogram"** worksheet is static and is the Monte Carlo output built with Excel's Histogram tool.

Exhibit A2 presents the interrelationships between the above worksheets. The "Assumptions" worksheet feeds the "Workings" one. It is also linked to the "Scenario Summary" worksheet. We used Excel's Scenario Manager to build into "Assumptions" worksheet the 3 scenarios by drawing some key output indicators from the "Workings" worksheet. The "Workings" worksheet in turn feeds all other dynamic worksheets like the "Control Panel", "Ratios", "Valuation", "Sensitivity Analysis", and "Monte Carlo Simulation" ones. At the same time the "Control Panel", "Sensitivity Analysis", and "Monte Carlo Simulation" worksheets feed some input variables into the "Assumptions" worksheet. Finally, the "MC Histogram" worksheet is static and is derived from the "Monte Carlo Simulation" worksheet.

2. OTHER EXCEL FILES PROVIDED WITH THE BOOK

Apart from the complete financial model described above the following Excel files are provided with the book and can be downloaded from the accompanying website. All of them have

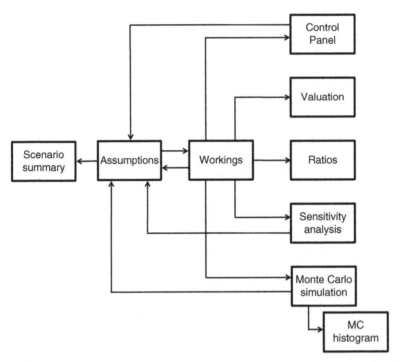

EXHIBIT A2 The interrelationships between the various worksheets of SteelCo's financial model built in the course of the book

been used as exhibits throughout the course of the book. They are presented according to the chapter of the book in which they appear.

Chapter	Excel File name	Description
Chapter 3	New Bond Loan Termsheet. xlsx	Presents sample terms and covenants of a bond loan.
Chapter 4	Depreciation schedule.xlsx	5 year CAPEX and depreciation schedule. The first 2 years are presented on a monthly basis and the rest on a yearly basis.
Chapter 4	Gompertz_Curve.xlsx	A model that presents diffusion on innovation based on the Gompertz Curve.
Chapter 4	WC Planning.xlsx	Working capital planning tool that calculates the level of receivables given certain turnover and credit terms.
Chapter 5	Betas.xlsx	Stock market data are used to estimate the *beta* of a company.
Chapter 6	Sensitivity.xlsx	A model performing 1-dimensional and 2-dimensional sensitivity analysis of a simple project's NPV.
Chapter 7	Scenario analysis.xlsx	A model performing scenario analysis of a simple project's NPV by using both Excel's Scenario Manager and the OFFSET function.
Chapter 8	Monte Carlo simulation.xlsm	A macro-enabled Excel worksheet that contains a model performing Monte Carlo simulation analysis of a simple project's NPV by using both Excel's NORMINV() and RAND() functions and a 4-line VBA code. The resulting histogram from this model is presented in Chapter 8 of the book.

Index